James P. Rushe

Carmel in Ireland

a narrative of the Irish Province of Teresian, or discalced Carmelites, A.D.

1625-1896

James P. Rushe

Carmel in Ireland

a narrative of the Irish Province of Teresian, or discalced Carmelites, A.D. 1625-1896

ISBN/EAN: 9783337300203

Printed in Europe, USA, Canada, Australia, Japan

Cover: Foto ©Andreas Hilbeck / pixelio.de

More available books at **www.hansebooks.com**

CARMEL IN IRELAND.

Permissu Superiorum.

Die 15ᵃ *Augusti,* 1897.

Nihil Obstat:

FR. HIERONYMUS MARIA AB. IMMAC.
CONCEPT., C.D.,
Provincialis.

Die 25ᵃ *Augusti,* 1897.

Imprimatur:

✠ HERBERTUS CARDINALIS VAUGHAN,
Archiepiscopus Westmonast.

Die 1ᵃ *Sept.* 1897.

(*Copyright*, 1897, *by the* VERY REV. JAMES P. RUSHE, O.D.C.)

CARMEL IN IRELAND:

A NARRATIVE OF THE IRISH PROVINCE
OF TERESIAN, OR DISCALCED
CARMELITES.

A.D. 1625–1896.

BY

FATHER PATRICK OF ST. JOSEPH,

O.D.C.

LONDON: BURNS & OATES, Limited.
NEW YORK, CINCINNATI, CHICAGO: BENZIGER BROTHERS.
1897.

TO

MY MOTHER.

PREFACE.

THE following chapters contain an account of the *Discalced Carmelites* in Ireland, from their first coming to this country down to the present time. To the Author, the writing of it was a labour of love, undertaken in the hope of supplying for a history now almost lost, owing to reasons that will be duly assigned.

The facts here collected are of general interest, and it is to be regretted that long intervals of time must be allowed to pass with brief remark, because of the frequent want of MS. material from which the record might be continued in a less broken sequence of events. However, the documents at my disposal were such as to enable me to carry out the purpose which I had in view—to show how intimately the Religious of the TERESIAN REFORM have been associated with the Faithful of Ireland for nearly three hundred years.

A notice on the Order of Carmel was necessary; I can only trust that no one will be disappointed in the subject-matter premised in the first chapter, nor in that to which the second has been devoted.

I have not verified each statement by literal quotation from the authorities; but, when necessary, the references are made in the usual way; and there is a list of the more important published works which I have had occasion to consult, together with the names of the Monastic Archives,—the chief sources of the information now submitted to the reader.

FR. PATRICK, D.C.

St. Mary's, Morehampton Road,
    Dublin.

CONTENTS.

	PAGE
PREFACE	vii
WORKS OF REFERENCE	xv

CHAPTER I.

INTRODUCTORY: THE REFORM OF CARMEL.

The Prophet Elias the Founder of the Carmelite Order—His spirit of zeal and prayer—The first written Rule—Carmel in Europe—How the Primitive Rule came to be mitigated—THE TERESIAN REFORM—St. John of the Cross and the first Discalced Carmelites—The Teresian Friars as missioners 1–20

CHAPTER II.

CARMEL IN IRELAND BEFORE THE TERESIAN REFORM.

St. Palladius and his companions—St. Patrick's devotion to the Prophet Elias—Early Irish Monasticism—Irish Carmelites of the thirteenth century—The monasteries founded in Ireland—Piety and generosity of the Founders—Distinguished members of the Order—Suppression of the abbeys during the reign of Henry VIII.—How the Faith was preserved among the Irish people—The first Penal Days 21–39

CHAPTER III.

ADVENT OF THE DISCALCED CARMELITES.

State of Ireland when Charles I. ascended the throne—The Irish in exile—Irish subjects in Teresian Monasteries abroad—Queen Henrietta Maria and the Discalced Carmelites—Revival of hope among the Catholics of Ireland—The Teresian missioners from Louvain—A friary opened in Dublin—The authorities aroused—Father Edward of the Kings—Success of the first foundation . . 40-55

CHAPTER IV.

THE PROVINCE OF ST. PATRICK.

The Irish Province—Several of the ancient Carmelite Abbeys granted, by Papal authority, to the Teresian Friars—The Foundations—Fathers Victor and Columbanus at Ardee—Interesting relics of the past—Father John Rowe, O.D.C.—The "Residences." . . . 56-70

CHAPTER V.

"THE REGULAR LIFE."

Everyday life in a Friary of Irish Discalced Carmelites when Charles I. was king—The object of "Visitations"—Influences of "*The Regular Life*"—The "Signs of the Times" in A.D. 1640—Puritan fanaticism—The Teresian Monastery of Kilkenny during the "Confederation"—Irish Fathers at the "General Chapters" . . 71-88

CHAPTER VI.

"WITH PALMS AND CROWNS."

The life and martyrdom of Father Thomas Aquinas of St. Teresa; of Fra Angelus of St. Joseph; and of Brother Peter of the Mother of God—Other martyrs of the Irish Province: Fathers Lawrence, Patrick, and Bede . 89-106

CHAPTER VII.

"THE OUTLAWED."

The Cromwellian persecution—Father Agapitus of the Holy Ghost as annalist of the Irish Province—The Teresian "*Outlaws*"—Horrors of the Transplantation—Father Agapitus and the Puritans—Failure of Cromwell's Irish Campaign—Some victories of "*The Outlawed*" . 107-123

CHAPTER VIII.

AFTER THE RESTORATION.

The "Black Act"—Ingratitude of Charles and Ormond—Prospects of St. Patrick's Province towards the close of this reign—Toleration under King James—Devotion of the Irish to the House of Stuart—After the Battle of the Boyne—The Teresian Friars at Loughrea—Another generation of Teresian "*Outlaws*"—Their mode of life during the Penal Days 124-139

CHAPTER IX.

ST. PATRICK'S PROVINCE IN THE EIGHTEENTH CENTURY.

State of the Irish Catholics during the reign of Queen Anne—The Hanoverian reversion—First Centenary of the Discalced Carmelites in Ireland—George II. and the Fathers of the Irish Province—The General Visitation of 1743—Opening of a friary in Stephen's Street, Dublin—A grand enterprise of the Archconfraternity—Death of two of the Teresian "*Outlaws*"—Eulogy of an Irish Discalced Carmelite in the *London Gazette*—Irish political movements in the reign of George III.—The French Revolution . 140-158

CHAPTER X.

"ST. TERESA'S CHURCH AND FRIARY"

PAGE

A new church and monastery built in Dublin—The foundation-stone laid by a leader of the "United Irishmen"—Historical list of generous friends—How the permission of the King and Parliament was secured—A lawsuit gained by the Friars—The Irish "Reign of Terror," A.D. 1798—The shock of the Union—"St. Teresa's" completed after many years—The past and the present—Interesting associations 159–177

CHAPTER XI.

O'CONNELL AND THE FATHERS OF ST. TERESA'S.

O'Connell's protest against the Union — Beginning of his friendship with the Discalced Carmelites—Public meetings held at "St. Teresa's"—"THE VETO"—Ireland's gratitude to the Teresian Friars—The source of O'Connell's power—Foundation of the Catholic Association—The "*Great Meeting*" of 1827—Father L'Estrange and the Ribbonmen—EMANCIPATION—O'Connell and the "*Young Irelanders*"—At "St. Teresa's" for the last time 178–197

CHAPTER XII.

REOPENING OF THE NOVITIATE.

The Abbey of Loughrea: past and present—Formal reopening of the Novitiate there—Numerous Vocations to Carmel—A General Visitation: Cardinal Gotti—The "REGULAR LIFE" at the Abbey—After Profession: the first *trial*. 198–212

CONTENTS. xiii

CHAPTER XIII.

"THE HOUSE OF STUDIES."

PAGE

The foundation of "St. Mary's"—Gayfield House—The "*Regular Life*" during the Scholastic Course—Blessing of the new college at Gayfield—The Discalced Carmelite schools of Philosophy and Theology—"The Studies"—Some scholastic exercises—The Science of the Saints 213–231

CHAPTER XIV.

A FRAGMENT OF THE "OBITUARY."

Loss of the "Obituary" of the Irish Province—Why the "Names of our Dead" are preserved—Father Serapion's task—Some Religious of St. Patrick's Province whose death occurred before that of Father Seraphim Power 232–267

CHAPTER XV.

"THE LIST OF OBITS" (*continued*).

CHAPTER XVI.

THE TERESIAN NUNS IN IRELAND: THEIR VOCATION.

Canonical establishment of a Carmelite Sisterhood—The blessed John Soreth—Irishwomen embrace the Teresian Reform abroad—A convent founded at Loughrea—How the Sisters lived during the Penal Times: evidences of their fervour—Vocations in Ireland at the present day—Influence of the Spirit formed according to the original "Constitutions" 268–283

xiv CONTENTS.

CHAPTER XVII.

OTHER CLIENTS OF CARMEL IN IRELAND.

PAGE

The Brown Scapular—Zeal of the Irish Teresian Friars in preaching this devotion—The Tertiaries—Foundation of "*St. Joseph's Monastery*," Clondalkin—Interesting historical associations—Drumcondra and its memories—The vocation of the Tertiaries 284-298

CHAPTER XVIII.

CONCLUSION: RETROSPECT.

The "difficulties" of the work—Present state of the Irish Province: its "Restoration"—The General Visitation of 1896—Ireland, Carmel, and Rome—The world and Monasticism in these latter times—THE END . 299-307

INDEX 309

WORKS OF REFERENCE.

Acta Sanctorum. BOLLANDISTS.
Aikenhead, Life of Mary. S. A.
Analecta. ROTHE.
Annals of Ireland (The Four Masters). O'DONOVAN.
Annals of Osney. Vol. iv.
Annals of the Sisters of Mercy, Leaves from the.
Annales de Dunstaplia. Vol. iii.
Annales des Carmes Déchaussés de France. R. P. LOUIS DE SAINTE-THÉRÉSE, C.D.
Annales du Carmel. No. 47.
Anne de Jésus et les Constitutione des Carmélites Déchaussées.
Anne de Jésus, Vie d'. R. P. BERTHOLD-IGNACE, C.D.
Anthologia Hibernica. (1794.)
Antiquities of Ireland. WAKEMAN.
Aphorismical Discovery. Vols. i., ii.
Archbishops of Dublin. DALTON.
Archives: MS. Documents from the, of the Discalced Carmelite Monasteries at Rome, Genoa, London, Dublin, and Loughrea.
Autobiographie de la V. M. Anne de Saint-Barthélemy. R. P. BOUIX.
Autobiography. ULLATHORNE.
Basil (St.), Works of.
Battle of the Faith in Ireland. O'ROURKE.
Bede (the Venerable), Works of.
Bibliotheca Carmelitana. R. P. COSMAS DE VILLIERS.

WORKS OF REFERENCE.

Blind, A Light to the (A Jacobite Narrative). GILBERT.
Breviarium Romanum Carmelitanum.
Britannia. CAMDEN'S.
Bullarium Carmelitanum. Vols. i.-iv.
Cambrensis Eversus.
Carmel, Annals of. LEZANA.
Carmelitarum Discalceatorum, Cong. Ital. Hist. General.
Carmes Déchaussés, Cong. d'Espagne, Hist. Générale.
Church History of Ireland. WALSHE.
——. LANIGAN.
Church, The History of the. DE GRAVESON.
——. ROHRBACHER.
Collectio Scriptorum Carmelitarum Excalceatorum. Vols. i., ii.
Complutenses; Opera Philosophica.
Confederation and War in Ireland, History of the. BELLINGS.
Confederation of Kilkenny. MEEHAN.
Constitutiones Carmelitarum Excalceat.
Cromwell in Ireland. MURPHY.
Cromwellian Settlement. PRENDERGAST.
Decor Carmeli. R. F. PHILIPPUS À STA. TRINITATE.
Distinguished Irishmen of the Sixteenth Century. Rev. E. HOGAN, S.J.
Documents relating to Ireland. GILBERT.
Doyle (J. K. L.), Life and Letters of Dr. FITZPATRICK.
Dublin, Chartularies of St. Mary's Abbey. GILBERT.
Dublin, History of. GILBERT.
—— *History of County.* DALTON.
Dublin Magazine. (1798.)
Enchyridion Chronologicum Carmelit. Discalceat.
England, History of. LINGARD.
——. HUME.
——. MACAULAY.

WORKS OF REFERENCE. xvii

English in Ireland. FROUDE.
Europe, History of. ALISON.
Fate and Fortunes of the Earls of Tyrone. MEEHAN.
Fleurs du Carmel de France. R. P. PIERRE, C.D.
Four Georges. THACKERAY.
Franciscan Monasteries of Ireland. MEEHAN.
Fundaciones de las Hermanas Descalzas Carmelitas. SANTA TERESA DE JÉSUS.
Hibernia Dominicana. DE BURGO.
Hibernian Magazine. Vols. i., ii.
History of Ireland. HAVERTY.
——. KEATING.
——. M'GEE.
——. PLOWDEN.
——. MITCHELL.
——. O'SULLIVAN-BEARE.
——. O'HALLORAN.
——. MACGEOGHEGAN.
Ibernia Ignatiana. Rev. E. HOGAN, S.J.
Ireland and the Irish. O'CONNELL.
Ireland, Topographical Dictionary of. LEWIS.
Ireland, the Kingdom of. WALPOLE.
Irish Names of Places. JOYCE.
Irish Nation, Rise and Fall of. BARRINGTON.
Irish Saints, Lives of the. O'HANLON.
Ital. Congregatio. A. R. P. EUSEBIO, C.D.
Jacobite War in Ireland. O'KELLY.
John of Jesus Mary, O.D.C., the Ven. Opera. (1771.)
John of the Cross (St.), Life and Works. D. LEWIS.
Leaders of Public Opinion in Ireland. LECKY.
Lives of the Saints. BUTLER.
Ménologe du Carmel. R. P. FERDINAND, C.D.
Monasticon Hibernicum. ARCHDALL.
Mores Catholici. DIGBY.

WORKS OF REFERENCE.

Newman's, Cardinal, Apologia and other Works.
O'Connell, Life of. FITZPATRICK.
——. DAUNT O'NEIL.
—— *Last Days of.* M'CABE.
—— *Life.* O'ROURKE.
——. FLANNIGAN'S.
—— *Centenary Record of.*
Papers, State.
Parliament, The Patriotic, of 1782.
Parliamentary, Irish, Reports, 1782-1800.
Patrick, St., Life of.
—— *Confession.*
Privilegia Fratrum Carmelit. Discalceat.
Recueil d'Instructions sur la devotion au St. Scapulaire de Notre-Dame du Mont-Carmel. R. P. BROCARD, C.D.
Regula Primitiva Carmelit.
Salmanticenses: Opera Theologica.
Secret Service under Pitt. FITZPATRICK.
Speculum Carmelitanum. FATHER DANIEL OF THE VIRGIN MARY.
Spicilegium Ossoriense. MORAN.
Succession, La, du St. Prophète Élie en l'Ordre des Carmes. R. P. LOUIS, C.D.
Teresa, St., Life of. D. LEWIS.
—— *Works of.* (Barcelona, 1887.)
Theologia Mystica. P. PHILIPPUS À STA. TRINITATE.
Thomas of Jesus, the Ven. Opera.
United Irishmen, History of the. MADDEN.
Viceroys of Ireland. GILBERT.
Vinea Carmeli. FATHER DANIEL OF THE VIRGIN MARY.
Ware's Bishops. HARRIS.

CARMEL IN IRELAND.

CHAPTER I.

INTRODUCTORY: THE REFORM OF CARMEL.

The Prophet Elias the Founder of the Carmelite Order—His spirit of zeal and prayer—The first written Rule—Carmel in Europe—How the Primitive Rule came to be mitigated—THE TERESIAN REFORM—St. John of the Cross and the first Discalced Carmelites—The Teresian Friars as missioners.

SAINT TERESA tells us that her own success in restoring the Primitive Rule among the Carmelite Friars was largely due to the edification which a holy and learned priest had derived from the perusal of the History of the Order. Having himself become a Discalced Carmelite, Father Jerome Gratian gave her much assistance in forwarding the object which she had at heart. While still a secular priest, he had devoted nearly all his leisure to the study of the Annals of the Church's most ancient Order. He had taken a deep interest in everything that related to the "Glory of Carmel"; it was his delight to be able to trace back the origin of this Order to a period little over a century less remote than that to which some historians attribute

A

the coming of the Milesians to Ireland; for the Prophet Elias was the Founder of the Carmelites.

About nine hundred years before the Birth of Christ, that "Man of God" dwelt on the mountain in Palestine from which his followers derive their name.[1] He was already practising—by vow according to many theologians—the virtues which are of Divine counsel in the Gospel of Christianity.[2] And he required *Obedience, Chastity,* and *Poverty* to be observed by those who had placed themselves under his spiritual care. Elias was pre-eminently a man of prayer and zeal. The time not spent in the discharge of the duty of his inspired mission was passed in solitary retreat, his soul in closest union with God. His disciples were taught to cultivate that self-same spirit; and he spoke freely to them of what had been revealed to him concerning the Mystery of the Incarnation. He encouraged them to have great confidence in the Mother of their Messiah; for he had seen her, in vision, rising like a cloud above the sea. Having built an oratory in her honour on the mountain-side, he used to assemble them there in order that they might meditate with him on the dignity and privileges of the future Mother of God.[3]

Such was the beginning of that special Devotion which the Carmelites have ever had towards the Patroness of their Order. From the very first ages of Christianity they were known as the "BROTHERS OF THE BLESSED VIRGIN."[4]

[1] *Vinea Carmeli.*
[2] *Thomas a Jesu Maria.*
[3] *Speculum Carmeli.*
[4] *Brev. Rom. Carmel. Excal.*

Controversies have arisen as to the authenticity of these assertions; but the Church herself deems the truth of them well established; and among the Statues of the Patrons of Religious Orders in the Vatican is one representing: "THE PROPHET, ST. ELIAS, FOUNDER OF THE ORDER OF CARMELITES."

Likely the great Thesbite's name will merely recall the scriptural account of his marvellous career. Yet many thousands of God's servants now assisting at the Altar of the New Law are recognised as the "SONS OF THE PROPHET," and daily invoke Elias's intercession in order that they, likewise, in their own generation, may advance "The Glory of the Lord of Hosts" by a spirit of prayerful zeal.[1]

The successors of the Prophets, who lived as hermits on Mount Carmel at the time of our Saviour's earthly mission, were converted to Christianity by St. Luke. The Evangelist assured them that Jesus of Nazareth was the Christ; that their mode of life was sanctioned under His Law. Receiving the "good news" with joy they were baptized. Afterwards, according to the tradition,[2] they heard the history of the Lord's Passion from the lips of the Mother of Sorrows, who dwelt near Mount Carmel some years before the Assumption. Continuing to follow faithfully in the footsteps of their holy predecessors, they observed the means that lead to evangelical perfection. A few centuries later on, they received their first Rule, written in Greek, from John, Patriarch of Jerusalem (A.D. 412);

---

[1] *Bullarium Carmelit.*   [2] *Vinea Carmeli.*

but it contained little more than the pious traditions handed down to them from the days of the Prophet Elias. And though somewhat similar to that obeyed in the monasteries established by St. Basil, its chief ordinances were directed to the formation of the spirit characteristic of the Carmelites ; and were to be found in no other code of Monasticism, whether in the East or in the West.[1] From that time the Religious dwelt in monasteries for the most part, their mode of life having received canonical approbation ; but the fact of their being regarded as *Monks* by the Church did not prevent many Carmelites throughout Palestine living as *Hermits* when called to the eremitical state. When, however, in the year 1207, St. Brocard obtained from the Blessed Albert a Latin compendium of the original Rule, it became obligatory on all the Religious of Mount Carmel to live in community.[2] Sometime after the first colony of Carmelites had come to Europe, the sixth Prior-General of the Order, St. Simon Stock, besought Pope Innocent IV. to make certain modifications in this compendium, and confirm it anew. The Pontiff did so, granting, moreover, to the Order of the Blessed Virgin all the privileges enjoyed by Mendicant Friars. Hence, even in modern history the Carmelites are alluded to more generally as Friars, but often as Monks, and even as Hermits occasionally.

It was St. Simon Stock's predecessor, the Blessed Alan, who permitted the Religious to

[1] *Thomas of Jesus Mary.*   [2] *Regula Primitiva.*

establish their Order in Europe; but as early as the year 1150 a Latin Prior-General had been elected: St. Berthold, who accompanied Godfrey de Bouillon on the first crusade, and eventually joined the hermits on Mount Carmel. In fact, Alan was compelled to withdraw most of his subjects from the East, in order to shield them from the fury of the Saracens, who were then in possession of the Holy Land (A.D. 1244).[1] It would seem that the Infidels had become childishly jealous of the Monks of Carmel for wearing a white mantle like the one which they considered distinctive of their own knights. And during the frequent persecutions in the East that mantle was dyed crimson in the blood of countless Carmelite martyrs. But it must not be thought that no missioners from Carmel had come to the West before the time of the Blessed Alan. We shall see that St. Patrick himself bore testimony to their zeal at the beginning of his own Apostolate in Ireland.[2]

The Rule, as approved of by Pope Innocent IV., was fervently observed throughout the Order until about the year 1431. Then, at the instance of Father John Faccus, the twentieth Prior-General, Pope Eugene IV. granted a mitigation in some of the austerities prescribed. This was owing to the fact of a number of Bishops having been anxious to bring the Carmelites into their dioceses; but were afraid lest the onerous duties to be entrusted to the Friars would prove too great a strain on Religious leading so mortified a life. Accordingly,

[1] *Ménologe du Carmel.*   [2] *Speculum Carmeli.*

Pope Eugene modified certain chapters of the Rule so that the Carmelites might be able to comply with the wishes of those Prelates. This action of the Sovereign Pontiff has often been sadly misunderstood. It was not called for by reason of any relaxation existing in the Order of Carmel; neither could it be an obstacle to the Religious in acquiring the spirit of their vocation as defined by the Primitive Rule. Furthermore, the Mitigation meant very little in itself, so far as lowering the standard of austerity was concerned; merely permission to use flesh-meat a few days in the week; a partial dispensation with regard to the fast that extends from the Exaltation of the Holy Cross (14th September) to Easter; and a less strict observance of silence within the cloister. Nor was it possible that these concessions could ever interfere with the exercise of true Carmelite zeal. In the beginning no one was compelled to accept, individually, the dispensations thus granted to all. And after a while great numbers of the Friars gladly embraced the reform introduced into the Order by the Blessed John Soreth, who became Prior-General of the Carmelites in the year 1451.[1] However, Divine Providence had predestined a weak woman to restore Carmel to its former fervour; as if to show the world clearly that far from impeding a work undertaken for God's greater glory, rigorous penances help to forward it all the more. That woman was TERESA OF JESUS, a Spanish Carmelite nun.

[1] *Ménologe du Carmel.*

The world has not been slow to applaud the success of this Saint's extraordinary labours; although her admirers outside the Catholic Church fail to realise what her spirit must needs have been. They attribute everything to natural qualities, judging Teresa wholly apart from God. They say very beautiful things about her influence on the age in which she lived; but never allude to the only source of that power which her resolution to observe the Primitive Rule had enabled her to wield; they overlook a truth which was constantly before the Saint's own mind from beginning to end of her grand career. "God suffices for all things; in working for Him alone not even the weakest strive in vain."

The daughter of Don Alphonso Sanchez de Cepeda, a nobleman of Avila in old Castile, Teresa had found a great attraction in the Carmelite Convent of her native city; and so desired to become a nun there when she felt herself called to the cloister.[1] She was then in her eighteenth year, having been born on the 15th March 1515. Her father at first opposed her design; neither was she herself anxious to leave the world. For the world seemed very bright to one who had everything in her favour to win its homage—station, wealth, and beauty. But she dared not resist the vocation-grace, and her sacrifice was all the more pleasing to Him Who had called her, because of her cheerful willingness when she found it so hard to obey. She left her father's

[1] *Life of St. Teresa: Written by Herself*, chap. iv.

house secretly one day; when he discovered her retreat, she was already a Carmelite postulant. Don Cepeda was himself a hidden Saint; he clearly understood the nature of his child's longing, and at once gave the needful consent in order that she might enjoy a peace that *must* be secured at any cost: the human heart having been created for such real happiness alone in time, and in eternity. And from the moment Teresa was clothed in the brown habit of the Carmelites until it became her shroud after nearly fifty years, she enjoyed that calm of spirit, despite all the struggles and trials, disappointments and afflictions which she was required to bear.

It is when convinced that this effect does surely result from the soul's union with God, we can best understand how St. Teresa could perfect a work, presupposing a zeal as enduring as that of the Prophet Elias. Indeed that self-same peace affords the simplest explanation of the wonders of her sanctity. Here, we may not allude to her visions and raptures and ecstasies, which only the pen of the Church's "Seraphic Doctor"—such the title given to St. Teresa on account of her Treatises on Mysticism—could worthily expound; but a knowledge of these extraordinary favours is by no means necessary to determine what her true spirit must have been. She herself attributes all to prayer; such prayer as any one might practise; because in her own case, at all events, it meant nothing more than persevering conformity to her Divine Master's Will. This is the reason which she would give for her life's success; and volumes might be written on the subject of the soul's progress heavenward, yet contain no safer principle for guidance in the spiritual way.[1] But St. Teresa's spirit was entirely opposed to that mere passive sentiment which modern Mystics (of the non-Catholic school) are wont to exalt; which is, in reality, nothing better than a sinful repugnance to contend, in Christian warfare, with the trials of daily life: a self-complacency in the consciousness of avoiding evil; as if there were no law relative to the doing of good. *Her* prayer enabled her to make that heroic Vow whereby she held herself solemnly bound before Heaven to choose always, under the direction of her superiors, whatsoever should seem to her the most perfect means of advancing God's Glory on earth.

Hence, knowing that the duty of one's particular state has first claim on obedience, she frequently declared that she would rather die a thousand deaths than willingly grow remiss in trying to acquire the object of her vocation. Her fervour regarding "*the little things*" was the beginning of her holy ambition to attempt greater, which her beautiful humility always caused to appear very small. So dear did she become to her Divine Master by being thus zealous in His service, that He permitted her unceasing occasion of advancing in His Love. Each new trial—it was by trials God drew Teresa to Him—was borne still more patiently than the last: "*to suffer or to die*" was

---

[1] *Relations*, i. par. 17.

her constant prayer, lest she should be forsaken, after all, in the end. But long before her death she received the Divine assurance that nothing thenceforth could separate her from Him to Whom she had ever given her heart's first place.

It is said that her death,[1] which occurred in October of the year 1582, was due rather to the physical effects of the Divine Charity in her soul than to any other cause. And among the very Seraphim she has received the meet reward of works achieved by her spirit of humble prayer.

Perhaps, the world would consider this the least satisfactory way of accounting for the success of St. Teresa's great enterprise; for the influence which she continues to exercise in the Church after more than three hundred years. But we hold that it was sufficient to have enabled her to rear even the splendid structure of the Reform of Carmel; St. Teresa's weakness, as a woman without human help or encouragement, being our argument for asserting that only her spirit of prayer could have prevented her undertaking so grand a labour in vain. Amid the difficulties that beset her, she never once lost hope. Having begun the work in God's Name, and seeking His Glory only, to Him she looked for the needful aid. She did not know how that assistance should come; nor did she grow weary awaiting the Divine good pleasure for years and years.

Meanwhile, she availed herself of a clause in the Decree of Mitigation, permitting her to live

[1] *Brev. Rom. Carmel.*

according to the Primitive Carmelite Rule. Her superiors did not interfere; her prudence, submission, and piety being well known; although her delicate state of health had often caused them serious alarm. Learned theologians were consulted, however, and they said that evidently Teresa was but humbly obeying the manifest Will of God. It was only when other holy nuns of the same community aspired to emulate her example that *people began to talk*. Unjust suspicions and cruel sayings were the beginning of a series of trials, which soon developed into a veritable persecution. The world outside the cloister was shocked. It was said that Teresa's spirit of perseverance was merely obstinate self-will. A practical knowledge of Christian self-sacrifice was needful to realise the object of her ambition in its true light; to appreciate the end of which *she* never lost view. Besides, Teresa was *sure* of herself; Grace was then not less efficacious than before her Divine Master's Advent, for which the children of Carmel had been preparing by that austere mode of life so conducive to zeal in His service, and to prayer. So she did not worry over the obstacles raised to hinder her project; while the evil things said about herself and her companions inspired them with neither fear nor shame: as is the way of the Saints, they had already formed a far worse opinion of themselves. And at length the world grew tired of assailing those defenceless nuns.[1]

[1] *Book of Foundations.*

When the crisis was reached, the Saint appealed to Rome; and her cause was warmly advocated by some of the most influential Prelates attending the Papal Court. The Sovereign Pontiff himself—St. Pius V.—was most favourably impressed; with the result that, in the year 1562, Teresa was enabled to found a convent in the city of Avila for those Sisters who, like herself, desired to renew their vows according to the Holy Rule which Pope Innocent IV. had approved for the Carmelites at the prayer of St. Simon Stock.

The world was wrong, once more; experience showed that that Rule was quite as suitable for St. Teresa's time as it had been in the past, and should be for every succeeding age. The number of vocations increased daily; and instead of having to exhort her spiritual children to fervour in the observance of that austere Rule, Teresa found herself constrained by prudence to moderate the longing of her novices for greater mortification. Her enemies deemed this fanaticism; her eventual success proved that the work was prospering under guidance of wisdom given her from above; and they became silently ashamed.

Thus far the Reform of Carmel was certainly assured, St. Teresa regarding the trials, which she had still to bear, as a guarantee of its future welfare. Yet she felt that her work would not be complete until the Primitive Rule was again observed by the Friars of Carmel—heirs to the Thesbite's zeal. She was wondering how God would deign to provide for His own Glory in this respect, when she heard of a young Carmelite Friar, who had been long following the Primitive Rule in secrecy, and was then about to embrace a still more austere mode of life. St. Teresa sent for him, and immediately recognised him as a Saint. She told him all about the Reform established in the convent which had just been founded by herself for nuns. What if he should try to introduce the same among the Friars? Father John of St. Mathias—such was the name that priest then bore; afterwards he became known as JOHN OF THE CROSS—believed God willed him to make the effort; but he could give no definite promise before he had sought counsel from the Most High in prayer. For the rest, he would leave himself absolutely in St. Teresa's hands. Now, she was well aware of his reputation among his brethren for learning and virtue; still she made no comment on such an expression of confidence in her own judgment; she went straightway to the oratory to return thanks, sure that Carmel would be restored to its pristine splendour. Thenceforth she spoke of that humble Friar as a Great Saint, whom it was a special privilege to know. Fra John's request was heard; it was revealed to him that the Teresian Reform was most pleasing in God's sight; and that in embracing it he himself could speedily attain the object of his own ambition: "*To suffer and be despised.*"

He was much consoled by this manifestation of the Divine Will in his regard; for it had sorely grieved him to think that he might be compelled to leave the Order of the Blessed Virgin in aspiring to the higher perfection to which he knew he was called. That would have been a bitter trial indeed, his love for the Queen of Carmel being so great. From his very childhood she had watched over him, coming to his aid visibly in the time of danger. And in gratitude he had devoted himself to her even when quite a child.[1] He was in the twenty-first year of his age when he at length joined, the Carmelites in the city of Medina del Campo, being already well known there for virtues which it was impossible for him to conceal.

Unlike the young Teresa de Cepeda, Juan de Yepes had none of those flattering prospects, so highly prized by the world, at the outset of his career. His parents were exceedingly poor; but he, their youngest child, early realised the true sense of the evangelical counsels which render self-renunciation so meritorious before God. However, he was richly endowed with the gifts both of nature and of Grace; so much so that he was only in his twenty-fifth year—having been born at Hontiveros, in the diocese of Avila, in the year 1542—when his fame reached St. Teresa. Although recently ordained a priest, his success in the schools had attracted the notice of his contemporaries. And now, having determined to follow St. Teresa's advice, he did not hesitate a moment in joyfully taking up the heavy cross which he had to bear until the year 1593, when he died.

[1] *Life and Works*, vol. i.

Had we only the *Life of St. Teresa* to follow in considering the "Reform of Carmel," probably we should think that her sufferings were the very severest test of human endurance in the Service Divine. But the part which ST. JOHN OF THE CROSS has taken in that glorious project shows with what loving solicitude God proportions the burden of trials to the circumstances of each one's state.

The threats used by the enemies of the Reform to terrify St. Teresa and her nuns were ruthlessly carried out in the case of St. John of the Cross. He a saint! There was ample evidence to prove him a hardened sinner. As such, at all events, he was visited with the harsh penalties which were customary during that age. This persecution included long imprisonment, together with other cruelties very painful to recall.

The first Foundation for the Teresian Friars was in a little cottage at Duruelo, a country place not far from Avila. It was poor in the extreme, consisting of a porch, which the Religious converted into an oratory; a garret, which they used as a choir; *one* room, which they divided into cells; and another very small apartment, out of which were improvised the refectory and the kitchen. But its poverty-stricken appearance and miserable accommodation enhanced the value of this house in the eyes of St. John of the Cross and the two other Friars of the Mitigation, who had come to dwell there by the permission of the General of the Carmelites, the Father-Provincial, and the Bishop of Avila; the Foundation having been cànonically made. The Friars were permitted to renew their vows according to the Primitive Rule; this they did on the morning of the First Sunday of Advent in the year 1568. They were allowed, moreover, to frame Constitutions which would enable them to observe the Holy Rule most strictly, and which form the basis of those followed by the Discalced Carmelites at the present day. Seemingly this was a very happy epoch in the early history of the Teresian Reform; though the privations then endured by the Religious were truly terrible: often after reciting the midnight office at Duruelo Fra John and his companions found their habits covered with snow; the glow of Divine Love in their souls rendered them insensible to the cold. No sooner did they commence to receive novices in that humble retreat than their trials began; every motive save the true one, which God saw, was attributed to St. John of the Cross; and those who were suspicious of the Teresian Reform hurried him on in the Footsteps of the Crucified. He never complained to the Saint herself when injury after injury was heaped upon him for his share in the work which she had begun; Teresa, however, was well aware of the persecution raised against him, but she could only pray. Still, as often as they had occasion to meet during those trying times, they had nothing to say of their mutual sufferings; for them the Cross was the clearest sign of the mercy and favour of God.

Rome spoke again, and now more decisively: the Reform of Carmel was for the edification of the Church. The first Province of the Discalced Carmelites—so called, because they wore sandals instead of boots, like the Fathers of the Mitigation—was established in Spain in 1580 by a Brief of Pope Gregory XIII. New Foundations had, apparently, multiplied by miracle, and it was necessary that those who made profession of the Teresian Reform should be under the immediate jurisdiction of a Provincial of their own. A few years after St. Teresa's death, Pope Sixtus V. sanctioned the election of a Vicar-General; the Congregation of Discalced Carmelites was then formally instituted; the Teresian monasteries already founded in Spain and elsewhere being divided into six full Provinces. From this time (A.D. 1587) it may be said that the two branches of the Vine of Carmel became quite distinct, one from the other: separate in all things pertaining to the exercise of the jurisdiction of the respective Superiors-General; yet as closely united as ever by that bond of fraternal Charity, in virtue of which both the Religious of the Mitigation and the Friars of the Reform are recognised as the "Sons of the Prophet," observing the Rule of Carmel with equal fervour, whether as restored by Teresa of Jesus, or mitigated by Pope Eugene. Indeed from the very beginning the Calced Fathers, generally, were themselves highly edified by St. Teresa's wonderful victory, knowing that her success could only redound to the greater splendour of Our Lady's Ancient Order.

Most of the features of regular observance,

whereby the Teresian Friars are distinguished from their Brethren of the Mitigation, arise from special statutes in the Constitutions of the Discalced Carmelites. As has been said, the dispensations granted by Pope Eugene were by no means a relaxation of claustral discipline; merely the moderating of certain austerities, still leaving the Rule exceedingly severe. This becomes more manifest from the well-known fact that both St. Teresa and St. John of the Cross could perfectly conform to the Primitive Rule without attracting very particular attention while living among the Religious of the Mitigation. There is one striking point of difference, however: the Calced Carmelites still retain the "*Ancient Rite*" in celebrating the Holy Sacrifice; but it was St. Teresa's wish that the Fathers of the Reform should adopt that of Rome.

Another earnest desire of our Saint was that the Religious should cultivate a great spirit of zeal for the Missions. At first there were certain difficulties with regard to the means of carrying out her most charitable purpose. Thus, for various reasons it was found expedient, in the year 1605, to form a Congregation of Discalced Carmelites, whose members would be bound "to go on the Mission for the conversion of Pagans or Heretics, wherever and whenever holy obedience should so enjoin." This was called the Italian Congregation of St. Elias, the first Prior-General being Father Ferdinand of St. Mary, who had the happiness of knowing St. John of the Cross intimately; and who had seen and spoken to St. Teresa. It would seem that the great ambition of Father Ferdinand's early life had been to meet the Seraphic Mother. Yet as often as the opportunity did occur, in order to mortify himself he never once raised his eyes.[1] The Superior-General of the Congregation of St. Elias was to reside in Rome with his four assistants, or Definitors-General, and was to have no jurisdiction over the Discalced Carmelites of the "Spanish Congregation." But the difficulties that occasioned this arrangement ceased in time, and all Teresian Friars are now subject to the same Father-General. It was to define more particularly the scope of the present work that reference has been made to this subject. For we have merely undertaken to give a historical review of the progress of one of the most successful colonies of Discalced Carmelite Missioners of the Italian Congregation.

A Teresian Friar must be wary lest his own enthusiasm should hinder him in the performance of this task. But the author feels he need not fear.[2] While the Church has constantly testified to the indebtedness of Christendom to the zeal of the children of Carmel, who call St. Teresa "MOTHER," the learned of every age speak of the Discalced Carmelite philosophers and theologians in terms of highest praise; even the sons of St. Dominic regard them as being the most faithful interpreters of the mind of the Angel of the Schools.[3]

[1] *Ménologe du Carmel.*   [2] *Bullarium Carmelitanum.*
[3] *De Graveson.*

Hence our object is simply to show what part the Religious of the Irish Province have taken in the propagation of the Teresian Reform, first introduced into this country nearly three hundred years ago. Neither will the Annals of this Province lose in interest because frequently identified with the History of Ireland.

But long before the Mitigation, sanctioned by Pope Eugene, was introduced into the Order of Carmel, many monasteries had been founded in this country for the "WHITE FRIARS," who lived according to the Rule compiled by St. Albert, and confirmed by Pope Innocent IV. And it was *after* the suppression of these houses that the Teresian Reform was first canonically approved. Hence we might not well begin to treat of the revival of the Primitive Observance in Ireland without paying a tribute (of reverent notice at least) to the memory of the predecessors of the IRISH DISCALCED CARMELITES.

CHAPTER II.

CARMEL IN IRELAND BEFORE THE TERESIAN REFORM.

St. Palladius and his companions—St. Patrick's devotion to the Prophet Elias—Early Irish Monasticism—Irish Carmelites of the thirteenth century—The monasteries founded in Ireland—Piety and generosity of the Founders—Distinguished members of the Order—Suppression of the abbeys during the reign of Henry VIII.—How the Faith was preserved among the Irish people—The first Penal Days.

WHEN St. Celestine was Pope, there came to Rome several Carmelite Monks from the Monastery of St. Anne's, near Jerusalem.[1] Their leader was called Palladius, a Briton by birth. He had been some years at St. Anne's, advancing rapidly in the way of Perfection, when he felt himself inspired to labour for the salvation of souls: this zeal was the fruit of his previous life of prayer. Submitting the matter to the holy Religious, who was Superior of the monastery, Palladius was advised to consult the Sovereign Pontiff himself, and abide by his decision. St. Celestine received the Monk's proposal with warm approbation ; and, after some time, consecrated him Bishop, and sent

[1] *Historia Generalis Ord. Carmel. Vinea Carmeli.*

him, together with the other Carmelites from St. Anne's, to preach the Gospel in the Western Isles.

The Missioners reached Ireland about the year 431, having endured many hardships during their long and perilous voyage. It would seem that the Irish people readily understood the object of these strangers in visiting their country; by reason of their commercial relations with foreigners, they had already heard of the Christian religion. Many conversions were made in a very short time, and even a few churches were built. But soon the Pagan priests became jealous of St. Palladius and his companions; and finally succeeded in having the holy Bishop driven from Ireland.[1] However, a number of the Saint's disciples still remained here, although they had to hide themselves in the wilderness owing to the persecution raised against them by the yet powerful Druids. St. Palladius, with some others, found a refuge among the Christians of Scotland; and there he died before the close of the year (A.D. 432).

Under direction of those fugitive Monks the practice of Asceticism was inaugurated among the Faithful of Ireland according to the method observed by the Carmelites in the East. And in the *Life of St. Patrick* it is recorded that, before his coming to evangelise the Irish nation, there were Christians who had already arrived at an eminent degree of sanctity.[2] He himself had a particular

[1] *Eccles. Hist. of Ireland* (Walsh).
[2] *Life of St. Patrick.*

devotion to the Prophet of Carmel. In his *Confessions* allusion is made to one occasion especially when he had recourse to St. Elias, who at once came to his assistance, and consoled him after he had been most violently assaulted by Satan.[1]

After this, it is not surprising that there should be evidence of that spirit of prayerful zeal, characteristic of the Carmelites, in the lives of the Saints of the early Irish Church. They acquired it, we are told, by the practice of austerities which have obtained for them throughout the whole Catholic world a name for Christian mortification not less renowned than that which has given such glory to the *THEBAID*. Virtue of this kind being the basis of true wisdom, the fame of Ireland's schools became equally wide-spread, as a matter of course. And as heretofore in the East, so now in the West, the severest mode of life followed by men, was not too harsh to be embraced by Irishwomen of every rank and age. An angel had to be sent from heaven to tell St. Ita, of the Decies, that pleasing as her spirit of penance was in the sight of God, He willed her to moderate the rigour of her mortifications (A.D. 570).[2]

Such being the traditions handed down in the Irish Church, generation after generation, it is easy to realise how eagerly the Faithful welcomed the Carmelite Friars to Ireland in the thirteenth century, a short time before the death of St. Simon

---

[1] *Speculum Carmel.*
[2] *Eccl. Hist. of Ireland* (Lanigan's).

Stock.[1] Monasteries were rapidly founded for them all over the country; and the life led therein seems to have had a very great charm for young Irishmen, whether of humble or of noble birth. As if jealous of the vocation-grace, the pious laity hastened to join the Confraternity of the Brown Scapular, in order to identify themselves with those Religious whose mode of life was so like that led by the Monks of old, when Ireland was known as "THE ISLAND OF SAINTS." Within the halls of those monasteries, when the Carmelite doctors were imparting knowledge to their eager scholars, care was taken to show how impossible it is to be learned and not holy. And in after life their disciples found themselves always influenced for the better by the practical lessons received while inmates of the cloisters of Carmel.

Neither did talents, which had been consecrated to God by the monastic vows, escape the notice of those responsible for the welfare of Church and State. The Friars were forced to leave their beloved Retreats, to take upon them the burden of the Episcopate, or the care of the Nation's affairs. Happily for us that it was so. Otherwise, we might search in vain for information regarding the ancient history of the Carmelites in Ireland; so complete was the destruction of the archives of the various communities at "the thorough uprooting" of Irish monasteries during the reign of

---

[1] A.D. 1260. But the Province was not established until A.D. 1303 (*Bullarium Carmelitanum*, vol. iv. p. 266. *Vide* note *infra*).

Henry VIII. But now the Annals of the Nation contain some of the names of the White Friars who occupied positions of highest dignity and trust.[1]

Among the Archbishops of Cashel we find mention made of a certain RALPH KELLY, a native of Drogheda, one of the Carmelites of the Abbey of Kildare. He had been educated in that famous friary and received the religious habit there at a very early age. He was Consultor-General of his Order in the year 1336; nine years later he was appointed to the See of Cashel by Pope Clement VI. We are told that he became a zealous and fearless Prelate, having only the interests of Religion at heart. He even rebuked the King, Edward III., for having dared to trespass on the privileges of the Episcopate; nor would he yield his own rights, or those of his people, although he had to suffer much in consequence of his heroic determination. This holy Prelate was the author of many treatises on Divinity and Canon Law; and remained a Monk, in spirit, to the end of his career (A.D. 1361).

DAVID O'BUGEY was another distinguished Friar of the Abbey of Kildare. He is called in history, "THE LIGHT AND GLORY OF IRELAND." Frequently elected to the most important offices of his Order, he discharged them with the utmost prudence and zeal. But he declined the ecclesiastical honours and State dignities offered him repeatedly by

[1] Compare *Walsh, Dalton, and Ware, treating of the Irish Episcopate.*

the successive Popes and Kings. However, his counsel was at the disposal of all seeking it; even the Government used to decide (most happily for the welfare of the people) matters of vital importance according to his advice. He flourished and died in the fourteenth century; but beyond constant allusion to his name, in terms of highest admiration, we are given no further particulars of his life.

Carmelites of the English Province were, also, called to fill vacant episcopal Sees in Ireland.

There was a Father WILLIAM DE PAUL, whom Pope John XXII. nominated to the Bishopric of Meath in the year 1327. A Religious of great fervour, he had taken his doctor's degree both at Oxford and Paris; and in the General Chapter held at Genoa (A.D. 1324) he had been elected Superior of the Carmelite Provinces of England and Scotland. He continued Bishop of Meath until his death in 1349.

King Richard II. having a very great opinion of Father RICHARD NORTHALIS, a Friar of the Carmelite Monastery of London (of which city Northalis's father was Lord Mayor), warmly recommended him to the Pope for appointment to the See of Ossory (A.D. 1386). The King's request was immediately granted, the merits of this Friar being well known in Rome, whither he had been sent on several occasions, as ambassador, during the pontificate of Pope Boniface IX. In the course of time he was translated to the Archdiocese of Dublin (A.D. 1396), and before his death (A.D. 1397) he became Lord

Chancellor of Ireland. His remains were interred in the cathedral of the metropolis, wherein he was long remembered as a great preacher, a most holy and learned clerk, and a prudent statesman. His successor was also a Carmelite, named THOMAS CRANLEY, who, previous to his coming to Dublin to take possession of that See in the year 1398, had been Chancellor of the University of Oxford. By all accounts he was a most popular Prelate: "fond of alms-deeds"; an excellent orator; a profound divine; and a "great builder," invariably improving the churches and other edifices placed under his care. He likewise filled the office of Chancellor of Ireland, and Lord Chief Justice (such duties being not unfrequently discharged by ecclesiastics at that time). It seems that he returned to England a few years before his death, which occurred at Farrington on the 25th May 1414. His body was removed to Oxford, and interred there in New College, of which he himself had been first warden.

In the year 1397 the See of Ossory was again governed by a Carmelite Bishop. This was THOMAS PIEREVILL, a member of a noble English family. He had been raised to the doctorate at the University of Oxford. Having spent some time in the diocese of Ossory, he was translated to Wales; and eventually to the See of Worcester. He had a great reputation for sanctity; the various dioceses over which he ruled successively being deeply indebted to his wise administration. He died at Oxford, probably, for he was buried in the

Church of the Carmelites, which then stood quite close to the University (A.D. 1418).

While thus briefly referring to those distinguished Carmelites, whose names are to be met with in Irish history, we are reminded that they did not hold themselves exempt from the observance of the Primitive Rule by reason of their exalted rank. On the contrary, they were among the humblest members of the Order of Carmel, which, by that time, had prospered in a wonderful way throughout the world. There were as many as *seven thousand monasteries* then in existence, the homes of at least *one hundred and eighty thousand* Religious ![1]

With regard to the Carmelite Abbeys founded in Ireland, we can only touch on the interesting history of those best known at the present day. Some writers state that there were originally twenty-five, others thirty-two.[2] Likely the former do not take into account the "CARMELITE CELLS," which were the small friaries dependent on one of the greater monasteries, and which may have served the purpose of "deserts" wherein the Religious could live yet further removed from the world. Such was the "cell" founded on Clare Island, Co. Mayo, by the O'Malleys, the ancestors of the celebrated Grace, or Granu - Weal ("Graine - ni - Mhaile ").[3] This foundation, like

[1] *Ménologe du Carmel.* [2] *Bullar. Carmel*, vol. iv. p. 266.
[3] A.D. 1224 is the date assigned for the foundation of this "cell." There may certainly have been Carmelites in Ireland at this time; but we are of opinion that no Community was canonically established before 1260. Vide *infra*.

most of the other Carmelite Monasteries, was dedicated to the Blessed Virgin.[1] In the course of time it became annexed to the Cistercian Abbey of Knockmoy, Co. Galway; for what reason it is impossible to tell. There was also an abbey for "WHITE FRIARS" at Borniscarra, Co. Mayo, of which few authors speak.[2] It passed into the possession of the Hermits of St. Augustine about the year 1412, Pope John XXIII. permitting this transfer to be made.

In a document written by the Mitigated Carmelites of Ireland in 1645, a list of the old abbeys is given; but we do not consider it complete.[3] The more satisfactory information to be had on this subject shows that there were Carmelite Monasteries at *Rathmullen, Co. Donegal; at Ardee, Athboy, Drogheda, Dublin, Kildare, Cloncurry, Ardnacrana, Frankford, Knocktopher, Little-Horton, and Leighlin-Bridge; at Ballywilliam, Ballingall, Castlelyons, Cork, Kinsale, and Thurles; and at Ballynahinch, Ballinismale, Crevebane, Knockmore, Galway, Loughrea, and Pallice*: in all *twenty-five,* the number on which most historians are inclined to agree.

The Abbey of RATHMULLEN was founded, probably, early in the fourteenth century by the MacSweeny Fannid, and placed under the invocation of St. Mary. It was built on a most picturesque site overlooking Lough Swilly — famous in Irish history.for its association with the episode

[1] De Burgo. [2] Walsh.
[3] *Spicilegium Ossoriense*, vol. i. p. 295.

which is more generally known as "*The Flight of the Earls*" (A.D. 1607). The ruins of the ancient church are still in a fairly good state of preservation, and contain some very fine specimens of the pointed style of Gothic architecture.[1] But not even an ivy-covered crumbling wall remains to indicate where the friary once stood. However, the Monastery of Rathmullen must have been built according to the plan adopted without exception (apparently) by the Irish Carmelites in founding their houses; so that it is easy to fancy a group of austere buildings rising beside the now ruined sacred edifice, and forming a quadrangle within which was the hallowed cloister. Main corridors led to the church and choirs; the proportions of the usual monastic offices — the library, refectory, dormitory (comprising the cells of the Religious), reception rooms, and hall — being limited to the requirements of each particular abbey.

Ralph Pippard endowed a house for White Friars at ARDEE, Co. Louth, in the reign of Edward I. The church of this monastery — crowded, alas, with men and helpless women and children — was burned down by the soldiers of Robert Bruce in 1315. But it was soon restored by the Faithful, and five years later a Provincial Visitation was held there by Father John Sugdæus; in 1489 a like canonical function again took place. A Synod was convoked in the hall of this abbey by Octavian de Palatio, Archbishop

---

[1] Compare *Lewis's Topog. Dict.* and the *Monast. Hiber.*

of Armagh, when the "Plague" was raging in Drogheda (A.D. 1504). The last of the Priors was a Father Patrick, whose office ceased at the suppression of Religious houses throughout Ireland in the year 1537.

Frequent reference is made to the Carmelite Monastery of DROGHEDA.[1] Yet regarding its foundation we can only learn that, sometime during the thirteenth century, the pious citizens of the city built an abbey for White Friars on the western bank of the Boyne, and dedicated it to the Blessed Virgin.

On the 17th October 1317 the Archbishop of Dublin, William de Londres, got permission from Parliament to offer the Carmelites the site of a friary at ATHBOY, Co. Meath. A church and monastery were established in that place soon afterwards; and Friar John Boxam made a Provincial Visitation[2] there in 1325. In 1372 the Friars of this house were prosecuted for having failed to observe some legal formalities on receiving a bequest of land. Another Visitation took place in 1409; and on the 31st April in the thirty-first year of the reign of Henry VIII., the Abbey of Athboy was confiscated, and granted to Thomas Casey, who had succeeded in winning the favour of the king. Part of the ruins still remain to bear silent testimony to that act of shameless apostasy.

[1] De Burgo does not allude to it, strange to say.
[2] Or it may have been the "Provincial Chapter" for the election of Superiors.

It is said that the present church and friary of the Calced Carmelites of DUBLIN occupy the identical site of the first monastery founded here for the White Friars. The Religious were not well received by the citizens in the beginning, owing to some dispute with the municipal authorities about the plot of ground for the proposed abbey. King Edward III. insisted on the Friars being allowed their claim; but it was only by the powerful intervention of Sir Robert Baggot that they were at length enabled to make the foundation in the parish of St. Peter. And once they had begun to build this monastery, dedicating it to "St. Mary," the pious people made full reparation for whatever pain their previous opposition had caused; they now exhibited a spirit of unbounded generosity (A.D. 1274). Among the chief benefactors of this house were Kings Edward III. (A.D. 1335), Richard II. (A.D. 1394); and Henry IV. (A.D. 1400), who saw that provision was made for the maintenance of the chantry. A charitable gentleman of Dublin, named John Beck, was also a great friend of the Friars. Provincial Visitations (or Chapters) were held by Father John Sugdæus (A.D. 1320); by the renowned David O'Bugey; and in 1367 (?) by Father Robert Searle. The Irish Parliament assembled in the hall of this monastery in 1333; and immediately after one of the sessions a tragic incident occurred. Murchard, the son of Nicholas O'Tothell, when passing through the courtyard, was stabbed to death, the assassin making good his escape. The Carmelites of the Dublin community seem to have taken an active part in trying to secure a university for Ireland. Father Edmund was Prior of "St. Mary's" in 1467; his successor at the time of the "Suppression" was Father William Kelly. The church, together with the buildings and abbey lands, was given to Nicholas Stanehurst in 1543; Sir Francis Aungier was in possession of the same during part of Queen Elizabeth's reign; and in the year 1732 a theatre stood on the site of the ancient monastery.[1]

About the year 1290, Richard de Vesci endowed a House of the Order of the Blessed Virgin at KILDARE. The present Carmelite Abbey of that place has been built on the original site. Father David O'Bugey was long a member of the community of this monastery; and did much to acquire for it that fame, as a school, which it had gained all over the world. There, also, he died—"full of years and honour," as the annalists relate—his remains being interred within his beloved cloister. Another historic Convent of the Order of Carmel was at CLONCURRY, in the Co. Kildare. It was founded in 1347 by a gentleman named John Roche, who had succeeded in procuring the royal sanction to carry out his pious project. During a battle fought in the vicinity (A.D. 1405) between the Anglo-Norman and native Irish septs, this abbey was almost destroyed by fire. The injury was afterwards repaired by the people themselves, as in the case of the Carmelite Monastery of Ardee.

[1] De Burgo.

On the 18th of January 1544 it was plundered by the King, and then granted for *ever* to William Dickson, to be held by military service. But when Queen Elizabeth came into power, it passed into the hands of Richard Slane, who was to pay a nominal rent for it to the Crown. Some of the walls of the ruined church may still be seen in the graveyard at Cloncurry.

The Furlongs of Wexford were the benefactors of the Carmelite Abbey at LITTLE-HORTON, founded towards the end of the fourteenth century; it was first given to Sir John Davis at the " Suppression," and to Francis Talbot later on. About the same time Robert Dillon of Drumrane built a Carmelite Monastery at ARDNACRANNA, Co. Westmeath. The Abbey of FRANKFORD was endowed by Hugh, chief of the Sept O'Molloy, who died on the feast of St. Remigius, A.D. 1454. He himself was buried in the church of this monastery. The death of one of the Priors, Father Edward Bracken, is also recorded as having taken place in the year 1467. A certain Robert Leicester got possession of the Carmelite Abbey and lands of Frankford in the reign of Henry VIII.

Some writers think that the Abbey of the Holy Saviour at KNOCKTOPHER, Co. Kilkenny, was the *first* monastery founded in Ireland for *White Friars.* It was built by a member of the Butler family, James, second Earl of Ormond. But we have seen that many of the foundations were made in the thirteenth century, and this monastery was not established until A.D. 1356. Father Henry Brown was Prior at Knocktopher in 1396; and Father William held that office when the abbey was suppressed (A.D. 1543), the lands and buildings falling to the lot of Patrick Barnewall. Part of the tower and one of the aisles still remain.

In a charming site, on the River Barrow, stand the ruins of another Carmelite Abbey, that of LEIGHLIN-BRIDGE, Co. Carlow. It was founded by the Carew family in the reign of Henry III. After confiscation, it was transformed into a military station, and in the seventeenth century it became the centre of martial operations, when the waters, flowing beneath its walls, reflected "naught save match-locks and iron skull-caps."

Not long after the building of the monastery at Leighlin-Bridge, the Carmelites throughout Europe resumed the wearing of their beautiful white mantle, which had been interdicted to them in Palestine. In alluding to this fact, the contemporary annalist of the ancient Abbey of Osney pays a very high tribute of praise to the "WHITE FRIARS," having occasion to allude to their reputation for holiness.[1]

The "Roches" were founders of a Carmelite Friary at BALLINGALL, Co. Limerick, in the fourteenth century. Father O'Daugane was last Prior there. In 1586 it was granted to the trustees of Trinity College, Dublin. There was another House of the Order at BALLYWILLIAM, in the same county; it was built by one of the Molloys. It is certain that the Carmelites had a friary in the city of Cork also sometime in the fourteenth century; but

[1] *Annals of Osney*, A.D. 1287, vol. iv. p. 312.

nothing is known of its history. The annalists are equally silent concerning the Carmelite Abbey founded by the De Barrys at CASTLELYONS, Co. Cork. In the town of KINSALE, at the north end, may still be seen part of the ruins of a monastery endowed for White Friars by Robert FitzRichard Balrayne, A.D. 1350. It was suppressed by Henry VIII. in the thirty-fifth year of his reign.

One of the Butlers gave another abbey to Our Lady of Mount Carmel in 1300, that of THURLES, Co. Tipperary; Thomas, Earl of Ormond, deprived her of his ancestor's gift, when the monastery was confiscated during the Priorship of Father Donagh O'Howleghan. Some ruins are still there, to remind us of the generosity of the faithful and the apostate's avarice.

In the west of Ireland, the Carmelites had an abbey at BALLINISMALE, Co. Mayo, built by the Prendergast family in 1356; also at BALLYNAHINCH, Co. Galway, endowed by the O'Flahertys about the same time. The De Burgos founded a friary for the Order at CREVEBANE, Co. Galway, and one within the walls of the city itself. The former was granted to the burgesses of Athenry, probably in the reign of Queen Elizabeth, who seems to have shown some favour to that once famous town. Lord Athenry, one of the Berminghams, was the founder of a Carmelite monastery in the same county before the end of the fourteenth century: the Abbey of PALLICE, which was given to John Rawson at the "Dissolution," A.D. 1589. In the Co. Sligo there was a convent for White Friars at

KNOCKMORE, the O'Gara being its benefactor. But the most important of the foundations made in Connaught was the Abbey of LOUGHREA, Co. Galway, built by Richard de Burgo in 1300, and granted to the Earl of Clanricarde at the "Suppression." The ruins of the ancient church are well preserved; close by is the modern Friary of the DISCALCED CARMELITES, who came to replace their brethren of the Mitigation in that town by the "Gray Lake," early in the seventeenth century.

From this very brief notice on the ancient Carmelite Monasteries of Ireland, there are two facts to which the reader's attention has been especially directed: the establishment of all those houses between the beginning of the thirteenth century and the close of the fourteenth; and their *Suppression* almost immediately after the rupture of Henry VIII. with Rome. It does not come within the scope of the present work to comment on this matter further than to recall the pious memory of those who gave such practical proof of their appreciation of the influences of Monasticism during the AGES OF FAITH, and to assign the only motives which an apostate king could have had in uprooting so many centres of learning, zeal, and prayer. For there is no need to introduce a wearisome digression on the cause of that monarch's revolt against the Church, nor in vindication of the mode of life led in the cloister. In the sad instance where a *Carmelite* of one of the English Monasteries became a creature of Henry's, receiving as his reward a *Protestant*

Bishopric in Ireland, even non-Catholic writers admit that that unhappy man's fall was entirely due to his want of perseverance in the virtues practised by his brethren,[1] *fifteen hundred* of whom had already been driven from their homes by his royal patron.[2] It was the King's object to justify his own criminal conduct before his subjects by attributing his most shocking deeds to scruples of conscience. But so long as the numerous abbeys throughout his dominions contained those who would continue to teach the TRUTH fearlessly, although sure of incurring the royal wrath, it was impossible for him to deceive the mass of the people. Hence, Henry began by proclaiming the Friars traitors; they had dared to oppose his will, and now all they possessed, nay, even their very lives, became forfeit to the Crown.

Here in Ireland, when the voice of prayer was hushed in the cloisters of the various Religious Orders, the tyrant's victims raised it more loudly than ever from their hiding-places among the forests and hills. And thither the Faithful came to be instructed, as formerly, in the one way of truth. They saw those who had yielded to the temptations held out to them richly rewarded out of the lands and goods of the plundered monasteries; yet they wondered how so poor a recompence could induce even the most avaricious to barter away the priceless treasure of their faith. For the most part, the libraries and monastic

[1] Ware's *Bishops*.   [2] *Ménologe du Carmel.*

archives were then destroyed, so that the best records of the Irish Carmelites of the MITIGATION we possess are the loving traditions of their devotedness to the people throughout the many persecutions which have arisen since that terrible reign.

Meanwhile the White Friars of the TERESIAN REFORM have established themselves in the country, and henceforth we shall merely treat of what concerns "*Carmel in Ireland*" as including only the Religious who observed the Restored Primitive Rule. By their fervour in this respect alone could they be deemed the worthy successors of those who had laboured on the Irish Mission before them, whether in the fifth century or in the fourteenth.

CHAPTER III.

ADVENT OF THE DISCALCED CARMELITES.

State of Ireland when Charles I. ascended the throne—The Irish in exile—Irish subjects in Teresian Monasteries abroad—Queen Henrietta Maria and the Discalced Carmelites—Revival of hope among the Catholics of Ireland—The Teresian missioners from Louvain—A friary opened in Dublin—The authorities aroused—Father Edward of the Kings—Success of the first foundation.

FROM the passing of that Act of Parliament for the suppression of Religious Houses in Ireland, to the time of Charles I., is an eventful epoch in the history of the Irish nation. Henry VIII. had still ten years to reign; Edward VI. succeeded; then Queen Mary ascended the throne, followed by Elizabeth; afterwards King James. So tried by persecution were the Catholics during those eight-and-eighty years (A.D. 1537–1625) that the annalists grow weary of recording the injuries which the people had received. Not alone were there many trials to be borne for conscience' sake: new schemes were constantly planned for plunder, and carried out in barbarous detail. We find those schemes alluded to under various titles: *" Plantations "* and *" Transplantations "*; *" Operations "* and *" Reductions "*; *" Immigrations "* and

"*Distributions*"; all implying a series of acts of heartless injustice. Even prejudiced English historians admit that there was very great misery in Ireland while each of the four last Tudors reigned; it was impossible for the country to prosper or be at peace. But it was quite different, we are told, under the government of James I., the people being then in the enjoyment of that twofold blessing of contentment and prosperity in a remarkable degree. By the "*People*," however, we are to understand not the native Irish, but a colony of strangers, who had recently settled in the land. Scotch and English "Planters" had purchased permission of Parliament to come over to Ireland and deprive the lawful owners of all their possessions, even of their very homes; and they were allowed to employ an armed force in this open violation of the most sacred rights. Thus it was at the cost of sorrow and suffering to thousands of inoffensive people, that the "Planters" secured for themselves the "peace and plenty" of which certain writers speak. And we read of aged members of those plundered families humbly begging to be allowed a last view of "*home*" before they died.[1]

Great numbers of the Irish were forced into exile; the mere fact of their being unwilling to submit to such wrongs was regarded as a spirit of rebellion; and further oppression on this account made it impossible for them to live, even as outcasts, in their native land. Seeking refuge

[1] *Cromwellian Settlement*, Preface.

on the Continent, they won for themselves respect and fame. Still the thought of Ireland was always before their minds; everything associated with the happier memory of their country was loved for Ireland's sake. The children of the exiles were made familiar with the nation's renown for learning and holiness; and special schools were established so as to preserve practically the cherished traditions of the Irish race. The Religious Orders received numerous vocations from among the young Irish students, whose dearest ambition on embracing the monastic state was to be permitted to return "*Home*" some day to labour for the persecuted Faithful in the "Island of Saints." As a matter of fact, many young priests, educated and ordained on the Continent, were risking their lives daily in this work of charity about the year 1625.

The TERESIAN REFORM had become famous throughout the world by this time; the Church had already given highest testimony to the virtues of the heroic Spanish nun, by declaring her a canonized Saint (A.D. 1622): later on the same token of approval was paid to the spirit of her companion, Fra. John of the Cross, by Pope Clement X.[1] Having heard of the Restoration of Carmel's Glory, and seen for themselves how the Teresian Friars conformed to the Primitive Rule, which had been observed in the abbeys of Ireland in olden times, many of the sons of the Irish exiles joined the order of Discalced Carmelites. In the austere mode of life practised within the cloister,

[1] Vide *Brev. Roman Carmelit.*

they found perpetuated the traditions which they had been taught to love so well. This may account for the fact of several young Irish priests dwelling in the missionary college at Louvain when Charles I. became king. This college had been recently established for the education of subjects for the mission both in England and in Ireland. It was under the immediate jurisdiction of the Superior-General of the Italian Congregation; Father Simon Stock being the first to hold the office of Prior there.[1]

Two of those priests seem to have belonged to Dublin families. They had already distinguished themselves in the professorial chair. In Religion they were known as FATHER PAUL of *St. Ubaldus*, and FATHER EDWARD of *the Kings*. No mention is made of their names in the world, which were renounced when they received the brown habit, as is customary with the Discalced Carmelites. Unhappily this beautiful practice—it signifies the absolute severance of the young Friar from his kindred, according to the Counsel Divine—may not be observed quite strictly in countries under a government that can still employ *legal* technicalities to the serious inconvenience of Religious Communities. Although Conventual Fathers of the Monastery at Louvain for some years, Friars Edward and Paul were only waiting a favourable opportunity to volunteer their services for the Irish Mission; and at length the occasion arose.

The Consort of Charles I., Queen Henrietta

[1] *Enchyridion*, p. 99. *Annales du Carmel*, p. 339.

Maria, was a Roman Catholic. She had great devotion to the brown scapular, and held the Teresian Friars in particular esteem. One of them, Father William Pendrick, used to wait on her at court while he was acting as chaplain to Lord Tynemouth. It is said that he even had the privilege of investing the Queen in the Sign that is the Pledge of Our Lady's protection. So we may presume that the King himself had this Father presented to him, and was well disposed towards the Order of Carmel. And soon we find Fathers Edward and Paul applying to the Superior-General for permission to be allowed to found a House of the Teresian Reform in Ireland. The Catholic religion was at least now tolerated, to a certain extent, in the country; and this was sufficient encouragement for the exercise of Carmelite zeal. While awaiting their Superior's decision, the two Fathers earnestly commended the matter to God in prayer; under obedience they could not mistake His Divine Will in their regard. Far from opposing their project, the Father-General did all in his power to assist them in so perilous an undertaking, and arranged that their proposed course of action should be in strict accordance with canonical procedure. He foresaw the difficulties of their enterprise, but he knew that no obstacles could hinder the success of a work directed to God's greater honour alone. Besides, he had confidence in the discretion and fervent perseverance of the missionaries. He appointed Father Edward *"President"* for the time being;

with the Discalced Carmelites, even for an undertaking wherein only two Religious are engaged, one of them must assume the burden of responsibility.

It was with many an earnest wish for their welfare that their Brothers in Religion bade Fathers Edward and Paul "God-speed" on setting out from Louvain for their long, weary journey to Ireland. (It is easy to imagine what the perils of travelling were over two hundred and seventy years ago!) That parting was very painful to the two Friars: the ties of affection, based on fraternal charity, are very hard to break. On the other hand, great was their joy on actually experiencing at length the first of the trials inseparable from their enterprise. Taking with them merely their habits and Breviaries, a few copies of the Holy Bible, and perhaps some other books, they had determined to go straight to Dublin. They arrived there safely in the course of the same year, A.D. 1625.[1]

This was a year of a General Jubilee, and should have seemed to them an auspicious time for beginning the work which they had come to do. But in Ireland, alas! there could be no outward sign of the universal gladness which the young priests had witnessed in the Church elsewhere. Their very worst forebodings were realised; persecution of the Irish Catholics was still carried

---

[1] De Burgo states that they came A.D. 1626, but the annalists of the Order are, naturally, to be followed by preference in this narrative.

on under the form of a *new "Plantation."* The office of consoler was the first sacred duty discharged by the Teresian Friars in Ireland. They had to use their utmost efforts to raise the faithful among whom they laboured from a state of despondency caused by an injustice for which there was no redress. They had to teach the cruelly tried people how to derive the needful support from their faith. And while thus engaged those Teresian Friars won a way to the hearts of the Faithful of Ireland, their influence becoming daily more evident as devotion to Carmel's Queen increased.

Meanwhile some Dublin friends had secured for the Fathers possession of a house in Cook Street, a locality which seems to have been a popular retreat for the Religious Communities then in the city : the Calced Carmelites, Franciscans, Dominicans, and Jesuits had convents there, or in the immediate vicinity.[1] This abode was very humble, indeed, reminding the Friars of the cottage at Duruelo. During the month of October of that year (A.D. 1625) the best room was converted into a temporary chapel; and, with Episcopal sanction of course, the Faithful were allowed to assist at Mass and receive the Sacraments there until such time as a suitable church and friary could be built. Poor as the pious frequenters of that little chapel were themselves, they contrived to find means of enabling the Fathers to found and complete the new monastery within a twelvemonth. To the astonishment

[1] *Hist. of Dublin* (Gilbert).

of the whole city—for the Catholic Religion was not yet tolerated publicly—the Teresian Church was formally blessed and opened, under the invocation of Our Lady of Mount Carmel, in the following October (A.D. 1626). No one interfered with the Religious. for some time, and Fathers Edward and Paul began to practise the "*Regular Life*" with that fervour which had given such edification to their brethren at Louvain. They wore the complete habit of the Order: the beautiful brown robe with scapular, cowl, and white mantle, the sandals and monastic tonsure rendering the entire costume becomingly austere. They were afterwards charged before the Justices with having dared to do so; for, according to the law, their conduct was a *crime*. But they had risked every penalty in order to succeed in a definite purpose, and they knew that the same could only be attained by the faithful observance of the Primitive Rule.

There must have been a secret charm in their way of life notwithstanding its austereness, seeing that they received application from many young Irishmen anxious to embrace the Teresian Reform. When the signs of the vocation-grace were satisfactory, the postulants were sent to some Novitiate of the Order abroad, more frequently to Belgium, so that they might eventually make their studies at Louvain. Father Edward must have shown admirable foresight in accepting those candidates, since, almost invariably, they were professed and ordained in due course. Meanwhile several other

Irish Discalced Carmelites returned from the Continent to assist in perfecting the work so happily inaugurated; and in the year 1627 Father Edward was canonically elected Prior of the first Community of Teresian Friars in Ireland. The Chapter was held in the monastery recently established at Dublin.[1]

This Father was spared to see the increasing popularity of his zealous subjects throughout the country; for the Discalced Carmelites were frequently invited by the various Bishops to co-operate with the secular clergy in the labours of the mission. So willingly did they comply with this request, that the people derived a certain confidence from the fearlessness of the Friars, although Irish Catholics had then very little reason to hope for religious toleration, as the unscrupulous Wentworth might persecute them as he pleased in the name of the King. However, the Faithful gladly availed themselves of the ministry of the Teresian Fathers; they desired to acquire that spirit of Christian fortitude which would make them still more steadfast in truth under the threatening trials.

As for the Religious themselves, except when thus engaged in the duty of Charity, they lived in the retirement of the cloister, studying how to forward the all-important interests of their own souls. But we shall see that in doing so they had, likewise, the welfare of the neighbour in view. Yet this love of seclusion did not enable them to

[1] *Enchyridion.*

escape the notice of those who had a jealous hatred of "*the foreign Friars.*" The Protestant Archbishop of Dublin, Lancelot Bulkeley, took it upon himself to put an end to the *prosperity* of the Religious Communities of that city; and he began by making a raid on the Carmelite Friary at Cook Street[1] (whether the *Calced* Carmelite Monastery, or *Discalced*, the Annalists do not say). It was his aim to establish his own power by harassing the Roman Catholics, whom he knew the King had reason to favour. Bulkeley wanted to show both the Friars and their benefactors that the Penal Laws were still in force; at the same time he could insult, with impunity, a queen who professed the Faith of Rome. He waited until the Christmastide of 1629 to put his plans into execution, receiving from the Lord Justices a warrant which left him free to act as he himself should deem most expedient while engaged "in the service of the King." Having pleaded the necessity of stamping out the sedition preached from the pulpit by the Friars, a troop of musketeers was placed at his disposal; and the Lord Mayor volunteered to accompany him in order to strike the offenders with greater awe.

Accordingly, on one of the holidays the Archbishop and his guard proceeded to Cook Street, and forced their way into the Church of the Carmelites, where the Faithful were assisting

---

[1] Some writers assert that the Prelate's first attack was against one of the other convents. Compare Gilbert, Meehan (*Franciscan Monasteries*), and Ware.

at Mass. The soldiers were told to destroy the statues and pictures adorning the sacred edifice; and to arrest the Friars and take them away to prison. For a moment the people were too amazed to resist; but no sooner did they realise that a horrible sacrilege was being committed, than they caused the Protestant Primate and his friend to regret their interference. They put the musketeers to ignominious flight, which Bulkeley and the Lord Mayor led through the streets of Dublin until they reached a place of safety wherein the Lord Justices happened to be assembled. The matter was immediately made a subject of serious complaint to the King and the Common Council of England; the successful self-defence of the Catholics having been set down as a Popish riot instigated by the Friars. So incessantly did the Justices clamour for the punishment of both the priests and people, that Charles was at length forced to yield; he was afraid of Bulkeley and his partisans. On the 31st of January following it was decreed that the Church and Friary of the Carmelites in Cook Street should be suppressed, and that the Penal Laws against the Roman Catholics should be rigorously enforced within the city of Dublin. By such means were those who would dare oppose "lawful authority" to be terrified. Nevertheless, after a few months we find the Discalced Fathers leading community life in their own monastery at Cook Street, as if no such incident had ever taken place (A.D. 1630). No doubt the order for "the total destruction of the friaries" had been given; but probably the vindictive Prelate and his friends were satisfied, for the time being at all events, with having compelled the king to champion their cause to the certain humiliation of his pious queen.

The Teresian Friars had previously experienced a trial far more grievous than any annoyance caused by narrow-minded bigotry. It was the death of Father Edward of the Kings; and his loss was as keenly felt by the people among whom he had toiled with most consoling results during his brief missionary career. His life's success was perfect, relatively to the end of his vocation —although it implied a holy ambition, the most exalted a man could have had on earth. No human motive was allowed to intervene. His every action had to be purified at its source; his intention ever directed towards God. This is what we understand the annalists to mean when they speak of him as a "*fervent Religious*." As Superior, he was *bound* to set his subjects an edifying example in the observance of the Rule; he had to teach them practically how they might make most rapid progress in the way of zeal and prayer. He did so, we are assured; and his authority weighed upon no one; he was so considerate, so patient, so kind. Knowing himself what it was to obey, the burden of office was less hard to bear when God willed that he should rule: his winning gentleness of disposition might have been traced to those virtues to which his biographers allude.[1] A master in the schools, he possessed the art of imparting knowledge; an art that requires the exercise of much prudence and tact, so that conviction may seem to result from a clearer perception of Truth, the arguments being almost concealed. Very useful, indeed, did Father Edward and his companions find their experience in this respect when explaining the Dogmas of Faith to those whose minds were biassed by prejudice. We may add that the attention of the Protestant Archbishop and of the Lord Justices was first attracted to the Teresian Friars of Dublin by the number of conversions already made.

We are not told whether Father Edward's first companion, Father Paul of St. Ubaldus, was at Cook Street when the Prior died. Being a senior Religious, likely he was in charge of a "*Residence*" in one of the Provinces; new foundations having been made within the first few years. Father Paul's fervent zeal on the Irish Mission is frequently spoken of; but without further allusion to his career.[2]

Father James Bricklane was, probably, the next Superior of the Friary at Dublin.[3] He was born in the north of Ireland; having been sent to France for his education, he joined the Discalced Carmelites there; and was one of those Friars who returned to share the labours of Fathers

---

[1] *Decor Carmeli. Annales du Carmel.*
[2] *Annales du Carmel.*
[3] *MS. in Archives of St. Teresa's,* Clarendon Street.

Edward and Paul. He did not survive his holy predecessor very long. When appointed Vicar-Provincial in Ireland, he was, at the same time, deputed to make a general Visitation of all the Houses of the Order in England; and while discharging that duty he died (A.D. 1636).

But the sorrow caused by trouble of this kind could not impede the work of the Irish Teresian Friars. Political affairs were becoming still more unsettled, affording the Religious frequent occasion for the emulation of their departed brethren's patient zeal. Neither could the Catholics of Ireland look forward to brighter prospects, while Wentworth's power continued to increase. He was soon to be created Earl of Strafford. Those Royal "Graces," which were, in reality, a most solemn pledge, binding Charles I. to render the condition of his Irish subjects bearable at least, could no longer be regarded except as a proof of the King's ingratitude and bad faith. Yet he had only been asked to protect a loyal people from the harrowing exactions made in his own name; to confirm the Catholics in possession of such property as they had been able to retain; and to allow them to obey the dictates of conscience in peace. For such gracious clemency, they had resolved to subscribe £120,000 towards the replenishing of the royal exchequer. They had found Charles disposed to make very generous promises in his pressing financial straits; but all they obtained for the large instalment of £40,000 was the painful knowledge of how easily that monarch could violate his word.

The disappointment had a very depressing effect on those deceived; and it was from the practice of their Religion alone that they obtained courage and solace under the trial. Consequently the Catholic clergy, both secular and regular, had to redouble their efforts in order to explain to the Faithful all the more convincingly that there was a happiness in store for them which Wentworth's cruelty could not affect, and which did not depend upon the favour of the King. So earnestly did the priests persevere, that they had the joy of seeing their people sacrificing even life itself, in after years, rather than be deprived of the consolations of their Faith.

For ten years after the death of Father Edward, aspirants to the brown habit of the Teresian Reform became daily more numerous in Ireland. There were also by this time (1630–1638), "*Residences*" in several counties; Fathers having been sent to various parts of the country to assist in comforting and encouraging those who were at the mercy of Strafford's "Discoverers."[1] It was by the ingenuity of his agents in *inventing* the so-called "*Defective Titles*," that the dread earl had plundered the Catholic landholders, until he reduced them to absolute poverty. Frequently the Friars were called to attend his victims in prison; often upon the scaffold itself. However, the time of retribution was at hand, when not even Charles could save his favourite from that power which had sprung up in England, and which was soon to

[1] *Cromwellian Settlement*, Introd.

usurp his own prerogatives as king. But long before the tragic end of Wentworth's career, the Irish Discalced Carmelites had so prospered, despite what they had to suffer in common with the Faithful, as to be in a position to make application at the General Chapter, held in 1638, to have the Houses of the Order in Ireland constituted into a Province, with all canonical privileges. This request was granted, and by a singular coincidence the new Province took the same precedence in the Teresian Reform—being the *eleventh* which had been erected—as that held in the Order by the Irish White Friars previous to the Mitigation.[1]

[1] *Enchy. Vinea Carmeli.*

CHAPTER IV.

THE PROVINCE OF ST. PATRICK.

The Irish Province — Several of the ancient Carmelite Abbeys granted, by Papal authority, to the Teresian Friars — The Foundations — Fathers Victor and Columbanus at Ardee — Interesting relics of the past—Father John Rowe, O.D.C.— The " Residences."

THE Father-General of the Discalced Carmelites is responsible for the supreme government of the Order, and is elected periodically in a Chapter composed of representative Religious from all parts of the world. He is titular Prior of the Monastery on Mount Carmel in Palestine, of which the Teresian Friars obtained possession, by Papal Brief, on the 3rd of December 1633. A local Superior is appointed there, because the General himself, together with his assistants (the four Definitors and a Procurator), resides in Rome during his term of office. In order that he may be able to exercise jurisdiction over his subjects throughout the world, the monasteries are divided into independent groups, called "*Provinces*," for the welfare of which special Superiors are elected, with whom he is in constant communication. Each of these "*Provincials*" has, likewise, four Definitors to consult; the Priors being also advised by three "*Discreets*" in the administration of the more important affairs of the particular community. The advantages of this economy are many and evident. But a full Province may not be established except under certain conditions; if these cannot be complied with, the Father-General appoints a Vicar-Provincial, who usually holds office for three years.[1] One of the conditions presupposes the existence of a requisite number of *Priories*, each containing at least six Conventual Fathers. Hence from the fact of the Irish Discalced Carmelites having been granted the request made at the General Chapter of 1638, it is manifest that the Teresian Reform had already progressed very rapidly in Ireland.

The newly erected Province was placed under the patronage of the National Apostle; Father Simon of St. Teresa being the first Provincial. Not much is known concerning the houses over which his jurisdiction extended; it is only certain that in one of them the Novitiate was canonically opened; and that another was used as a college for the education of the young Religious after profession. The Postulants were no longer sent on the Continent, the Catholics being *now* permitted to profess their faith openly in Ireland. Within the next few years (1638–1643) we find that there were *nine* Teresian Friaries in the Irish Province, in each of which dwelt a community sufficiently large to carry out the "Primitive Observance" with edifying exactitude.[2] Besides the Conventual Fathers, there were Lay-brothers who attended to

[1] *Const. Carmelit. Excal.*, Pars iii. [2] *Enchyr.*

such domestic duties as would have prevented the Choir-Religious assisting at the Divine Office or in the church, or undertaking the labours of the mission. There were several "*Residences*," also, wherein two or three Fathers and a Brother endeavoured to follow the "Regular Life" as fervently as circumstances would permit. But as soon as Priests could be spared elsewhere other Friars were sent to these houses; that is, when it was the intention of the Superiors to form a new priory or vicariate.

In all probability the first monasteries of the Province of St. Patrick were but plain, commodious buildings when founded expressly for the Discalced Carmelites. Sometimes a private dwelling-house was enlarged for the purposes of monastic life, either by the Fathers themselves or by their generous benefactors. And in *four* instances the ruins of ancient abbeys of the Order were transferred to the Teresian Fathers by Papal authority.[1] It would seem that the friends of the Religious succeeded in purchasing these ruins from the descendants of the apostates to whom the monasteries had been granted in the sixteenth century. There was some doubt as to the lawfulness of accepting such a gift, and several Irish Bishops applied to Rome to have the matter decided by the Pope himself. It was immediately declared that the Discalced Carmelites were perfectly justified in their claim to the ruins, which they had received

[1] *Bullar. Carmelit.* (Ital. MS. from Archives of London Monastery).

by sanction of the Holy See; for permission had been already given them to take over and restore those friaries, originally founded for Religious who, like themselves, had observed the Primitive Rule.[1] We have positive proof that two of the four monasteries were those of Ardee and Loughrea; probably the others were the old abbeys of Drogheda and Athboy. In the year 1646, the Teresian Fathers had again to appeal to Rome to have their title to these foundations confirmed, and once more the decision was in their favour; thenceforth their rights could not be called in question.[2]

But it is not likely that these friaries were then in a habitable state; however, with the assistance of the Faithful, they were soon put into such repair as enabled the Religious to lead the "*Regular Life.*" At first serious inconvenience had to be endured; but the "Homes" which Divine Providence had thus given to the Friars were easily improved upon, or rebuilt in the course of time. Indeed, no matter how unpromising the new foundation seemed, the Discalced Carmelites had never long to wait until they were provided with the necessary monastic offices, including the choir, library, parlours, refectory, and cells.

Here we may also repeat what has been said with regard to the monasteries of the Irish Province of White Friars established at the beginning of the fourteenth century. Having informed us that the Teresian Carmelites had houses in Dublin,

[1] *Bullar. Carmelit.* (Ital. MS.). [2] *Spicil. Ossor.*, vol. i. p. 308.

Athboy, Drogheda, Ardee, Galway, Limerick, Kilkenny, Kinsale, and Loughrea, before the year 1643, the annalists do little more than record the destruction of these friaries during the Cromwellian persecution.[1] Each monastery was the centre of Carmelite zeal and prayer, and as such could not escape the fanatical fury of those who well knew how the faithful of Ireland were encouraged to persevere in the truth by the influence of the monastic profession. So long as the "Monks" were free to preach "the sedition" of the Catholic Religion, the people would remain indifferent both to threats and bribes. And in order that the suppression of the Religious Communities might be thorough indeed, the contents of the conventual archives were invariably committed to the flames. We find the loss thus occasioned to the Irish Discalced Carmelites deeply deplored at the General Chapter of 1646. The Fathers were aware that many of the documents destroyed in the plunder of the monasteries of St. Patrick's Province were of the utmost importance, whether considered from a historical point of view, or as an authentic source of information regarding the martyrdom of the Religious who had already died for the faith in Ireland.[2]

Like the monastic archives at the present day, those of the first houses of the Irish Province contained "Books" in which was written a simple account of transactions deemed worthy of special note; together with the documents pertaining to the

[1] *Enchyr.*
[2] *Enchyr. Annales du Carmel. Gen. Hist. of Discal. Carmel.*

rights and privileges of the various communities. There were "*Books*" for the minutes of "General" and "Provincial" Visitations; also a summary of the acts and decisions of Chapters convened for any particular purpose. There was a record of every canonical election, likewise of each profession; and there was a list of all the "Obits." From such sources the Annals of a Province are chiefly compiled; consequently, were it not for the forethought of the Fathers assembled in the General Chapter of 1646, we should know very little about the establishment of the Province of St. Patrick. They ordained that the formal testimony of contemporary witnesses, still living, should be taken; and that facts authenticated by them should be carefully preserved for insertion in a future " History of the Order."[1] Time after time some Friar would also write an account of his own experience on the Irish Mission, giving an interesting insight into the state of the Province during the Penal Days. Several of these narratives are now extant, and afford us considerable assistance.[2]

The Novitiate was first opened by the Irish Teresian Fathers in their monastery at Dublin. Most of the Religious who laboured on the mission throughout the Puritan persecution were received into the Order and professed there. As has been seen, this friary was situated in Cook Street. Later on the community were driven thence to

---

[1] *Ibidem.*
[2] *Enchyr. Decor Carmeli. Annales du Carmel. Ital. MS. Vide, also, Spicil Ossor.*

find a temporary refuge in Hammond Lane; afterwards at Wormwood Gate ; then in Stephen's Street, where the Fathers remained for nearly forty years. Towards the end of the eighteenth century they secured possession of the present site of their church and house in Clarendon Street. The archives of this monastery contain a number of documents written by a Discalced Carmelite, who was a member of the community at Stephen's Street. They are the result of his praiseworthy efforts to repair the loss of the original records of the Irish Province. Although very incomplete, throwing hardly any new light on the history of the Teresian Reform in Ireland, the information which they convey could only have been acquired by much diligent research. We shall have occasion to refer to these papers, more at length, in one of the subsequent chapters.

Following the authorised order of Foundations, the first colony of Discalced Friars from the monastery in Cook Street appears to have gone to Athboy, Co. Meath, to take over the old Carmelite Abbey of that place. The enterprise was successful, for soon the Religious consented to come to DROGHEDA also, to found a house there among the ruins of another ancient monastery of the Order. This became the college, wherein the newly professed Choir-Religious were to make their studies for the priesthood. The fourth place is assigned to the Friary of ARDEE, Co. Louth, but it was not established until the year 1638. It bore the title of " *The Annunciation.*" The

Provincial, Father Simon of St. Teresa, had been asked to undertake the foundation, for which purpose some benefactors had already obtained for the Discalced Carmelites the ruins of the ancient abbey. In an Italian MS.[1] of the seventeenth century great pains are taken to show that the Teresian Fathers had a strict right to the land and buildings which the Faithful of Ardee had generously bestowed upon them, and we have seen that the Holy See allowed the Order to accept the gift. In the beginning the Father-Provincial could send only two Religious to acquire formal possession of the "Abbey," and to provide accommodation for the community that was to follow later on. One of these Friars was a priest, named Father Michael of St. Victor; his companion was Brother Columbanus, a student who had recently completed his studies and was then waiting to be ordained. Further mention will be made of both Religious when treating of the "*Regular Life*" as led in the Province of St. Patrick.

A relic of this monastery still exists, and happily in one of the houses of the Irish Discalced Carmelites. It is a curious historical work, entitled " MONS HANNONIÆ," which was once in the library of the Teresian Friars of Ardee. From an inscription on the title-page we learn that it had been presented to the Irish Fathers by their brethren in Belgium sometime in the year 1640.

[1] From the archives of the Order at Rome. It seems to be a fragment of a history of the Irish Province.

Frequent reference is made by the annalists to the Discalced Carmelites of GALWAY. This is owing to the fact of the members of the Order in that city having taken a very decided part in the controversy between a number of the Confederate Catholics and Cardinal Rinucini. It seems that the Religious publicly resented the Nuncio's arbitrary mode of proceeding in the sequel to a most painful episode in Irish History —the proposed treaty with Inchiquin. However, we must receive with prudent reservation the statements holding the Cardinal alone responsible for the violent persecution to which the Teresian Carmelites of Galway were subjected on that occasion, as well as those censuring the conduct of the Fathers themselves, and made with equal bitterness. No doubt there must have been some grounds for complaint, since one of the gravest charges against the Prelate, in an appeal made to the Pope, was his treatment of the Teresian Friars of Galway. Yet, it is very hard to realise that the relations between the Nuncio and the Discalced Carmelites could have been so strained at any time, since we find Cardinal Rinucini promising a little while afterwards to use his influence at Rome to forward certain interests of St. Patrick's Province, and applying, moreover, to one of the Irish Fathers for a report on the state of the country under Cromwell's Protectorate. In furnishing the required evidence, the Religious thus honoured often bears testimony to the spirit of fraternal charity which existed among the clergy of Ireland, both secular and regular, during that perilous time.

The Friary of the Order at KILKENNY receives much notice, also, for a like reason. Father John Rowe, the Provincial of the Irish Discalced Carmelites in 1644, was a conventual there; and it was he who had been chosen to take the Appeal of the Nuncio's adversaries to Rome. He was likewise deputed to defend the cause of those recently excommunicated by the Cardinal. Hence, we are prepared to have his conduct criticised according to the prejudice of writers, who either regard the projected alliance with Inchiquin as a policy of prudence, or consider it an action of unpardonable rashness. Some are of opinion that nothing but evil could have resulted from friendly intercourse with one who had wantonly persecuted the Catholics of Ireland; others think that the well-nigh desperate state of the Confederates would have justified them in adopting such a measure.[1]

Father Rowe had long to wait for the more favourable issue of the task imposed upon him. He seems to have returned to Ireland in the meantime to attend to the duties of his office as Provincial. Likely he was recalled to Rome a few years after Cromwell's dread campaign, for mention is made by some authors of a "*Father John of the Mother of God*," who was Provincial of the Teresian Carmelites of Ireland about the time of the Catholic Confederation. This Religious (Father Rowe pre-

[1] Compare *Haverty, De Burgo, Meehan, Prendergast, Bellings, Ital. MS., Aphor. Discov.*, &c.

sumably) wrote "*A History of the Irish Province,*" when at length he had been compelled by age and infirmities to withdraw from the labours of the mission.[1] As for the part which he had taken in that grave political crisis, we can only say that certainly it never proved an obstacle to the discharge of his monastic duties; otherwise, no matter how anxious Father Rowe himself might have been to comply with the wishes of those desirous of forwarding the interests of the Confederation, the Superior-General would have forbade him undertake what was opposed to the spirit of his vocation. This makes it all the more difficult to understand the precise state of affairs in this country when Father John consented to lay the grievances of a large body of the Irish Catholics, clergy and laity, before the Sovereign Pontiff at Rome.

With regard to the Teresian Monasteries founded at KINSALE and in the city of LIMERICK, they prospered for some years, but were eventually pillaged and destroyed by an army of Puritan adventurers, who had the express sanction of the English Parliament to plunder the people of Ireland.[2] Having paid a price to secure the goodwill of Government in the carrying out of this nefarious project, the fanatics seized the property of the Roman Catholic inhabitants of several towns in Munster. The fate of the communities of those two friaries was such as might have been expected at the hands of mercenaries, whose hatred of the true faith was quite as intense as their greed for the land and homes

[1] *Ital. MS.*   [2] *Cromwellian Settlement*, Introd.

of the King's Irish subjects. The "blood of the martyrs" was now shed freely; three of the Discalced Carmelites being among the first victims of the Puritan persecution (1641–1643). The character of the persecutors is manifest from a horrible incident which occurred near Dublin about this time. The soldiers boasted that having captured a priest, they cut him in pieces "*as small as flesh for the pot.*"[1] It is recorded that whenever the Teresian Friars had succeeded in escaping the sword on the arrival of the Puritans, they used to remain concealed in the various districts in order to provide for the spiritual wants of the Faithful.[2] They knew that their presence would be a consolation to the suffering people; and the risk they ran in remaining was, after all, only that of a violent death to themselves. Still they waited on in hope, thinking that when this season of trial had passed their beloved Province would be speedily restored, and they themselves permitted to follow the "*Regular Life*" in peace once more.

The House last established by the Teresian Fathers was at LOUGHREA. The ruins of the old abbey and church were in possession of the Clanricarde family at the time of the Confederation. The friends of the Discalced White Friars had some influence with the Earl (who was *a Catholic*), and prevailed on him to rent the dilapidated friary and an adjoining plot of ground to the successors of the Monks, whom the most celebrated of his own ancestors had been proud to assist. Apparently

[1] *Prendergast.*   [2] *Enchyr.*

that nobleman was favourably disposed towards the Fathers, and granted the request. And there is a tradition to the effect that the Teresian Friars were never afterwards denied their right of possession; not even when outlawed with a price upon their heads. Although suppressed, like all the other Houses of the Order, when Cromwell was in power, several members of the community of the abbey remained in the neighbourhood until the Restoration, their claims being at once recognised by the Clanricarde family. At the time of the battle of Aughrim four or five Religious still resided there, but secretly, of course, their profession being no longer tolerated in Ireland. Likely the priest-hunters never thought of those ruins as a comparatively safe retreat for the fugitive Friars. A silver chalice was discovered there, concealed in one of the walls; it had been presented to the Irish Discalced Carmelites in 1641, as may be seen from the Latin inscription which it bears. This sacred vessel is now used daily in the Holy Sacrifice by the Teresian Fathers at present in Loughrea. Another chalice, which had belonged to one of the communities of St. Patrick's Province in the seventeenth century, was found in Drogheda some years ago; it was handed over to the priest in charge of one of the parish churches.

It would seem that there was also a House of the Irish Province at YOUGHAL, Co. Cork; but no mention is made of this foundation in the official list of monasteries. *De Burgo* says that Father Patrick Donovan, O.D.C., resided there as *Superior* in 1626. It may have been merely a "*Residence*"; for in alluding to this Father, the author of the "HIBERNIA DOMINICANA" twice calls him "*President*," a title used among the Discalced Carmelites to designate the Religious who holds the office of local Superior by reason of seniority of profession.[1] In a contemporary History, under date of the 8th June 1644, we find reference made to Father Donovan as "*one of the Friars of eminent quality.*"[2] Neither do the annalists speak of the Monastery of ARDBRECCAN, Co. Meath, of which Father Corry was sometime Superior. The "*List of Obits*" of the Friars of the Irish Province records his death as having taken place there in the year 1752. Evidently this house also was a temporary "*Residence*," established early in the eighteenth century, when the Religious had begun to come forth from their "hiding-places" throughout the country, and to live in community.[3] There must have been several other "*Residences*" of this kind in Ireland during the Penal times; for in an Ordination made at the "General Visitation" of 1743, the communities in Dublin and Loughrea were expressly mentioned; and then allusion made to all other "*Residences*" in the kingdom. The annalists do not notice these houses, because they had not been canonically founded like the nine friaries which formally constituted the Province. They were simply the "*Humble Homes*" of two or three Fathers whom the Bishops of different dioceses had invited to

[1] *De Burgo.*   [2] *Hist. of Cath. Conf.*
[3] *MS. Archives of St. Teresa's.*

take charge of certain districts in which the Faithful had been long deprived of the consolations of Religion by the restrictions of the cruel laws. There is conclusive evidence to prove that the Irish Discalced Carmelites had been often asked to cooperate in the work of the mission in such wise; and that they always gladly complied. When the secular clergy became more numerous, the Religious left the "*Residences*" in order to rejoin the larger communities either at Dublin or Loughrea.[1]

This brief review of the establishment of the Irish Province is to show what foundations had been made in this country by the Discalced Carmelites, and how the Teresian Reform continues to flourish here notwithstanding the terrible trials of a persecution lasting several hundred years. Further details of its history in Ireland during so long an epoch will be given in the course of our narrative; we have yet to speak more particularly of the labours of the Friars of St. Patrick's Province among the people, before passing on to a season of peace for the long-persecuted Irish Catholics. However, the references hitherto made rather bear on the *temporal* welfare of the Teresian Friars for over a century; we shall now see that in the constitution of a Province of the Order nothing is deemed of real importance except what conduces to greater fervour in the observance of the Primitive Rule, by which is to be understood the practice of "THE REGULAR LIFE."

[1] *MS. Archives of St. Teresa's.*

CHAPTER V.

"THE REGULAR LIFE."

Everyday life in a Friary of Irish Discalced Carmelites when Charles I. was king—The object of "Visitations"—Influences of "*The Regular Life*"—The "Signs of the Times" in A.D. 1640—Puritan fanaticism—The Teresian Monastery of Kilkenny during the "Confederation"—Irish Fathers at the "General Chapters."

THE Discalced Carmelites of St. Patrick's Province were very faithful, we are told, in the observance of the *Restored* Primitive Rule. In this respect, they gave great edification to their brethren on the Continent; and the annalists are loud in praise of them for having attempted successfully to lead the "*The Regular Life*" amid the difficulties to be encountered by Religious in Ireland when Charles I. was king.[1] For, if the Catholics were not then actually persecuted in the cause of religion, we know what they had to suffer by reason of Wentworth's dreadful policy of Plunder. The harsh treatment of the Carmelite Friars at Dublin illustrates the uncertainty of the *toleration* which the Irish people were then *supposed* to enjoy.[2] But such trials do not seem to have interfered with the strict observance of the Car-

[1] *Enchyr.*   [2] *Prenderg.*

melite Rule. Just as St. Teresa herself felt assured of the success of the Reform, after having witnessed the obstacles which St. John of the Cross and his companions were engaged in surmounting at Duruelo; so were the Fathers of St. Patrick's Province never disheartened by adversity; never forced to relinquish "*The Regular Life*" so long as they were allowed to remain in their monasteries.[1] Far from availing themselves of certain Dispensations provided by the Constitutions for those on the mission in countries subject to heretical government; *even* while in prison for their faith and profession, there are instances to show that the Religious endeavoured to conform to the austere practices of the cloister.[2]

Whenever a new foundation was proposed to the Superiors of the Province, they had first to consider whether the circumstances were favourable to the "Observance"; satisfied on this point, they rarely hesitated to comply with the wishes of their benefactors, if it were at all possible to spare a few Fathers to form the nascent community. So that no matter how poor and humble the nine Houses of the Irish Province may have been in the year 1640, it is manifest that in each of them the Friars could lead "*The Regular Life*"; and although, at times, there may have been various grave inconveniences to contend with, it is very edifying to find two or three Religious quite as intent as a large community in trying to carry out exactly everything prescribed by the Rule and Constitu-

[1] *Annales du Carmel.*   [2] *Enchyr.*

tions.[1] Particular mention is made of the fervour of Father Victor and Brother Columbanus from the hour of their arrival at Ardee.[2] Indeed, an outline of their everyday life there in the beginning can be given with as much precision as if written in the year 1638 by a contemporary annalist. Rising at an early hour — before dawn — they recited part of the Divine Office, and afterwards passed some time in mental prayer. Father Victor then said Mass (formal possession of the new foundation could not be taken until the Blessed Sacrament was placed in the Tabernacle).[3] By seven o'clock, or a little later, the Friars were free to devote their attention to the repairing of the ruined abbey. Were they not so occupied, they might have retired to their "Cells" for study. Working hard with the labourers, sent to assist them by some thoughtful friends,[4] they had to retire before noon in order to continue the Canonical Hours, and to make the midday examination of conscience. Now, for the first time that morning, they might break their fast— presupposing they had already obtained food for an exceedingly meagre meal. A brief recreation followed; it was spent, no doubt, by Father Victor and his young companion in the further improvement of their new "Home." If the priest had not been called away to discharge the functions of his sacred ministry in the meantime, Vespers were

[1] *Ital. MS.*
[2] *Annal. du Carmel.*
[3] *St. Teresa's Book of Foundations.*
[4] A gentleman named "Gerard Colley" was one of their chief benefactors (*Ital. MS.*).

said at two o'clock, various duties occupying the remainder of the afternoon until the evening Meditation. After Compline they partook of a frugal collation; then other monastic exercises were gone through ere they might take a much-needed rest. But neither the toils nor anxieties of a day thus passed could hinder them, once they were free, spending a few hours in the study of Theology, Holy Scripture, or Canon Law; of course this meant a curtailment of the repose, which was to be interrupted at midnight for recital of the Matins of the morrow.

The two Religious were not bound to this strict practice of "*The Regular Life*," considering the circumstances of the foundation at Ardee. But we are assured of their sanctity; and with the Teresian Carmelite there is but one standard of perfection: persevering faithfulness to the Holy Rule. In after years Fathers Victor and Columbanus became renowned both in Ireland and on the Continent—the former for his success as a missioner; the latter for learning, which he employed to great advantage in the college of his Order at Rome. But only indirectly do the annalists allude to the fame of these Friars: when speaking of their fervour in religious observance.[1]

Once established, each of the nine Monasteries of the Irish Province seems to have been well adapted to the purposes of "*The Regular Life*." There was the required number of Fathers to fill the usual conventual offices. And it was the

[1] *Enchy.* (*Ital. MS.*).

Provincial's duty to see for himself, from time to time, that all the Religious under his jurisdiction were exact in so important a matter; this being his own surety of their earnestness in acquiring the twofold object of their vocation. If necessary he might have made "*Ordinations*" to ensure greater diligence in this respect; and these Ordinations would have been binding on the members of the particular community. With a view to the same end, the Superior-General himself had to make a "Visitation," in person or by deputy, of all the Provinces of the Teresian Reform during his term of office.[1] We have seen how an Irish Provincial, Father Bricklane, had been delegated to fulfil that canonical function in England; nor is the fact of his having died in the performance of so sacred a trust more pathetic or edifying than the zeal of the many Superiors who came hither from Rome to discharge this duty at the imminent peril of their lives.[2] In the "*Book of Visitations*" of the Irish Province we find that entries had been made when the Penal Laws were in full force; and they are, for the most part, earnest exhortations of the successive Fathers-General to perseverance in the true Carmelite spirit of prayer. By such means alone ministry of the Friars could be made efficacious among the Faithful; so that the Superiors-General of the Order would thus insist always on the pressing need of "*The Regular Life.*"

In the year 1640, the Fathers of the Irish Province were more assiduous than ever in im-

---

[1] *Const. Carm. Excal.*   [2] *MS. in Ar. of St. Teresa's*

pressing upon the people the value of the gift of Faith. The King's affairs were now becoming quite alarming; his Scottish subjects were in open revolt. Three years previously the trouble had commenced in that kingdom when Charles tried to introduce there the Liturgy of Archbishop Laud.[1] In 1639 the Parliament of Scotland had abolished Episcopacy; the King attempted to assert the royal prerogatives by force; but the Scotch, crossing the Border, succeeded in defeating him,—not to the regret of his English Parliament, historians say. The Earl of Strafford, having been recalled from Ireland to assist in checking that rebellion, had raised an army of Irish soldiers, mostly Roman Catholics, to defend the Stuarts' cause. He knew that he might rely on their loyalty and bravery, notwithstanding his own treachery towards them as representative of the King. The Earl's failure in that expedition was seized by Charles's enemies as a motive for the favourite's impeachment; they hated Strafford for his apparent sincerity in the service of his royal master. One of the most serious charges made against him was that he had been too tolerant of the Irish Catholics, and had even allowed them recently to bear arms in defence of the King! But Strafford's answer to the accusation proves that his only reason for not having *persecuted* the Faithful of this kingdom, as relentlessly as the Puritans would wish, had been to further the royal interests

---

[1] Such interference may be regarded as the primary cause of the King's unpopularity.

in Ireland.[1] Still Charles could not save him from the scaffold; the unhappy monarch had himself to sign the Earl's death-warrant. Soon afterwards the "*Grand Remonstrance*" against the King's own conduct was drawn up by the House of Commons; and then the *end* was very near.[2]

Towards the close of the same year, 1641, "*The Regular Life*" was interrupted by the destruction of several Friaries of St. Patrick's Province.[3]

Seeing that the English Parliament was no longer obedient to the King; and that absolute suppression of the Catholic Religion was spoken of as being merely a matter of a very short time, the people of Ireland had no alternative but to appeal to arms in self-defence. The Northern Irish, under Sir Phelim O'Neill, were the first to move in this serious crisis. No sooner did their action become known at Dublin than the Lords Chief-Justices gave orders for a rigorous persecution of the Roman Catholics within that city.

The garrison was then composed of Puritan soldiers, several regiments of whom had been lately brought over to Ireland; and these were most eager for the opportunity to exercise their fanatical zeal. The Teresian monastery in Cook Street was pillaged and wrecked, the members of the community having barely had time to escape with their lives. In Drogheda, also, a similar fate befell the Friars who were leading "*The Regular Life*" there in 1641; that place being another stronghold of

---

[1] *Trial of Earl Strafford.*   [2] *Hist. of England* (Lingard's, &c.).
[3] *Enchy. Prenderg.*

the Puritans. When driven from those two convents, some of the Religious made their way to the other houses, but several always managed to remain concealed near the scenes of their former labours, until they were either captured or slain.

Although the Novitiate and the College of the Irish Discalced Carmelites were thus suppressed at the first outbreak of Puritan fury, the Fathers continued to receive postulants in Ireland, special arrangements having been made to meet the emergency which had newly arisen in their Province. So far as their own spiritual welfare was concerned, the Friars could not have been put to a disadvantage, or taken by surprise. From their noviceship upwards they had been taught to regard the monastic exercises merely as a means to the end of their vocation, which could likewise be attained by them if "*outlaws*" in the country. Later on, bands of the fanatical soldiery invaded the South, and then "*The Regular Life*" also ceased in the Teresian Friaries of Limerick and Kinsale.[1]

The persecution now raged fiercely, and it was carried on in the name of the King. The rack and other horrible instruments of torture were freely employed in Dublin at this time to extort from Roman Catholic victims confessions which might afterwards be used in prejudicing the English against those who professed the true faith. Numbers of defenceless men, women, and children were put to death by the pitiless Puritans,

[1] *Prenderg. (Ital. MS.).*

whose leaders excused such barbarity on the plea of retaliation for the *many massacres* of Protestants which had been perpetrated by the Irish people. Parliamentary pamphlets, containing reports to this effect, were spread broadcast in England and Scotland, while every published refutation of such calumnies was instantly seized and destroyed. Hence those historical fictions transmitted by contemporary writers who gained favour with unscrupulous statesmen by perverting facts, or by inventing falsehoods injurious alike to the cause of the Catholic religion and to the Stuart dynasty.

It was only when driven to their last resource that the people of Ireland resolved to fight for their rights, encouraged by the decision of the Provincial Synod held at Kells, under the presidency of Hugh O'Reilly, Archbishop of Armagh (A.D. 1642), such a course of action being then declared lawful and inevitable. A most earnest exhortation was also made by the clergy there assembled to impress upon the leaders in this movement the necessity of true Christian mercifulness on their part during the war about to ensue. Here we have a striking illustration of the assertion made in our own times by an eminent English Prelate when speaking of the spirit of the Irish people: "*The Catholics of Ireland never persecuted their Protestant neighbours. The children of martyrs are not persecutors.*"[1]

As representative Irishmen throughout the country desired to forward the enterprise, a

[1] *Life of Cardinal Manning*, vol. ii. p. 621.

national Synod was afterwards (1643) convened at Kilkenny, in order that a responsible committee might be selected, and everything calculated to bring the momentous struggle to a successful issue definitely arranged. Then was formed the association known as the "CONFEDERATION OF THE CATHOLICS OF IRELAND." The members bound themselves by oath to strive to attain the object which they had in view : the defence of the Catholic Religion, the safety of "the prerogative and royal rights of King Charles and his gracious Queen," the protection of "their own lives, lands, and possessions." All the Faithful of the kingdom were exhorted to take this solemn pledge, since the "Confederation" was now their only hope. Its "Council" was composed of officials, ecclesiastical, civil, and military, who were held responsible to the nation for the right administration of affairs until a permanent Government could be established by the King *sincerely* confiding in the loyalty of his Irish subjects, whom he still regarded and treated as rebels.

A great army was soon raised, principally from among the Anglo-Irish Catholics of the Pale and the native Irish of the North under Sir Phelim O'Neill. Even many young women came, in disguise, to be enrolled, and on being discovered they said they would rather die on the field of battle than fall into the hands of the Puritans! The English Parliament was now in a position to publish its intentions with regard to the Catholics of Ireland ; *they were not to be tolerated;* the lands of the rebels were already confiscated, and promised to the soldiers in payment for military service. Thus encouraged, the Puritan fanatics committed the most revolting crimes with impunity, the cold-blooded murder of countless unoffending Catholics, often women and children by choice, being by no means the most terrible of their inhuman excesses.

The "Confederates" appealed to Catholic courts on the Continent, and assistance was readily promised them. A special Nuncio was sent from Rome to take part in their deliberations, and not only was their cause approved of and blessed by the Sovereign Pontiff, but large sums of money were contributed towards the expenses of the campaign out of the Papal treasury. At length Charles I. was very glad to accept their still proffered allegiance; for in the year 1643 the English Parliament took the Covenant of the Puritans of Scotland, thereby making open profession of principles entirely opposed to the prerogatives of the Crown. Just before the King had been thus compelled to make terms with the "Confederate Catholics," the political situation assumed a strange aspect in Ireland. Although engaged in fierce conflict with each other, the Royalists and Parliamentarians were equally intent on oppressing the Faithful in this country. The interests of either party were upheld, moreover, by the representative of an ancient Irish family. The Marquis of Ormond, one of the Butlers, had succeeded to Strafford as favourite of the King, and was now the leader of the Royalists, while an O'Brien of Thomond, the notorious "Lord Inchiquin," had become commander-in-chief of the Puritans. Ormond advised Charles to enter into a treaty with the "Confederates," who had by this time gained several important victories, privately suggesting that any concessions promised to the Irish in such circumstances could be thought over more maturely when his Majesty had defeated his enemies. Naturally, the Catholics were doubtful of the adviser's sincerity and the King's good faith; however, it was finally decided to co-operate with Ormond in upholding the cause of royalty. And in 1648 we find even Inchiquin separating himself from the Parliamentarians to assist Charles, his action causing a crisis in the history of the Confederation which resulted in that deplorable state of affairs already alluded to, when we had occasion to speak of the Provincial of the Discalced Carmelites at the time being, Father John Rowe.[1]

The city of Kilkenny was the scene of some of the most important events of a truly thrilling drama. Yet in the Teresian Friary of that place "*The Regular Life*" was followed as calmly as if the nation enjoyed perfect peace. Knowing that each day's "*Observance*" was complete in itself, the Religious could have no more efficacious method of preparing themselves for the trials, which their brethren had recently encountered in various other parts of the kingdom. Occasionally they were joined by Fathers who had escaped from the Puritans after the destruction of the monasteries elsewhere, and from

[1] *Hist. of Ir. Confed.*

those fugitives they heard of the cruelty of their persecutors, into whose hands they were liable at any moment to fall. But if they listened with pain to a terribly graphic account of the sufferings of those confessors, they rejoiced when told of the glorious triumph of members of their own Order who had already gladly laid down their lives for the faith. It would seem that often, while the Teresian Friars were being put to death, the intense hatred which the heretics bore them became manifest. They were accused of having been so zealous in exhorting the Faithful to reject "the pure Gospel" of the fanatics, that it was impossible to propagate it among the Catholics of Ireland.[1] Neither were afflictions and privations of any avail; the people appeared to be quite happy in being called upon to bear them, and the Puritans were amazed, not knowing how soothing a peace of mind had been acquired by this heroic profession of faith. The Discalced Carmelites humbly thanked God for their own share in the great work of the nation's perseverance; but if the Irish people had been enabled by their ministry to prize Religion above anything which the world had power to give or to take away, the Fathers were well aware that their own success among their countrymen could only be attributed to what they themselves had received from the fervent practice of "*The Regular Life.*"

Yet even the bravest of those Religious might have trembled at the thought of the fate of their martyred brethren—a fate which the Puritans had

---

[1] *Ital. MS. in Archives of London Monastery. Enchyr.*

certainly in reserve for all Friars falling into their power. The majority of the Parliamentarians were ignorant fanatics of a most dangerous type, fancying that their leaders had no other end in view in fighting against their King and his adherents save the defence of their "*Liberty of conscience,*" *insidiously* threatened by the Royalists. They were assured that they were engaged in a "*Religious War*"; and told that their enemies should not be spared, being determined to resist the "*Pure Word of the Lord.*" It was no unusual sight to see a band of those ruthless warriors grouped round one of their number, who, with blood-stained hand, was turning over the pages of his Bible, searching for a "Text" to justify deeds that had been done by the sword. Even the Puritan women were possessed of the same spirit of fanaticism, and at times could be more brutal in their wanton cruelty than the men. One of them murdered a Teresian Friar under particularly revolting circumstances. The Confessor (whose name is unknown) was a young lay-brother who had been engaged in attending to the temporal wants of the Fathers then secretly discharging their sacred duties in Dublin. Of course he had to use a disguise, and having met this shameless woman, she made proposals to him which he at once rejected by revealing his religion and profession. In her rage at the discovery she took immediate revenge, and struck him a fatal blow.[1] But she seems to have had remorse; instead of boasting of her crime, as was usual with the Puritans when

[1] *Annales du Carmel.*

they had slain a "Monk," she expressed deep sorrow to the Fathers who had come to take the Confessor's body away; and she promised not to betray them on being told that they themselves were, also, Teresian Friars in disguise.

Another very edifying evidence of the fervour of the Irish Discalced Carmelites in the practice of "*The Regular Life*," during the seventeenth century, was the efforts which they made to assist at the General Chapters of their Order. Three representatives of each Province were required to be present, and this presupposed the long, dangerous journey either to Rome or to Genoa, as it was in one or other of these cities the Fathers were wont to assemble. In the Chapter of 1641, convened in the Teresian Monastery of "Our Lady of Victory" at Rome, Fathers Patrick of St. James, Malachy of Jesus, and Simon of St. Teresa, were the Religious from the Irish Province. They then succeeded in having the transfer of those four ancient abbeys ratified both by their own Superiors and the Father-General of the Calced Carmelites.[1] It must have been while they were absent that the Puritan persecution broke out in Ireland; for the annalist who records this Act of the Chapter does not allude to the recent interruption of "*The Regular Life*" in St. Patrick's Province. Two of these Friars held the office of Provincial, Fathers Simon and Patrick (the Religious entitled to vote in the General Chapter being the Provincial, Ex-Provincial, and an elected Socius; in *semi-*

[1] *Ital. MS.*

Provinces, however, only the Vicar-Provincial is summoned to attend). Father Patrick's memory is still revered in Italy whither he retired, like Father John Rowe, after an eventful career on the Irish Mission. It is said that the Puritans had actually led him to the scaffold for execution; but he escaped quite miraculously before the halter was placed round his neck, and afterwards devoted himself with all the more zeal to the duties of his holy profession. It is to be regretted that so little is known of the Teresian Carmelites of Ireland thus incidentally mentioned by our annalists. Commenting on this, Father Isidore of St. Joseph, a celebrated writer of the Order (1666), says that the reason why the work of the missioners has not been spoken of at greater length in history, was owing to the fact that those Religious would not recount what they themselves had suffered for the faith. And if through obedience they had to describe their own trials and labours, they always carefully suppressed their names.[1]

Three Fathers of the Irish Province had been called, as usual, to the General Chapter of 1646, but they did not arrive at the appointed time, and no one could account for the delay. News travelled very slowly in those days, so that likely the true nature of the persecution then raging in Ireland was not yet fully realised abroad.[2]

One of those Irish Fathers—Father Cyril of St. Joseph—presented himself eventually, and gave a thrilling report of how he and his two com-

[1] *Ital. MS.*   [2] *Enchyr.*

panions had been pursued over the seas by the heretics. He had escaped by the merest chance, but knew nothing of the fate of the other priests. Various important documents concerning the Irish Province had been given him to lay before the General Chapter; unfortunately Father Cyril had been obliged to cast all his papers into the sea to save his life when the ship was captured by the Puritans. The heretics suspected that there were Friars on board; a most rigorous search was made, and to his own presence of mind the Father owed his escape. The Chapter, on hearing his narrative, ordered no pains to be spared in trying to replace those documents, particularly such as related to the death of the Religious who had recently died for the Faith.[1] Father Cyril became Provincial in Ireland in the course of time (A.D. 1656), and rendered great service to the persecuted Irish Church during Cromwell's Protectorate.[2] But then the "*The Regular Life*" was no longer followed in St. Patrick's Province; not even *one* of the nine monasteries remained.

Before considering other phases of the Puritan persecution, we must show how "*The Regular Life*" enabled the Teresian Friars to die. Happily we can give a more detailed account of the careers of several of the Discalced Carmelites who received their "Crowns" in Ireland previous to the final revolt of the English Parliament, while Charles I. still thought to win his Scottish subjects to his cause by confiding in their loyalty. He went so

[1] *Enchyr.* [2] *MS. from London Arch.*

far as to trust his person among them, and they promptly delivered him up to the Parliamentarians for £40,000! The last act of the "Tragedy" did not take place, however, until the 30th January 1649, after which Oliver Cromwell — the most guilty of the murderers of the King — openly assumed the rôle of Dictator, his will being virtually absolute in all matters, military, civil, and religious; while his attitude towards the Catholics of Ireland was one of fiercest persecution. This we shall soon have occasion to see, when inquiring into the state of the Irish Province after the Irish Teresian Friars had been compelled to relinquish the "*Observance*" for a time.

CHAPTER VI.

"WITH PALMS AND CROWNS."

The life and martyrdom of Father Thomas Aquinas of St. Teresa; of Fra Angelus of St. Joseph; and of Brother Peter of the Mother of God—Other martyrs of the Irish Province: Fathers Lawrence, Patrick, and Bede.

IN the Monastery of the Discalced Carmelites at Linz, Austria, there is a fine old oil-painting of three Teresian Friars put to death by the heretics in Ireland. Their names are inscribed on a scroll beneath the picture; and over their heads the artist—a talented lay-brother who lived in that house towards the end of the seventeenth century—has represented angels holding the symbolical "Palms and Crowns."[1] The fate of these Confessors is better known than that of the many other Religious of the Irish Province who suffered for the faith during the Puritan persecution. One of the three Friars was a priest, recently ordained; another, a student, preparing for the sacred ministry; the third was a lay-brother.

I. FATHER THOMAS AQUINAS OF ST. TERESA.[2]

The signs of the vocation-grace must have been very evident in a postulant anxious to embrace the

[1] *MS. from London Archives.*   [2] *Enchyr. Ménol.*

Teresian Reform at Dublin in the year 1635. For he was at once received into the community, being thenceforth known as Fra Thomas Aquinas of St. Teresa. The young novice was then in the twenty-third year of his age; his parents being Catholics, and residing in Dublin probably. From childhood Fra Thomas had been encouraged to devote himself to God in Religion; but it was after he had obtained a thorough education, and distinguished himself at college, that he felt called to the cloister. His fervour during the time of probation was most exemplary; not even the austerities of the Primitive Rule could satisfy his desire for mortification, which had, nevertheless, to be moderated by Obedience,—a virtue considered to be the basis of Religious perfection by the Discalced Carmelites. Having taken the Solemn Vows, Brother Thomas was sent to Drogheda to study for the priesthood. He must have been ordained there before the year 1641; because at the outbreak of the persecution in that city, he had already gained fame as a distinguished preacher.

The Puritans vainly thought that by arresting this popular Friar, and making an example of him, they could intimidate the resolute Catholics of Drogheda. But it was no easy matter to effect their purpose, as the Faithful grew daily more anxious for Father Thomas's safety; indeed his retreat might never have been discovered were it not for the treachery of a heretical servant.

Among the converts, whom the young priest had received into the Church, were the members of an influential family; a gentleman, his wife and son—an only child. On making open profession of their faith, the father and son were seized and cast into prison. Distracted with grief, the lady was on the point of simulating the errors of her persecutors, knowing that by doing so she could at least save the lives of her husband and son. Father Thomas heard of her deplorable state, and risking every peril, hastened at once to her assistance. He explained to her the grievous sinfulness of her design, which she immediately renounced, resolving to trust those dearest to her to God's loving care. And, acting on her director's advice, she resolved to escape the vengeance of the Puritans by flight. The annalists do not say whether so beautiful a spirit of Christian resignation was rewarded on earth by the happy reunion of those fervent converts.

While Father Thomas was still engaged in discharging this duty of charity, one of the lady's own servants summoned the soldiers of the garrison, who came and surrounded the house silently. Yet, the Friar might have eluded all their precautions, had he not the welfare of others to consider. They had searched for him in vain, and were about to set fire to the building, when he himself appeared and bade them desist. They did comply; surprised at this unexpected event, and giving loud expression to their grim satisfaction at having captured him so easily. They treated him most barbarously as they dragged him back to Drogheda to await there in prison his certain doom.

Having then much work of a like gruesome kind

on hand, the fanatics left Father Thomas to endure for a time the horrors of a cruel captivity. But in this they were disappointed. One of the Confessor's fellow-prisoners was a Franciscan Friar who had obtained favour with the governor, and who now secured for Father Thomas several of the privileges which he himself enjoyed; among others that of visiting the Catholics suffering for their faith, and of *saying Mass almost every day*. This zealous son of St. Francis was also able to procure the Teresian habit for the young Carmelite, who was very anxious to die clothed as became the members of his Order. Hence we may infer that there were other Discalced Carmelites in Drogheda with whom the Franciscan Father held secret communication.

Early on the morning of the sixth day of his imprisonment a messenger came to tell Father Thomas that he had been sentenced to death, and that the soldiers would be ready to lead him to the scaffold within an hour. Happily he had just offered the Holy Sacrifice; so, merely inclining his head, in meek submission to God's will, he continued his prayer. He looked upon such a death as an exceeding great act of mercifulness; his life's work was well accomplished, nor could he reproach himself with having left anything undone. His only regret was at being taken away from the Faithful, who sadly needed the poor comfort his words could give them in the hour of trial. On hearing of his terrible fate the Catholic prisoners raised a wail of bitter grief, and even many of the

Puritans were touched with pity, so calm and fearless did the young Friar seem. But a crowd of heretics had assembled outside, clamouring for his death, and scoffing at his constancy. A number of pious people had also come to receive his blessing, for which they knelt, unmindful of the threats of their persecutors.

When on his way to the place of execution, Father Thomas saw them lead forth a wretched woman who was about to suffer death for some crime. To his horror he distinctly heard the Puritans offer her life, and freedom, and wealth if she would only renounce her faith. Calling out to her, he warned her to beware lest she should forfeit eternal happiness by accepting those things that must pass with time. His zeal was well rewarded, for even before he himself reached the scaffold that woman's soul was safe with God.

And yet his executioners tried to bribe him with the very allurements he had just exhorted a weak woman to despise! But he silenced them by asking whether they could think him so foolish as to reject doctrine which he knew to be infallibly true, in exchange for the mere invention of human caprice? He reminded them, moreover, of the dangers of their own state, and implored them to return to that Church to which their ancestors had once been so loyal. This filled them with unspeakable rage, making them still more eager for the Teresian Friar's death.

The scene at the foot of the gibbet is not difficult to realise: the fierce soldiers dressed in buff jerkins, and wearing caps and breastplates of steel; in their midst the young priest, clothed with the lovely habit and mantle of Carmel, a crucifix and beads in his hands, his lips moving in earnest prayer; and the instrument of death reared against a fair summer sky.

The Puritans themselves being the executioners, the final preparations were hastily gone through. The cord was fastened in its place, the signal impatiently given and eagerly obeyed. But Father Thomas did not die. The strong halter was wrenched in twain to the astonishment of all present, whose surprise gave place to awe when another rope yielded like the first, and they beheld the Confessor standing still uninjured before them. Raising his voice he asked them why they had condemned him to death, and he guilty of no crime. Then they accused him of being a *Catholic*, and a *Priest*, and a *Monk*. He joyfully admitted the charge, saying that he was *now* ready to lay down his life in testimony of his faith. They instantly placed him under the gibbet again, and, with a prayer for the conversion of his persecutors, this time Father Thomas received his Crown.

The Catholics took his body away, no one trying to prevent them, and they interred it within the ruins of an Augustinian abbey, beyond the walls of Drogheda. They kept watch by the Confessor's grave until late in the evening, when soldiers were sent to drive them forth from that hallowed place. Late at night one of the sentinels saw the old abbey brilliantly lighted up by torches which appeared to be suspended in mid-air over the place where he knew the body of the martyred Friar had been laid, and having drawn a comrade's attention to the strange sight, they both deserted their posts, and hastened to report the matter to the officer in charge. Instead of reprimanding them for their cowardice, the captain went to see those lights for himself, but no sooner had he beheld them than he also was seized with a great dread. However, he dissembled his fear, and assigned an absurd reason for the apparition. Accompanied by the more courageous of his men, he paid a visit to the ruins to make sure that the Catholics had not removed the martyr's body. They found the grave undisturbed, and clearing away the loose stones and clay, they gazed once more on the young Friar's face, still most beautifully composed in the happy death-sleep. The soldiers then declared that a just man had been slain without cause, and while one of them took possession of the crucifix which Father Thomas had held clasped to his breast on the scaffold, another-claimed the white mantle. And we are told that neither of the Puritans could ever be persuaded to part with those relics, although they had previously deemed Father Thomas worthy of death for having persevered in his holy profession.

II. Brother Angelus of St. Joseph.[1]

The Teresian student slain by the Puritans was known in the world as George Halley. He was an Englishman, the member of a Catholic family of Herefordshire. An Irish Discalced Carmelite had been the first entrusted with his education, and when at a very early age the youth found himself called to embrace the Religious life, he himself ambitioned to become a Friar of the same Order. He received the brown habit at Dublin in the year 1640, taking the name of Angelus of St. Joseph, which, we are told, was admirably significative of his gentle disposition. He hoped to be allowed to return to England after his ordination to labour there for the conversion of his countrymen. God willed otherwise, and now Ireland numbers him among her Confessors, as it was here he shed his blood for the faith.

Fra Angelus was professed in due course, having given great edification to his brethren during his noviceship. He had begun by resolving to remain ever indifferent to such things as could win for him human esteem; we shall see how his conduct was influenced by the same good purpose to the end. Hardly had he arrived in Drogheda to begin his studies when all the Friars had to leave that city owing to the fury of the Puritans. Brother Angelus escaped in the beginning, but he was subsequently arrested and taken back to the town. During his imprisonment he suffered

[1] *Enchyr. Mēnol. (Ital. MS.).*

great annoyance from the heretical ministers who tried to harass him by objections against the faith. On hearing them allude to the "Pure Gospel" of their sect, he quietly remarked that he knew the Law of the Lord must indeed be undefiled, and for this very reason he abhorred the errors of all fanatics.

His spirit could not be broken by the cruelest privations; he was always wishing for yet greater trials. And keeping himself recollected by the practice of mental prayer throughout his long captivity, he was able, from time to time, to give prudent advice to the Faithful imprisoned with him for the Catholic cause. Contrary to all expectation, he was one day released on condition that he should leave Drogheda forthwith. This was an unaccountable act of leniency on the part of the Puritans. They must have had some political motive in view; perhaps it was their fear of Owen Roe O'Neill, who had succeeded Sir Phelim as leader of the Confederate army, and who was determined to besiege the city.[1]

There was a certain Father Nugent, a Capuchin Friar, who knew Brother Angelus intimately, having often contrived to visit him in prison. This priest informs us that it was the intention of the young Religious on his release to join his brethren who were still leading "*The Regular Life*" in a place not very far distant (probably Ardee), which was still protected by an Irish regiment. On his way thither Brother Angelus met a little band of nuns

[1] *Haverty.*

proceeding in the same direction, and having a "*Safe-conduct*" from the Puritans: an extraordinary favour, surely, considering how women devoted to God were hated by the heretics of the seventeenth century.[1] One night they found refuge in a fort held by the Confederates; but before morning it was taken by the enemy—the fanatical soldiers of Lord Moore.[2]

Brother Angelus appears to have had a presentiment of his approaching doom. He was told that there was a priest in the fort; and that the Holy Sacrifice could be offered secretly without any great risk. Availing themselves of the opportunity, the Religious — Fra Angelus and his companions—made arrangements to assist at Mass the next morning, and to receive the Blessed Eucharist. Wonderfully strengthened by this great consolation, the young Friar proposed that the nuns should present their "*Safe-conduct*" to Lord Moore. Naturally they were terrified at the thought of meeting a Puritan general; but there was no other means of escape, and they were reassured when Brother Angelus said he was coming with them himself; for they imagined that he also would be allowed to leave the place in virtue of their passport.

Lord Moore received the nuns with much courtesy, telling them they were free to depart whenever they pleased. But he instantly recognised their companion as the monk who had been so *leniently* dealt with at Drogheda. A court-martial

[1] *Prenderg.* [2] *Enchyr.*

was summoned to decide *his* fate, and of course he was condemned to death. If Brother Angelus would avert this dread sentence, and even ensure the general's patronage and friendship, he had only to deny his faith. This he could not do; and it enraged the Puritans to hear him request, quite calmly, that his execution should not be delayed, as he longed to celebrate the grand privilege of the Blessed Virgin by dying for the Catholic faith. It was the Feast of Our Lady's Assumption.

A file of soldiers were ordered to take him apart, and shoot him. He knelt when they presented their firearms at his breast; but in this instance, likewise, Heaven intervened, several volleys having been fired in vain. However, the Puritans were determined to silence the voice that still invoked the holy name of Mary; like the Pagan tyrants, in the early ages of Christianity, seeing the failure of the executioners the general commanded them to have recourse to the sword. Brother Angelus was beheaded on the 15th August 1642. Lord Moore himself was shot dead soon after, having previously suffered the disgrace of an ignominious defeat.[1]

The nuns, who had been the witnesses of the martyr's victory, communicated all the circumstances to his brethren later on. At first his body was interred by the Faithful of the district in a secret place, and in more peaceful times they removed it thence to a church with every mark of pious veneration for the slain Friar's memory.

[1] *Hist. Irish Conf.*

Brother Angelus's virtues were well known to them; although very young "*he had been made perfect in a short space, thereby fulfilling a long time: because his soul pleased God.*"[1]

III. BROTHER PETER OF THE MOTHER OF GOD.[2]

The lay-brother, the third of our Confessors, was Peter of the Mother of God. He was received into the Order at Dublin, his native place. It was his vocation to sanctify himself by solely attending to the domestic affairs of the monastery, never ambitioning the state of his brethren who had been called to undertake the duties of the priesthood. He knew it was not necessary to pass through the schools in order to acquire the science of the Saints: the study of his crucifix and rosary-beads was sufficient for him throughout life. And we shall see that with the knowledge thus obtained he was able to refute the sophistries of those who tried to rob him of his faith. He was most zealous in the discharge of his various offices; prudent and pious; and always cherished a very tender devotion to the Blessed Virgin.

After the Teresian Friary in Cook Street had been suppressed, Brother Peter gladly remained in the city to provide for the temporal wants of the Fathers who were daily exposed to the horrors of the persecution. Having rendered them invaluable

[1] *Sap. IV.*
[2] Some say "*Of St. Andrew.*" Compare *Enchyr., Ménol.*, &c.

service in their perilous mission, his reward was the martyr's crown. He was captured by the Puritans early in March of the year 1643. Almost worn out by past toils and privations, his health gave way completely under the cruel treatment he received in prison, so that it was only a relief to him when told his sufferings should cease on the Feast of the Annunciation, the day assigned for his death. Before the end, however, he was haunted by a dread of that *shameful* doom. It was the conflict between nature and grace, and very fierce while it lasted, but, through the intercession of his patroness, the Queen of Carmel, he gained the victory. His heart was now filled with peace; he gloried in the thought of his approaching struggle. This marvellous change was brought about by the special grace mercifully granted to the weak when their burden is heavy to bear. Hitherto Brother Peter had been timorous and despondent, now he possessed the martyr's confidence and strength. Those who had seen him in affliction wanted him to appeal to the pity of his persecutors, but he begged them to spare him their kindly remonstrances, as he was himself most eager to die. There were some Catholics among the prisoners, and these he implored to unite with him in praying God to pardon his cowardice, and grant him the needful courage to persevere. He had but one desire, he told them, to prove himself a loyal son of Holy Church—worthy of the habit which he wore. Accordingly, the whole night preceding his execution was passed by him and his friends in the recital of the Litany, Rosary, and other prayers.

He seemed very happy in the morning as the appointed time drew near. He continued still more earnestly to call upon the Mother of God, thanking Her, in the name of all men, for having been so humbly obedient to the Divine Will at the Annunciation. On hearing him speak thus one of the heretical ministers—several had come to try to pervert the heroic Confessor—rebuked him for attributing such honour to Our Blessed Lady. Brother Peter reminded his tormentor how Mary had been praised by the Holy Ghost in her own inspired words of the "Magnificat"; and this answer gave the Puritan a subject for serious reflection until they arrived at the scaffold, which had been set up in a most frequented part of Dublin to intimidate and mortify the Faithful. But the pious people regarded this as the "*shame of the Cross*," in which Christians glory; instead of producing fear it afforded them new constancy and hope, recalling to their minds the reward of those who die in the cause of religion. When about to ascend the steps, Brother Peter prostrated himself to the ground in sign of his unworthiness to rank with the Confessors of the faith; he also kissed the halter with great reverence, making in the meantime fervent acts of contrition, and renewing his religious profession. The Puritans still persisted in telling him that it was folly to sacrifice himself for such convictions; he replied that there was a wisdom which the world could not understand. And in the thirty-third year of his age, on the 25th of March 1643, he suffered a violent death—the last proof of the firmness of his own belief.

Braving the wrath of their persecutors, the Catholics took possession of the Confessor's remains, and bore them with all honour to the grave. In fact, they seemed to ambition that Teresian lay-brother's terrible fate; but the Puritans were satisfied, for the time being, with the revenge which they had taken on one whom the Faithful had long revered for his spirit of self-sacrificing zeal.[1]

Besides these three Confessors and that other young lay-brother killed by a Puritan woman, we find casual mention of several more of the Discalced Carmelites who died for the faith in Ireland. Indeed, "*many*" must have received the martyr's "*Palm and Crown*" during that dread persecution, because there are traditions in various parts of the country relating to the martyrdom of Teresian Friars, to whose memory only passing allusion may now be made. A tree is pointed out in Longford as being that on which "*the Carmelites were hanged*"; and we are assured, moreover, that three members of the Order met a like fate together in Dublin, at St. Stephen's Green. In an appeal to Rome in the year 1647, the Irish Fathers speak of three of their Religious who had been recently slain by the Puritans.[2] But there is no means of ascertaining whether these were the Friars put to death in Stephen's Green, or those whose martyrdom we have just recorded; or, perhaps, others

[1] *Ital. MS. Enchyr. Ménol.*   [2] *Spicil. Ossor.*

who are to be numbered among Ireland's unknown Confessors of the Faith. It is equally impossible to say whether a Father Patrick of the Irish Province, who was another victim of the Puritan persecution, is to be identified with the Friar of that name alluded to in several documents as one of the Irish Provincials. The annalists also speak of an Irish Father named Bede, who merited the "*Palm and Crown*" about the same time.[1]

In a letter written to the General of the Order on the 21st of November 1656, mention is made of a Father Lawrence of St. Thomas who, likewise, claims a brief notice in this place, since it is distinctly stated in another document that his death resulted from a malady contracted while in prison in Ireland for the faith. He had been already on the mission elsewhere before coming to St. Patrick's Province in June of the year 1657. Although the fury of the Cromwellian persecution was then less violent, the Friars were by no means secure, and Father Lawrence's zeal soon made him an object of bitter hatred to the Puritans. He managed to avoid them for nearly six months, the diocese of Meath being the principal field of his labours. He celebrated Mass almost daily, and frequently preached to the Faithful. Often, too, he would disguise himself and visit the heretics, many of whom he succeeded in winning back to the faith. But on the 11th of September 1657, he was taken by the soldiers in the very exercise of the sacred ministry. He was kept rigorously

[1] *Annales du Carmel.*

confined at Drogheda for three years. However, this vigilance on the part of the Puritans did not prevent him communicating with his Catholic fellow-prisoners, and even with the Faithful of the city. For a long time there was no other priest in the neighbourhood; so that the people had no means of obtaining the solace of religion except by availing themselves of every favourable opportunity of seeing Father Lawrence. At length, the dreadful privations of his prison-life brought on a disease so painful that his persecutors, sure of his helplessness, released him on parole.[1] The remaining few years of his life were passed in great suffering until he died at Dundalk on the vigil of the Feast of St. Teresa, 1667, his brethren on the mission bearing highest testimony to his fortitude, patience, and zeal.

A Father Kieran of St. Patrick was equally zealous; he was arrested in another part of the country when Father Lawrence was seized in Meath; and for the six long years of his captivity he attended to the spiritual wants of the Faithful who came to visit him in prison. He was one of those priests afterwards "transported beyond the seas": a fate justly considered more terrible than that of his brethren who had happily obtained their Crowns by martyrdom in Ireland.[2] There was also Father Patrick of St. Brigid,[3] who escaped as the Puritans were about to fix the rope round

---

[1] *MS. from Lond. Arch.*
[2] *MS. Arch. of Lond.* and *Spicil. Ossor.*
[3] Or, "*of St. James.*" See p. 85.

his neck! Afterwards he became famous in Italy, where the remainder of his life was spent, for his great fervour in perpetuating the traditions of the Teresian Reform according to the spirit of the Seraphic Virgin and of St. John of the Cross. He died there towards the end of the seventeenth century.[1] Then we have "Our Outlaws," who risked every peril to assist the persecuted people. We find them referred to as Fathers of the Irish Province, who had lived in caves, suffering many hardships in order that they might carry on the work of their mission : to guard Ireland's treasure of the faith.[2] One who had himself personal experience of their mode of life has left us an interesting account of their trials and struggles while he is treating of the state of the Irish Church under Cromwell's Protectorate ; and thus, indirectly, furnishes much important information concerning St. Patrick's Province.

[1] *Ital. MS.* [2] *Enchyr.*

CHAPTER VII.

"THE OUTLAWED."

The Cromwellian persecution—Father Agapitus of the Holy Ghost as annalist of the Irish Province—The Teresian "*Outlaws*"—Horrors of the Transplantation—Father Agapitus and the Puritans—Failure of Cromwell's Irish Campaign—Some victories of "*The Outlawed*."

A COUNCIL of State, formed of Parliamentarians, assumed control of affairs in England immediately after the murder of the King (A.D. 1649). Oliver Cromwell was appointed Lord Deputy and military leader in Ireland, where a desperate struggle was still being made in favour of Charles II., whom Ormond had at once proclaimed lawful heir to the English throne. But it was thought that a vigorous campaign, conducted by Cromwell in person, would effectively put an end to the Royalist cause in this country; and in little over a twelvemonth the most sanguine hopes of Parliament were fully realised. The new Lord Deputy came with the express purpose of defeating the enemies of his own party, it is true; however, he was equally determined, and he candidly said so, to suppress the Catholic religion by every means in his power; if necessary the entire Irish race could be extirpated, and the kingdom given to other colonies of Puritan Planters.

His method, we are told, with grim humour, by the most enthusiastic of his modern apologists, was one of "*moral surgery*," as instanced in the massacres of Drogheda and Wexford : helpless women and children being chiefly the victims of his inhuman deeds.[1] The Irish army had by this time lost the spirit of heroic resistance hitherto fostered by union among its leaders, and too soon the victorious Lord Deputy was free to entrust the dread work of the campaign to his lieutenants, he himself having been recalled to crush the hopes of the Royalists in Scotland, where ardour in the cause had been revived by the presence of the young King. Cromwell was again successful; and being now in a position to name his own reward to Parliament, he was invested with absolute power, and given the title of Lord Protector (A.D. 1653). This was the object of his ambition from the beginning; but he was too prudent to reveal it until he could confidently rely on the support of the army.

The persecution of the Catholics of Ireland became fiercer than ever; the "Act of Settlement" was now in operation, for the soldiers had to be paid. As for the disbanded Irish troops, they were forced into exile to the number of nearly forty thousand, so the people could no longer look to them for aid. The Friars who had escaped "*being knocked on the head*"—it was Cromwell's way of disposing of the Religious—were "*Outlaws*"

[1] *Carlyle.*

in the land, and as such relentlessly pursued by the Puritans.[1] When captured, they were usually put to death without any form of trial, a barbarous penal statute of Queen Elizabeth's reign to that effect having been re-enacted against them; or, worse still, they could be sold to the West-Indian planters as *slaves*. Among the Teresian "*Outlaws*" at this time was a Father Agapitus of the Holy Ghost, who has left us an account of some of his own experiences on the Irish Mission, dating from the "Transplantation," which he considers fully explained by the infamous "ACT OF SETTLEMENT." This scheme meant the wholesale plunder of the people of Ireland, who were driven from their homes in midwinter in order that their lands and possessions might pass into the hands of Cromwell's adventurers. The inhabitants of three other Provinces had to migrate into Connaught, and dared not return thence under pain of death. Father Agapitus had been asked to furnish an official report of the state of religion in Ireland during this terrible epoch, and his document contains that reference to the Irish Discalced Carmelites.[2]

Even when most diligent search was being made for them by the Puritans, the Teresian Fathers not alone remained in the country, but actually continued to receive postulants, whom they afterwards sent to monasteries of their Order abroad, incurring

[1] *Cromwel. Settle.*
[2] *Ital. MS.;* also in *Spicileg. Ossor.*, but without the author's name.

thereby all the penalties attached to the crime of high treason. It was the grand desire of those aspiring to the brown habit to return to their native land as "*Outlaws*" when ordained. In one instance we find a candidate permitted to pass his noviceship, and even make his profession in Ireland before leaving for the Continent. The circumstances merit special mention, for that young Friar is now known to the Catholic world as FATHER LAWRENCE OF ST. TERESA, a famous Teresian theologian.[1]

He was born in Drogheda in 1625, his parents being fervent Catholics, and generous benefactors to the Discalced Carmelites. His father held a command in the army of Charles I., but was killed in action before the more serious troubles of that unfortunate monarch's reign. And now it was the widowed mother's earnest hope to see her son a priest. Her prayers were heard; the future divine had only attained his sixteenth year when he begged to be admitted to the Order of Teresian Friars among the members of the community that had been provided with a refuge at Drogheda, by a relative of his own, after the outbreak of Puritan fanaticism in that city (A.D. 1641). Owing to the then disturbed state of political affairs, the Fathers there could not at first comply with his request, although they themselves were still leading "*The Regular Life.*" Later on they did receive him, and arranged that he should take his Vows in accordance with the usual canonical formalities, after he

[1] *Opera Theol. Collect. Scrip. Ord. Excel.*

had undergone his term of probation. He was eventually sent to France for his studies, to which he devoted himself with extraordinary success. Having completed his scholastic course in the College of the Province of Aquitaine, he was ordained priest; he then got permission to go to the missionary seminary at Rome, in order to prepare himself thoroughly for his duties in Ireland. But having defended his public "Thesis" in 1650, he was told that instead of returning to St. Patrick's Province, as he so keenly desired, he should have to undertake the serious task of training others for the labours of the "*Outlaw's*" career. His humility prevented him seeing in this decision of his superiors the evidence of their highest appreciation of his virtue and learning. The Father-General had him affiliated to the Province of Lombardy, and he was soon appointed Professor at the College of Bologna.

Father Lawrence taught there, and also at Cremona, for a number of years. He held, moreover, the important office of Definitor-Provincial; and was afterwards Prior of the Missionary College of St. Pancratius at Rome. Renowned as a spiritual Director, it is said that several communities of Carmelite nuns made rapid progress in the way of perfection under his prudent guidance. His death occurred at Rome when he was only in the forty-fourth year of his age, November 1670. A Religious who had been one of Father Lawrence's students, and who succeeded him as Professor—Father Adeodatus of Saints Peter and Paul—was appointed to prepare his holy predecessor's writings for publication. These works fill five folio volumes, which were printed at Rome about the year 1682, and bear the title "ELUCIDARIUM THOMISTICUM." All the great theological questions, both dogmatic and moral, are to be found treated therein most profoundly, yet with an admirable simplicity of style. Father Lawrence also composed a short Treatise on Mystical Theology. The great divines of the seventeenth and following centuries speak loudly in his praise as a theologian; and while reading his Works it is impossible to withhold one's affectionate esteem from an author who could thus expound the "*Difficulties of the Schools*," while his heart was with his "*Outlawed*" brethren, so much more favoured than he, in being called to labour among the Faithful of his native land.

Father Agapitus was in Rome in 1662, at the time Father Lawrence was Superior of the Monastery of St. Pancratius, but he does not speak of him when alluding to the other Irish Teresian exiles. However, his document deals more directly with the state of the Catholics of Ireland in the year 1653. The country was then overrun by the Cromwellian adventurers, who not alone seized the lands of the defenceless people, but were empowered by Parliament to traffic in Irish slaves with the planters of Barbados and other colonies. The Penal Laws were certainly then stringent enough to render the lives of the outlawed Friars miserable in the extreme; yet Father Agapitus assures us that the clergy of Ireland, secular and regular, suffered deepest anguish at the thought of their own powerlessness to alleviate the sorrows and afflictions of the Faithful. He himself had seen many noble families, who had been driven from their homes during the winter months, living in rude tents until such time as a place of residence should be assigned them amid the wilds of Connaught. Still they never complained of their hard lot; they accepted it in a spirit of Christian resignation as being a divinely permitted opportunity for the fervent profession of their faith. It was his own and his outlawed brethren's most painful duty to try and console them at every personal risk (when captured, the Friars were already doomed " *to be hanged, drawn, and quartered*"). But what words of comfort could they find to soothe the grief of a man who beheld his "gently nurtured" wife and little ones suddenly exposed to such want and perils? or the woe of a widowed mother when her husband was brutally murdered, and her children sent over the sea to be sold as slaves? Night after night Father Agapitus would visit an encampment of the "Transplanters" in order that they might avail themselves of his presence among them to receive greater courage and strength from the Sacraments. In this he had to use the utmost caution lest he should do them a temporal injury by the exercise of his sacred ministry; because it was deemed a very heinous crime to harbour a priest, or to assist him to escape the penalties of the law. But he seems to have been particularly fortunate in this respect, although the Puritans were even more than usually vigilant in his case, having frequently heard of how he succeeded in opposing the efforts of their ministers to propagate the "pure Gospel" in Ireland. He had been actually arrested, but happily made good his escape before they could carry out the death-sentence which he had incurred.

At first the heretics were quite confident that their idolised Protector, Cromwell, would succeed in the chief object of his Irish campaign. And Father Agapitus says that very few Catholic priests were left in the country to ward off the danger of apostasy, for many of them had been already either slain or transported; only the "*Outlaws*" remained. He knew but one Prelate, the Venerable Bishop of Kilmore, who was hiding in the woods, like the other "*Outlaws*"; being too old and infirm to fulfil his episcopal functions, the Faithful, who were acquainted with his retreat, provided him daily with the means of support. However, it soon became known to the authorities that numbers of the "*Felon Friars*" of the various Religious Orders had come back to Ireland from over the seas. The Puritans, therefore, considered it an easier and better way of dealing with the Irish priests to imprison them in future on the island of Innisboffin. Slavery in the plantations of the West Indies was quite a luxury compared with captivity in that place. Still, not even the dread of being sent there could prevent the "*Outlaws*" continuing their labours; and Protestant historians are often loudest in praise of the heroic spirit of the Catholic clergy during the Penal Days. Nor was it the vengeance of their persecutors only the "*Outlaws*" risked in discharge of their sacred duties; there was a famine in Ireland most of that time, accompanied by the awful plague. Contemporary writers attribute these two scourges to the "Act of Settlement," which was thus likely to prove what its originators intended it should be, an instrument for the extermination of the Irish race. Many priests were among the victims of the dread visitation; they died uncared for in some hovel or cave when they were no longer able to move about and assist the stricken people.

Father Agapitus speaks of the stratagems to which the "*Outlaws*" had recourse in order to administer the Sacraments. A disguise was always necessary; he himself adopted that of a Puritan soldier. Frequently he would join a regiment on march, taking care that the Faithful in the various districts should be told of his coming, so as to meet him whenever he had an opportunity of leaving his companions, who used to think, and rightly, that he had gone in search of "recusant papists." For there was a heavy fine imposed upon those refusing to attend the religious service of the Puritans; and part of the money was distributed among the more successful soldiers.

Between Christmas-tide and the following Easter, Father Agapitus was enabled to visit fully three thousand Catholics who had fled from the towns to the woods and hills. At first a few ignorant people thought it no great harm to present themselves at the Conventicles, thereby hoping to escape plunder and imprisonment; but when their error was explained to them, they protested that they would rather die the cruelest death than betray their faith. In the time of adversity the value of this treasure was more clearly realised. From time to time Father Agapitus would recognise, beneath some ingenious disguise, one of his own brethren, or a member of another Religious Order, or a secular priest, actively engaged in his missionary duties. When arrested himself, a Franciscan and two of the secular clergy were captured with him; and on a certain occasion both he and Father Charles Nolan, the Vicar-General of the diocese of Leighlin—a very learned man, and most devoted to the Faithful—barely avoided the Puritans three several times the same day by fleeing to the woods.

While still in the garb of a soldier, Father Agapitus had an extraordinary adventure; although the hero of it, he speaks of himself in the third person—as "*one of our Discalced Carmelites whom I knew*"—and this for the reason already assigned by Father Isidore, the humility of the missioners. Hearing, on his arrival in Dublin, that one of the Puritan ministers, a favourite preacher, had just been called away from his Conventicle when about to begin the usual fanatical harangue, Father Agapitus hastened to the place and offered to say a few words in his stead. The congregation were pleased; an exposition of the "*pure Gospel*" by an honest soldier was always in season. A very *seditious* but most successful sermon was then delivered by the Friar, who had the great happiness of receiving every one present into the Church. The new converts, the majority of whom were "*Adventurers*" of importance, concealed the priest among them until he had instructed them thoroughly in the faith. Finding himself deserted by his once devoted flock, the minister felt sure that a "Monk" had outwitted him, and he vowed to take speedy revenge. Thus we see how in a few hours one of the Teresian Carmelites was instrumental in causing more heretics to renounce their errors than there were apostates among the Faithful during the entire Cromwellian persecution. Because Father Agapitus assures us, "before God," that *hardly forty* wretched Catholics had yielded to either the threats or the allurements of the Puritans.

Furthermore, in the space of a week he knew one of his own brethren to convert as many as *twenty* fanatics in the Co. Wicklow alone. Nay, he was sure that altogether over a thousand of the "*Adventurers*" became Catholics, while he himself was in Ireland, owing to the zeal of the Teresian Friars; and *at least three thousand more* were instructed and received into the Church by other Irish priests. Evidently Cromwell's method of "*moral surgery*" was a failure, remembering the purpose which he had in view; the "*Outlaws*" were certainly entitled to the victory.

According to Father Agapitus, the more *scrupulous* of the soldiers refrained from "priest-hunting" on Sundays. The "*Outlawed*" were, on that account, able to do a great deal of missionary work on the day of rest. Week after week, for five consecutive years, he himself was accustomed to say Mass every Saturday at midnight in some far-off mountain retreat, well known to the Faithful, but which the Puritans would be least likely to suspect as the resort of "Recusants."

Before celebrating, he heard confessions; when required, he administered the other Sacraments, having faculties to do so; and never dismissed the crowd of earnest worshippers without exhorting them to perseverance in a short, fervent discourse. Such was the general practice of priests on the Irish Mission at that time. As they were thus engaged, Fathers Lawrence of St. Thomas and Kieran of St. Patrick were captured, and Father Agapitus heard that three Franciscans and five secular priests had been arrested in Meath on the same day. Previous to his departure from Ireland, he had occasion to visit nearly all the dioceses; and he remained in each place so long as his presence there was necessary to the Faithful. Hence the value of his information regarding the state of the persecuted Irish Church.[1]

He says that he had met many of the "*Outlaws*" in Dublin, among whom were two members of his own Order, several Dominicans, a few Jesuits, three Franciscans, and one secular priest —a Father Patrick Relly (?), who was a native of that city. The Catholic clergy became quite

[1] *Spicileg. Ossor. Ital. MS.*

numerous there in the course of time, and were under the jurisdiction of Dr. James Dempsey, the Vicar-Apostolic, a zealous Prelate, who even held "Conferences," that he might have the benefit of the advice of his brother "*Outlaws*" in furthering the interests of the diocese, and bringing about the conversion of heretics.

So great were the wants of the Catholics in Wexford, that Father Agapitus had to spend over two years in that place. He was at length relieved by two secular priests, two Franciscans, and a Teresian Friar; so that the people were thenceforth enabled to assist at the Holy Sacrifice and communicate more frequently. In Kildare and Meath, he was intimately acquainted with several priests. A nephew of the late Bishop of the latter diocese was then Vicar-General; several of the parishes were, however, in charge of the "*Outlawed*" Friars. Dr. Antony Geoghegan was subsequently appointed Bishop of Meath, and Father Agapitus, who was several years in the diocese, bears testimony to this Prelate's solicitude for the Faithful. He knew the Bishop to have confirmed the people by thousands at a time; and to have received a great number of Puritans into the Church. Even many priests were ordained, and other candidates for Holy Orders sent abroad in order that they might become perfectly qualified for the duties of the Irish Mission, by a full course of theological studies.

Father Agapitus found that there were some of the "*Outlawed*"—both secular and regular—in the Co. Kilkenny from the beginning; one of them was Vicar-General. Likely a few of the members of the Community of Discalced Carmelites of that place had escaped death and transportation, and were then assisting the local clergy; for he himself did not remain there. Travelling farther south, he met three other "*Outlaws*"—a secular priest, a Franciscan, and a Dominican—who had been recently imprisoned in Cork. They told him that there were a good many clergymen through Munster, all working as zealously as if they had nothing to fear from the Puritans.

There were Teresian Friars always in or near Drogheda, where, together with several other priests, they administered to the wants of the Faithful. Each of the Northern Dioceses was under the jurisdiction of a Vicar-General, and Father Agapitus mentions one of these dignitaries in particular—the Very Rev. Philip Croly. This was a man of great learning, and endowed with a remarkable prudence, which he employed in availing himself of political crises to advance the cause of religion in Ireland. He had been banished, and on daring to return had been confined in a Dublin prison for two years. He was then released on parole by Henry Cromwell, the Protector's fourth son, who, it is said, was constrained to persecute the Roman Catholics against his better judgment. After the Restoration Father Croly obtained his freedom unconditionally, like Father Lawrence, one of the Teresian "*Outlaws.*"

In the west of Ireland the horrors of the "Transplantation" should have been deemed sufficient to overawe the Faithful banished beyond the Shannon. Yet here, as in other parts of the country, "priest-hunting" expeditions were frequently raised by the Puritans, and many of the missioners were captured. The dioceses were fairly well supplied with clergy, a Vicar-General being usually in charge. Father Agapitus says that the Vicar-General of Elphin was a friend of his own; he also speaks of Father James Fineach of Roscommon, who had a great reputation for holiness; so much so, that *innumerable* conversions were attributed to the exercise of his miraculous power. Indeed, although the persecuted people never wondered to see crowds of the heretics renounce their errors, still Father Agapitus tèlls us that the Irish Church was shocked and grieved when it became known for certain that two faithless Catholics had publicly taken the Cromwellian Oath of Abjuration, denying the Papal Supremacy, the Real Presence, and the true nature of the Christian priesthood. One of them repented almost immediately, and made due reparation for the scandal given by his crime of apostasy. Even at the present day the Faithful of Ireland would deplore such a fall, and think it only natural that *four thousand Puritans* should yield to the "*Outlawed*" within three years, during which time the persecution had reached its most terrifying phase!

The state of Ireland just before the Restoration of the English Monarchy did not prevent a Visitator-General coming to discharge the duties of his office in St. Patrick's Province; his presence, however, was merely to encourage and console the "*Outlaws.*"[1] The Religious derived hope from the manifest failure of the "Protectorate," also, and were now looking forward to a season of peace in the near future, when they might resume the practice of the "*Regular Life*" once more. But nothing could be attempted in that respect while Cromwell still lived and was in power; though there were signs to show that his more than regal sway was becoming as irksome to the great majority of the Puritan party as to the Catholics of Ireland. The very soldiers were growing weary of his despotism; only the end was approaching, they might have *complained.* It would seem that he was tortured by a dread of assassination; some say he was also haunted by the thought of his share in the murder of the King. Nor would it have been strange if he saw in another persistent, unpleasant vision the victims of his Irish campaign! Cromwell died about six years after the completion of his work of "*moral surgery*" in Ireland; his son Richard succeeded him, to resign in a very short time. Parliament no longer feared the army, and there was anarchy in England for a while. Men soon realised how necessary it was for the welfare of the nation that the royal fugitive should be recalled. Accordingly in the year 1660 Charles II. returned to take possession of his throne, and nothing marred the enthusiasm of the welcome given him save, perhaps, the scowl on the faces of the late Lord Protector's "Ironsides," which reminded

[1] *MS. Lond. Arch.*

him of the tragedy at Whitehall. It was at last in his power to reward the unswerving devotion of his loyal Irish subjects.

This year, also, Father Agapitus came to Rome, and was commissioned to write in Latin an official account of his experience on the Irish Mission. He was then Conventual at the Monastery of Our Lady of Victory, where in all probability he died.

Many of his brethren had by this time returned to Ireland, and were hoping against hope to be soon able to exchange the perils and distractions of the "*Outlaw's*" life for the calm if austere retreat of the cloister. On his way to the Eternal City, Father Agapitus had himself conveyed the good news of the "Restoration" to the young Teresian exiles who had been sent abroad for their studies, and these were now eagerly waiting to be summoned to the labours of the mission in their native land.

CHAPTER VIII.

AFTER THE RESTORATION.

The "Black Act"—Ingratitude of Charles and Ormond—Prospects of St. Patrick's Province towards the close of this reign—Toleration under King James—Devotion of the Irish to the House of Stuart—After the Battle of the Boyne—The Teresian Friars at Loughrea—Another generation of Teresian "*Outlaws*"—Their mode of life during the Penal days.

CHARLES II. acknowledged his indebtedness to Ireland in his very first speech from the throne. Beyond this he did not trouble himself to give any practical proof of his gratitude; on the contrary, he soon began to complain of being annoyed by the frequent petitions of the Irish. And instead of any good resulting from that one expression of royal favour it only caused the Puritans to cry out against the "*growing power*" of the hated Catholics. Fearing that they should have to restore the plundered property to its rightful owners—the King's Irish subjects—they lost no time in persuading Charles that his safety absolutely depended on his adopting Cromwell's policy towards Ireland. All the old accusations were repeated more shamelessly than ever, until at length the King was terrified into assenting to a new "Act of Settlement," by which the people of this country were for ever deprived of the right of appealing to the Throne against the injustice of their oppressors. By that "BLACK ACT" the forfeited estates became vested in the Crown; and Charles granted them anew to his father's murderers! Nor was it ever possible for the victims of this wanton wrong to plead their own cause in the royal presence; not even a letter could he receive if its contents were such as might lead him to think that he was being duped by those who pretended to advise him. Should claimants be discovered in the act of forwarding him a memorial they were instantly seized as conspirators; and once in the power of their enemies there was no danger of their repeating the offence. No longer harassed by complaints from Ireland, the King entered on a career of profligacy which, seemingly, some of the *austerest* of the Puritans might not always *consistently* condemn.[1]

While this state of things lasted the Catholic clergy dared not venture forth publicly from their places of concealment; in the year 1661, we find an Irish bishop, Dr. Antony Geoghegan — Father Agapitus's friend — writing to Rome from his "*Cave*." A little toleration was shown the Faithful in the course of time; and many who had been imprisoned for their religion were released — among them several Discalced Carmelites; and, in fact, the priests everywhere resumed the exercise of their sacred calling with less danger of arrest.[2] Periodically, however, an

[1] *Prenderg.* [2] *Spicileg. Ossor.*

alarm was raised, and the Penal Laws had to be again rigorously enforced. In these circumstances the Teresian Fathers could not attempt the re-establishment of their Province in Ireland. Not until the panic of the "*Popish Plot*," invented by the notorious Titus Oates to incense ignorant heretics against their Catholic fellow-subjects by rumours of a French invasion, had ceased might the regular clergy safely open their churches in Ireland once more. For the persecution was likely to be renewed at any moment; the conspirators had only to show a Latin document to the fanatics, and say that it contained treason, in order to stir up the flame. Some of the Irish Bishops had to destroy the very Briefs of their Consecration to prevent an outbreak; and for a similar reason the members of the various Religious Orders then in the country could rarely communicate with their Superiors-General at Rome. The Venerable Oliver Plunkett, Archbishop of Armagh, was one of the last victims of these heartless intrigues; after his martyrdom (A.D. 1681) Irish Catholics were treated somewhat more leniently.

Like his royal master, the Duke of Ormond—who had been appointed Lord-Lieutenant of Ireland at the Restoration—remained long unmindful of his personal obligations to this nation. Far from using his influence at court in behalf of the Faithful, he rivalled Coote and Broghill (their most inveterate persecutors, whom Charles II. made Lords Justices) in oppressing them on every occasion. But suddenly reminded that a monarch's favour is not always a shield against the malice of one's enemies by the miscreant Blood's impeachment of his own loyalty, Ormond made some effort to repair his past ingratitude; at all events thenceforth his policy towards Ireland and the Roman Catholics became more tolerant. Charles himself was now well inclined towards his Irish subjects, having had long and bitter experience of the nature of the allegiance professed by the Scotch and English Puritans; it was well known that he had to appeal to Louis XIV. of France for aid, expecting that the people of England would regret, as indeed they did, having restored him to his throne. To the end of his reign it was a struggle for the mastery between him and his Parliament. But interesting as a more lengthy digression into these historical details might be, they are beyond the scope of our present task, and are merely touched upon inasmuch as they help us to trace the progress of the Teresian Reform in Ireland. Besides, those political agitations were very foreign to the spirit of the Discalced Carmelites, whose every ambition was centred in the cloister. Rarely had any of the Fathers, by reason of their office as Spiritual Directors, to concern themselves with the affairs of the world while they were leading "*The Regular Life*," and at the same time attending to the salvation of souls: never might they interest themselves in projects which could have hindered them attaining the object of their vocation. We have dwelt on this subject in another place when speaking of Father John

Rowe's relations with the Council of the Irish Confederate Catholics. And at the very epoch we now treat of there was a beautiful illustration of the Teresian spirit of retirement to be had in one of the monasteries of France. We are told that a lay-brother called Lawrence of the Resurrection, for whom Fénelon had a profound affection and esteem, was far happier, and considered himself much more usefully occupied in the *kitchen* or *garden* than in the parlour with his "*dear friend*," the Archbishop of Cambrai.[1]

This love of the cloister seems, moreover, to have inspired the Religious with tenderest devotion to their country. They never ceased to pray for the nation's welfare, all the more earnestly while waiting the issue of each new crisis in Charles II.'s reign. It never gave them a moment's thought, unless, perhaps, to thank God for their own *greater privilege*, that, although they themselves were living as felon-fugitives, the habit and mantle, which they dared not wear, were a welcome sight in nearly all the courts of Europe.[2]

A few years before the death of Charles II. the members of Religious Orders in Ireland were permitted to live in community. The Discalced Carmelites appear to have been then quite numerous in Dublin, Drogheda, and Loughrea, but although there were several "Residences" also, they had not yet reopened either the Novitiate or House of Studies.[3]

---

[1] *Ménol.*   [2] *Ibid.*
[3] MS. in *Archives of Dublin Monastery*.

The King died in 1684, undoubtedly a Roman Catholic. He was succeeded by his brother, the Duke of York, who had long been a devoted son of the Church. The accession of this prince was received with unfeigned joy by the Faithful in Ireland especially, and after events showed that they had grounds for the newly awakened hope. James II. began his reign by solemnly declaring that all his subjects should have perfect liberty in matters of religion. Even the Puritans rejoiced in this proclamation, and joined in praising the King for his good intentions; still they were enraged at his assisting at the Holy Sacrifice publicly, and at his making much of the Friars, who now began to wear again the habits of their several Orders.

Great was the change in Ireland. Churches were speedily repaired, to be thronged by the Faithful who had often waited with eager expectancy for the coming of one of the "*Outlaws*" to assist at the Mass which he would offer at the peril of his life. The Primitive Rule of Carmel was observed once more as fervently as if the interruption to "*The Regular Life*" had occurred but yesterday, not half a century previously; and the sight of the brown habit consoled and reassured the pious people. The reorganisation of the Irish Province was only a matter of time, and then the necessity for sending subjects abroad for ordination would be happily removed.

Alas, the spirit of intolerance was too deeply rooted among the narrow-minded fanatics to permit the Irish Catholics a lengthy enjoyment of these prospects of prosperity and peace. The acquittal of the "Bishops" in 1688 was the surest sign of the rising storm. These heretical prelates had refused to subscribe to the "*Declaration of Indulgence,*" whereby the King, in virtue of his royal prerogative, merely wished to repeal some of the existing Penal Laws. A little while, and his rebellious subjects brought James II. to a condition quite as deplorable as that to which his murdered father had been reduced a short time before his tragic death. Ireland alone remained loyal to the Crown—the Irish Catholics; for the "Adventurers" were up in arms at the bare mention of religious toleration, fearing the effects of such a policy on their own interests, having no established claim to the lands which they held throughout the country. The throne being thus deemed vacant again, the King's own son-in-law, William, Prince of Orange, was invited to take possession of it by invading England. His enterprise was more successful than that of the unfortunate Duke of Monmouth, who, nevertheless, had found many to uphold his cause for no other reason than his well-known hostility to the Catholic faith. James II. fled to the court of Louis XIV. on the approach of William's formidable army, having already commissioned the Earl of Tyrconnel to apply to his Irish subjects for support.

There is something pathetically romantic in Ireland's devotion to the Stuarts. It is said that this extraordinary loyalty—extraordinary, seeing how it had been requited by the successive representatives of that fated dynasty—sprang from the people's high sense of the duty of patriotism. The nation had always clung to the tradition that Edward Bruce was the last crowned " King of Ireland," and the Stuarts were descended from his brother, the hero of Bannockburn.[1] Beautiful as this sentiment was, those most deeply indebted to the spirit of self-sacrifice which it called forth often received it with a sneer; but the Irish were ever ready to forgive and forget when appealed to in the sacred cause of their religion, their country, or their *King*. And now, while James II. was imploring the aid of France, they strained every possible resource to raise an army in his defence. By their efforts principally was he enabled to come to Ireland in person the following year (1689), confident of ultimately regaining his crown. Indeed, James II. thought the final victory assured on first witnessing the enthusiastic determination of the Catholic soldiers, and it was on their valour he relied to suppress the fanatic discontent which had driven him from his throne. Still was he slow to sanction an Act passed by Parliament (that which he himself had convened on his arrival in Dublin) providing for the protection and relief of his Roman Catholic subjects; he was afraid of displeasing the English Puritans, now in open revolt. We hardly wonder that even his most ardent supporters were driven to despair.

Terrified at his defeat in the Battle of the Boyne, James fled to the Continent again, to seek

[1] *History of Ireland* (Haverty).

further assistance; while his generals, both Irish and French, bravely continued the struggle in Ireland. The frequent repulse of the Williamite besiegers at Athlone, the action at Aughrim, and the defence of Limerick show what the issue of the war might have been under another king. A want of resolution caused James II. to forfeit his throne, and with it the loyal esteem, if not the pity, of his Irish subjects, whose bravery and self-sacrifice his own timidity had rendered all in vain.[1]

It is said that after the battle of Aughrim (A.D. 1691) the body of St. Ruth, who had been one of the slain, was borne secretly from the fatal field, and interred in the old Abbey of Loughrea, in presence of several of the Discalced Carmelites.[2] The Teresian Friars were certainly living in community there at the time; but we have only a local tradition for the statement that the obsequies of the impetuous French general were celebrated by the Fathers of that monastery. However, it is probable that some of the Religious were among the priests who used to attend to the spiritual wants of the Irish army; and, after "Aughrim," they may have suggested the old abbey as the most convenient place wherein the body of St. Ruth could receive the rites of Christian burial. This was the only tribute of respect that might be paid to the dead general's memory; nor was it likely to have been omitted by his soldiers as they passed through Loughrea on their retreat still further west.

[1] *Jacobite War in Ireland.*   [2] *A Light to the Blind.*

The annalists often speak of the heroic endurance of the Irish people during the Jacobite war. But nothing could compensate for a spirit of disunion among the leaders of the King's forces, although in justice it must be said that the Irish were always willing to yield their own views if by so doing they could in any way forward the cause of the Stuarts. Neither were the French in the right mood for an *Irish* campaign against the Prince of Orange, whose soldiers had likewise invaded France. Hence we find King James's foreign allies hastening to embark from Ireland, leaving a remnant of the Irish army at bay in a beleaguered city of Munster. Even when reduced to such straits, the Jacobite soldiers would insist on their own terms, and obtained from the victorious enemy a treaty most advantageous to the nation: on no other condition could the intrepid garrison of Limerick be prevailed upon to withdraw from the struggle, which certainly had not failed through any fault of theirs.

William and Mary were now in undisputed possession of the English throne, and they were both solemnly pledged to ratify a solemn compact made with their subjects in Ireland. By the "*Treaty of Limerick*" the Irish Catholics were entitled to a measure of religious toleration which would, at all events, have prevented the renewal of the horrors of past Penal days; briefly, it ensured for the Faithful of this kingdom peace. Nearly all the soldiers—fully twenty thousand—had entered the French service immediately after the capitulation of Limerick; and by their subsequent devotedness to King Louis they richly repaid his generosity to the House of Stuart. But it was a woeful day for the country when they left; no sooner had they sailed away, in those ships so eagerly provided by the English Government, than a cry was raised against the terms of a treaty, which the Protestants considered entirely too liberal to be carried out with the vanquished. It was openly declared that no faith need be kept with a people acknowledging the supremacy of the Pope of Rome. No matter how well disposed, the King and Queen were powerless to respect their royal word, and the persecution of the Catholics was again renewed.

As in former times, it began by the confiscation of property in Ireland; all who had sworn allegiance to James II. being now declared guilty of high treason. About four thousand of the leading gentry were thus proscribed and driven into exile. New "Planters" were sent over to colonise the country, while William himself took a royal share of the plunder for his favourites, notwithstanding his admiration of a people whom his very first Parliament was trying to extirpate. Another means adopted during this reign for suppressing the Catholic religion in Ireland was just as barbarous as the worst which Cromwell had employed. Bishops and priests, secular and regular, were ordered to leave the country before the 1st May 1698; if they should dare remain, it was at the peril of their lives. To harbour a priest or Bishop was also regarded as a crime, to be punished by heavy fines, imprisonment, or death, at the discretion of those who had been appointed to enforce the infamous law. The priest-hunter's office was now regarded as a patriotic duty, and tempting rewards were held out to encourage the efforts of wretches engaged in the gruesome task. And in order that the Exchequer might not be burdened with the payment of these expenses, the Catholics of districts wherein a victim had been seized were to furnish the required amount. Thus, some four hundred and twenty-four of the regular clergy alone were captured and banished even before the time assigned.

A good many of the Discalced Carmelites of St. Patrick's Province were then advanced in age, and unequal to the hardships of an "*Outlaw's*" life. These were recalled to Rome by their Superior-General, and a number of young Religious came to Ireland in their stead, having been recently ordained on the Continent. Many of the names of this new generation of Teresian "*Outlaws*" are to be found in the "*Obituary.*" Theirs was a great sacrifice, coming forth from the secure retreat of the cloister to risk the dangers of such a career; but the young missioners did not think so; they had gladly chosen this duty of charity among the Faithful of their native land in preference to a share in the fame of their brethren, who were at that time renowned in other countries as philosophers and divines.[1] Their only regret was to have to doff the beloved habit of their Order for a necessary disguise; since the brown

[1] *Menol.*

robe of the Teresian Carmelites might not be worn in Ireland again for more than a hundred years. However, they themselves and the Faithful generally still retained the small scapular which is the prescribed livery of Carmel's Queen; and often it proved a *sign* of protection to them amid the terrible trials which they had to bear. There was little danger in concealing this sacred badge about the person; although the Friars could not venture to carry with them anything else pertaining to their sacred profession. The Breviary was considered ample proof of guilt when discovered on one suspected of being a cleric. Dr. James Fallon, of the "*Noble Sept*" that has given so many saintly Prelates to the Irish Church, had his "*Office-Book*" used in evidence against him. And it is a significant fact that a very small-sized edition of the various manuals of the Order should have been published in the year 1693 by the Superiors-General of the Discalced Carmelites. Some copies then used by the Fathers on the Irish Mission are still to be had.[2]

The life of the Teresian "*Outlaws*" during William's reign hardly differed from that of their predecessors under Cromwell's Protectorate. They tried to perpetuate faithfully the fervent zeal characteristic of the Fathers of St. Patrick's Province in the past. Their own sufferings were quite forgotten when they saw the persecuted people derive much consolation from their presence among them in this hour of woe. As usual, the

[1] Vide *Cerem. and Constit.*, A.D. 1693, with inscriptions.

Visitators-General came from Rome periodically to encourage the missioners themselves; and we find the "Exhortations" given by them even at that time, just as if the Religious were practising "*The Regular Life*" in the secure retreat of their monasteries.[1]

When at all possible two or three Fathers, disguised either as labourers or peasants, dwelt together in a little cabin beyond the priest-hunter's easy reach. They made this poor hut the centre of their missionary labours, and spoke fondly of it as their friary. In the towns they contrived to secure a humble abode in one of the less frequented streets, so as to exercise their sacred duties with less danger of being suspected by the secret agents specially employed for their discovery.

A few years before King William's death, several Teresian Fathers were in Dublin, occupying a tenement in Hammond Lane.[2] They remained there for a considerable time; and were very fortunate in thus evading the vigilance of the authorities, who would prevent young men leaving Ireland with the *criminal* purpose of joining a Religious Order on the Continent. But the Discalced Carmelites continued to receive Irish postulants; and made every effort, moreover, to instruct poor Catholic children doomed to ignorance by the law. Often, too, the Fathers assisted more promising pupils to enter the universities abroad, where they were afforded opportunities of cultivating natural talent under guidance of the greatest masters

[1] *MS. in Arch. of St Teresa's.*   [2] *Ibid.*

of that age. These most efficacious means were, likewise, adopted by many other priests throughout Ireland to counteract the designs of Government. There was an alternative, but *impossible* to the Irish people: conformity to the "*Religion of the State.*"[1]

The glimmer of hope remained to the nation while James II. still lived, not that the dethroned monarch had gained the confidence of the Irish, but because he was supported by Louis XIV. as the lawful claimant to the English crown. In all his wars with England, the King of France had ever in view the ultimate restoration of the Stuart dynasty. In fact, English people were themselves now heartily tired of William III., whose affections were with the Dutch rather than with those who applauded every fresh mortification which he received from a refractory Parliament. Besides, King William was *too honest* to dissemble his feelings when he saw that he had no control over the rival parties—the "Whigs" and "Tories"—who were called in turn to the veritable exercise of the royal prerogatives, according to the humour of the hour. As a refuge from political strife, he spent most of his time in the camp with his soldiers, even taking an active part in the foreign campaigns. And then did he encounter once more those brave Irish foes who had yielded him so poor a victory at the Boyne, and whose heroic bravery now caused him to deplore his own inability to repeal the laws which gave such allies to France.

[1] *MS. in Arch. of St. Teresa's.*

The death of James II. occurred only a short time before that of his son-in-law and rival William III. (A.D. 1701). His son, James Edward Stuart, was immediately proclaimed heir to the throne of England at the courts of France and Spain. This was a painful humiliation to King William, who seems to have been keenly sensitive with regard to his title to the crown. Having survived Mary II. about eight years, he died in 1702, and was succeeded by his sister-in-law, another daughter of James II., Queen Anne.

But these events did not improve the state of the Faithful in Ireland. The "*Outlawed*" would be well inured to privations of every kind before a favourable crisis in English politics made Religious Toleration a happy necessity, bringing relief at last to the long-tried Catholics, priests and people.

CHAPTER IX.

ST. PATRICK'S PROVINCE IN THE EIGHTEENTH CENTURY.

State of the Irish Catholics during the reign of Queen Anne—The Hanoverian reversion—First Centenary of the Discalced Carmelites in Ireland—George II. and the Fathers of the Irish Province—The General Visitation of 1743—Opening of a friary in Stephen's Street, Dublin—A grand enterprise of the Archconfraternity—Death of two of the Teresian "*Outlaws*"—Eulogy of an Irish Discalced Carmelite in the *London Gazette*—Irish political movements in the reign of George III.—The French Revolution.

LIKE her sister Mary, Queen Anne was a Protestant, and most bitterly prejudiced against her Roman Catholic subjects. During her reign they were treated with appalling severity, not that she herself had power to succour them did she so please; but an expression of sympathy on her part might have checked the eagerness of her Parliaments, both English and Irish, in increasing the number of the Penal Laws. As it is, Anne's name in Ireland, at least, has become associated with that of Queen Elizabeth for a particularly barbarous persecution of those who professed the true faith. Not content with having reduced the people to abject poverty and misery in the preceding reign, the Protestant party still continued to importune

Government to take more stringent measures for the suppression of the Catholic Religion in Ireland. These demands were nearly always successful, because urged most persistently by an intolerant Home Parliament. In 1703 a grandson of the Duke of Ormond—the adviser and favourite of two Stuart kings—was appointed Lord-Lieutenant, and became primarily responsible for the sufferings which the Faithful had now to endure. A Bill for their oppression was introduced; but of so vile a nature, that members of both Parliaments protested against it as being uncalled for, and excessively harsh. Notwithstanding all this, it is remarkable that in an age of conspiracies against the Queen and her friends, the loyalty of the Irish Catholics could not be questioned even by their enemies. However, the "*utter extermination*" of the "*Papists*" was still loudly advocated; and those bent on forwarding this object were soon able to profess themselves quite satisfied with the rigour of the laws. Under the new "Code," parents were placed at the mercy of apostate children; Catholics were rendered incapable of receiving annuities, or of purchasing lands, or of taking long leases, or of inheriting property, except in rare instances; and they were deprived of the right of voting at elections. They had to pay a fine of £20, or undergo imprisonment for two months, if they did not inform when they knew Mass had been celebrated; or if it could be proved against them that they had failed to disclose the place of refuge of a priest. Moreover, any one could obtain a reward of £50 for betraying a Roman Catholic Bishop or Prelate; £20 being the sum offered for each secular priest or Friar. Other equally infamous clauses were contained in that "Code," and judges and magistrates had to enforce those statutes with the utmost strictness, if they would not incur suspicion of disloyalty to the Crown. It followed that priest-hunters and spies were held in higher repute than ever by Government.

Despite such threatened dire penalties we find that the Irish clergy were indefatigable in the exercise of their sacred duties. They were not in the least intimidated by that "*machine of wise and elaborate contrivance for the oppression and degradation of the nation*" which is one description of what the Penal Laws against Roman Catholics had attained to during the reign of Queen Anne. But such was the perseverance of the priests that in the end they *had* to be permitted to live in Ireland, on condition that they should have their names registered " and *give security for their good behaviour.*"[1]

The Teresian Friars at this epoch shared the lot of the other priests and indeed of the Faithful generally. They now occupied a house at Wormwood Gate in Dublin; and also a little cottage beside the ruins of the old abbey at Loughrea. When ordained, the young "exiles" returned from the Continent, and were sent to either of these centres to devote themselves to the labours

[1] Haverty's *Hist. of Ireland.*

of the active life, not forgetting, meanwhile, how much depended on their progress in the contemplative.

The reign of Queen Anne was neither long nor happy. During those twelve years she was painfully conscious of her usurpation of her stepbrother's rights. She even took part in a truly pitiful intrigue to bring about the succession in his favour, but, being a Roman Catholic, "James III." declined to secure a crown by the denial of his faith. The Queen was most urgent in her entreaties: yet the royal conspiracy did not succeed. Anne died in 1714, and was succeeded by George I. The new King's accession was all the more triumphantly proclaimed lest the thoughts of the English people should turn to the nature of his title to the crown. He himself accepted their allegiance for what it was worth; but resolved that his German favourites should enjoy the confidence which he could not place in the Parliament of England.

Next year (A.D. 1715) another effort was made in Scotland to restore the Stuart dynasty. Although the Irish Catholics took no part in this revolution, it was used as a pretext for persecuting them with increased violence. Strict orders were issued by the Lords Justices, insisting on the more rigid enforcement of the Penal Laws. A great many Catholic noblemen were arrested, and had to suffer all the miseries of a long imprisonment without there being the slightest criminatory evidence against them. The priests were seized at the very altar. And before transporting them it was customary to clothe them in their sacred vestments to be ridiculed by the Protestant soldiery.[1] The most shameful measures proposed for the suppression of Catholicism came from the Irish Parliament; but that assembly had now reached the lowest stage of moral degradation; void of all sense of national independence, it was in proper keeping with the corrupt state of " Society " in King George's reign. The Faithful of Ireland alone seem to have escaped the venality and profligacy so prevalent among those by whom they were persecuted and despised. It is truly said that the Irish Catholics were rather strengthened in their religion by trials; for even their worst enemies had to admit that they were endowed with virtues such as those recorded of the early Christian martyrs.

If, however, the Protestants were thus instrumental in bringing much misery upon the Catholics of this kingdom, it was at the cost of their own prerogative of freedom. They were themselves but the servile creatures of the King and Parliament of England. Their every legislative act was performed with fear, lest it should not be according to the wishes of their English taskmasters. Not until Dean Swift's scathing denunciations brought home to them how despicable their conduct was before the civilised world, did they begin to realise the criminal folly of those long-cherished fanatical prejudices. The famous satirist's exposure of an

[1] Haverty's *Hist. of Ireland.*

injury about to be done to the nation by one of the King's favourites, was the first attempt made to unite all classes and creeds of Irishmen in the sacred cause of patriotism. But George I. did not live to see the final issue of the hostile reception which Wood's project (of debasing the coinage) met with throughout the country.

Two years previous to this monarch's death (A.D. 1725) the Teresian Friars of St. Patrick's Province kept the centenary of their coming to Ireland; and notwithstanding the extreme poverty of the Fathers at that time, they have left us a beautiful memorial in commemoration of the event. It is a solid silver monstrance still constantly used in the Church of the Discalced Carmelites at Dublin. The inscription shows that a Father James of St. Bernard was then in charge of the poor friary at Wormwood Gate; he was also Vicar-Provincial; and there are some documents extant which give ample proof of his piety, learning, and zeal.[1] Knowing that the Religious depended on the Faithful for support, of course we may regard this monstrance as a generous acknowledgment of the people's gratitude to the Fathers for their labours of one hundred years.

No sooner had George II. ascended the throne (A.D. 1727) than he was called upon to sanction an addition to the Penal Statutes against Irish Catholics. The new Bill was intended to deprive them of the few remaining constitutional rights allowed them in former reigns. But happily this

[1] *Arch. of St. Teresa's.*

measure was loudly, if ineffectually, condemned by many patriotic Protestants, who were now emulating the example set them by Dean Swift. Indeed, the wretched condition of the Catholic population became such, within the next ten years, that it appealed to the most bigoted of their enemies. Owing to various laws—particularly that sanctioning the system of extortion by tithes —the Irish farmers could take no interest in agricultural affairs; their only ambition being to raise the crops needful for food; and should these fail, as the potato did in 1739, a famine was inevitable. It is stated that fully *half a million* people died in Ireland of actual starvation between the years 1739 and 1741! As usual, the priests had now to pass through a terrible ordeal: to witness sufferings which they were powerless to relieve. Yet they saw their devoted people dying by tens of thousands in great contentment and peace—and of *their own free will!* For, sad to relate, there was food in plenty for those who would deny their faith.

In the General Visitation of the Irish Discalced Carmelites, held by Father Hilarion of St. Mary in 1743, there is allusion to the deplorable state of the country. That same year the Vicar-Provincial, Father Robert Mary of St. Joseph, made some wise regulations by which the Fathers were afforded greater facilities for the exercise of the office of Consoler.[1] But suddenly all the Catholic churches had to be closed, and the priests were diligently sought for by "spies" all over the

[1] *MS. in Arch. of St. Teresa's.*

country. This was on account of the rumour of an invasion of England by the French in 1744. So carried away were the more bigoted Protestants by their fanaticism, that it was seriously contemplated to get rid of the Irish Catholics, once for ever, by a general massacre! The Teresian Fathers in Dublin had recently changed to Stephen's Street, where they had built a more spacious church and friary; and soon after this "Outbreak" they received permission from the King himself to reopen "their chapel," a favour granted under most interesting circumstances. Early in the year 1745, Viscount Nicholas Taaffe, who was then Austrian Ambassador at the English court, and a particular friend of George II., paid a visit to Dublin. He wished to hear Mass in the Church of the Discalced Carmelites, but on going to Stephen's Street, found the doors nailed up, and was told that the same harsh treatment had been extended to all the other priests in the city. Lord Taaffe immediately wrote a bitter complaint to the King, saying that it was a hard case he was not allowed to worship according to his conscience, in his own native land. It seems George II. smarted under the rebuke, and gave peremptory instructions to have the Viscount's request instantly respected.[1] In the course of the same year Lord Chesterfield, for motives of his own, gave a like permission to the Irish clergy generally. In view of the crisis caused by the Scottish Rebellion of 1745, it was Chesterfield's policy to conciliate the Catholics of

[1] Taaffe's *History of Ireland*.

Ireland, not knowing but they also were preparing to assist the grandson of James II. In fact the army of Prince Charles Edward was largely composed of Irishmen who had enlisted in his service in France. And it is said that as many as *four hundred and fifty thousand* soldiers of Irish nationality had died fighting the battles of Louis XIV. and those of his immediate successor, from the violation of the Treaty of Limerick to this invasion of Scotland by the new claimant to the English throne. But Prince Charles failed, his cause having become hopeless after the battle of Culloden, in which he was utterly defeated, in 1746.

At this epoch the Protestant Primate of Ireland used to take a very active part in the government of the nation, in order to ensure the ascendency of those opposed to the Roman Catholics. After the recall of the Earl of Chesterfield in 1746, Archbishop Hoardley was appointed one of the Lords Justices; next year he was succeeded by that most unprincipled of men, George Stone. This Prelate employed revolting, immoral means to corrupt the Irish gentry; and, of course, was the chief patron of the so-called "Charter Schools" which Primate Boulter had inaugurated in 1727 for the purpose of proselytising Catholic children. Fortunately Stone's zeal in the latter respect was frustrated to a great extent by an influence which the Government does not appear to have considered; certainly, the far-reaching effects of the same were unforeseen by those endeavouring to deprive the helpless little ones of their faith.

Presuming a good deal on "*the royal favour*" obtained for them by Viscount Taaffe, the Teresian Fathers of Dublin reorganised the Archconfraternity of the Brown Scapular in the Church of "Our Lady of Mount Carmel," Stephen's Street. This was an exceedingly dangerous enterprise at the time, since Roman Catholic associations, of whatsoever kind, were subjected to constant espionage by Government; the members being exposed to the constant danger of arrest as "conspirators."[1] Under the Father-Provincial's own watchful care the "Brothers" were not interfered with; although it must have been known to the Castle officials that a very large number of laymen were accustomed to meet at the Friary of the Discalced Carmelites. These pious clients of the Queen of Carmel led a most edifying life, aiming at a high degree of holiness by the fervent practice of the Christian virtues while engaged in the occupation of their everyday lives. Not content with attending thus seriously to the work of their own salvation, they sought occasion to help their fellow-citizens, both spiritually and temporally; for they had learned to appreciate the value of a true Carmelite's vocation of prayerful zeal. Seeing the peril that threatened the children of the Catholic poor of Dublin from those detested "Charter Schools," they took upon themselves the burden of educating and providing for as many orphan boys as the voluntary subscriptions of "the Brothers" would permit: a heroic project that developed itself wonderfully in

[1] *MS. in Arch. of St. Teresa's.*

the course of time. In the simple record of the "MONTHLY MEETINGS" of the members of the Archconfraternity, frequent reference is made to the progress of this undertaking: how the number of pupils continued to increase in the "School"; what satisfaction the boys already "*apprenticed out*" were giving to their masters; and new plans for the extension of their labours were discussed by the good "Brothers." The "*infants*" were sent into the country to be reared; and we are told that at times it was very hard to provide them necessary food and clothing. Commonplace as they seem, we now regard these transactions of the "Monthly Meetings" as topics of absorbing interest. For those zealous "Tertians" have certainly merited the admiration of posterity for the efforts thus made to resist the action of the Courtier-Prelate Stone, who was trying to deprive the children of Ireland of their birthright of the faith. And they persevered in their self-sacrificing labours for many years; until happily at length, Catholic institutions were founded in Dublin and elsewhere, to carry out the selfsame purpose which the "Brothers" at Stephen's Street had in view.[1]

From 1741 to 1746 the Teresian Fathers of the Irish Province lost several of their number by death. Father Antony Coleman, who had been one of the "*Outlaws*" in the reign of William III., died at Loughrea in 1741; a companion "*Outlaw*" of his was Father Nicholas of St. Angelus, who survived him six years. Both priests had laboured

[1] *Ibid.*

on the Irish Mission before the battle of Aughrim. The death of Father Hilarion of St. Teresa occurred at Stephen's Street still later; this Friar had the extraordinary distinction (considering the anti-Catholic spirit of the age) of having his name mentioned "*with honour*" in the "*London Gazette*." He was called a "*Benefactor*" of his country, having rendered much service to the sick and wounded in the time of war. This notice in his praise appeared two years after his death,[1] which had occurred in 1754.

Towards the close of the reign of George II. (A.D. 1757-59) the Irish Faithful, under the leadership of a Catholic physician of Dublin—Dr. John Curry, who had already ably vindicated the national cause by his historical writings—tried to obtain redress of their grievances. A favourable reply was given to a petition made to the Crown; but soon afterwards, owing to a great riot caused by Protestant patriots in Dublin, it was first seriously contemplated to unite this kingdom to England, doing away altogether with the Home Parliament, as in the case of Scotland. The Roman Catholics were again accused of disloyalty, the suspicion being confirmed by the rumour of another French invasion. Later on a few vessels did actually arrive, under command of the gallant Thurot. Carrickfergus was seized and occupied for a short time; but the expedition ended most disastrously. George II. died the same year (1760) quite suddenly; and the realisation of the recent sanguine

[1] *MS. St. Teresa's.*

hopes entertained by the Catholics was deferred indefinitely once more. Their condition at this time—by reason of the legal hindrances to Irish commerce, and of the premeditated ruin of those industries on which the prosperity of the nation depended to a very great extent—was such as to justify the boast, that they dared not breathe in their native land save by the gracious connivance of Government! In some districts the pressure of their trials had become intolerable, chiefly because of a barbarous method of exacting the tithe-tax; and secret societies were first formed in the country to resist violence of this kind by physical force. But in the course of the present reign it was found more expedient than ever to conciliate the Catholics of Ireland. The King himself, the grandson of George II., seemed friendly disposed towards them from the beginning; it is said that he had escaped the contamination of the shocking licentiousness of his profligate predecessor's court, so that his heart may not have been entirely hardened to the sufferings of his Irish subjects; besides, Irishmen still made very good soldiers; and whenever war was waged against England the exiles sought service under the hostile flag, longing to avenge their country's wrongs. Consequently, after the Declaration of American Independence by the French in 1778, the English Government deemed it prudent to try the policy of slightly relaxing the Penal Laws in Ireland. Next year the country was menaced by yet another foreign invasion, and *forty-two thousand Irishmen* enrolled themselves as *volunteers* to ward off the threatened danger. Before laying down their arms they wisely resolved to insist on the rights of the Irish people being established according to the constitutive principles of "perfect nationhood." These rights were interpreted by Henry Grattan and other Protestant patriots in presence of a *now* attentive Parliament; and in 1782 the victory was gained, when all claims, including the demand for liberty of conscience, were unconditionally allowed. Alas, that this glorious triumph should have been rendered absolutely in vain by the revival of an irrational spirit of bigotry! The great majority of the Protestant party would have excluded their Catholic compatriots from an equal participation in the privileges of freedom thus secured. It was easy to foresee the result. True patriotism has its origin in a strict sense of justice; and having lost sight of that virtue, the Irish Parliament sacrificed honour and honesty to a spirit of avaricious jealousy ever opposed to the welfare of those professing the faith of Rome. Grattan's thrilling eloquence could not stay the rising tide of the nation's ruin: the once *dreaded* volunteers were no longer feared.

Meanwhile (A.D. 1760-1786) we learn that the Teresian Carmelites were unwearyingly engaged in forwarding the twofold object of their vocation. Deeply as they were interested in those crises of vital importance to their country, they were *bound* to grow daily more fervent in the practice of the monastic virtues, and in the discharge of the pressing duties of the mission. Documents, preserved in the various archives, show that year after year the Province was governed as if it had been actually reorganised, although the Religious might not yet so much as wear the habit of the Order within the cloister of their humble friaries. Mention is made of only three houses—Dublin, Loughrea, and the residence of Ardbreccan in Meath; and Superiors were elected or appointed in each of these, just as the constitutions prescribe.[1] Of course the Religious were now able to have much more frequent communication with their Superiors-General at Rome, and indeed with the monasteries of the Order all over the Continent, since the Irish postulants had still to be sent out of the country for ordination. Many of the young Friars, as in the case of Father Lawrence, the theologian, were not allowed to return to Ireland, their services having been required in some of the Provinces abroad. The most responsible offices were entrusted to them; instance Father Seraphim Power, who died in 1776. He was Provincial of Aquitaine, and his memory is still revered in that Province; but he had also acquired fame throughout France, and Spain, and Italy, for his holiness and learning.[2]

In a Provincial Visitation, held in the year 1787, Father Eliseus of St. Patrick made a special ordination relative to the disturbed state of Ireland.[3] So many outrages had been recently perpetrated upon the Catholics by fanatical Protestants, that it was thought another persecution had set in; and, follow-

[1] *MS. in St. Teresa's.*   [2] *Ibid.*   [3] *Ibid.*

ing the example of his predecessors, Father Eliseus exhorted those under his jurisdiction to prepare for the trials which they should have to endure while attending to the wants of the Faithful. The intolerant members of the "Orange League" were now the oppressors, but they were openly supported by Government. They harried the people into taking measures for self-preservation; and then cried out against them as rebels. As a matter of fact, the express purpose of that organisation of Protestants and Presbyterians, as inaugurated in the year 1784 (the "Orange Lodges" as such were not opened until 1795), was to drive the Roman Catholics from the north of Ireland, in order to obtain possession of their lands; nor was this object ever lost sight of in after years.

In 1778, an event occurred which is generally assigned as the remote cause of a great national disaster. George III. became insane, and the Prince of Wales was appointed Regent, but with powers restricted to suit the party purposes of the Prime Minister, Pitt. A Bill was framed and, as the merest formality, presented for acceptance to the Irish Parliament. To the astonishment of the nation, and to the very keen mortification of the Prime Minister, that assembly declined most positively to be dictated to; and, in the exercise of its inherent independence—too long forgotten— voted for a Regency without limitation.

The King recovered unexpectedly, before Pitt had time to bribe the majority to favour his motion; but he was determined to humiliate the

Irish people profoundly for even this *one* praiseworthy act of their Home Parliament.

Henceforth, from the year 1791, the Roman Catholics of Ireland began to use every constitutional means to free themselves from their legal disabilities. They might not yet avail themselves of the full benefit of the slight relaxation already made in the Penal Laws, except by taking the Oath of Allegiance, which contained certain clauses altogether opposed to their religious convictions. During the month of May of this year, the Catholic clergy held a conference in Dublin to pronounce formally on the question, the Prior of the Teresian Carmelites at St. Stephen's Street, Father Patrick Ward, being one of the priests invited to assist as theologians.[1] Seeing such resolution on the part of the Catholics, and well aware of their loyalty, the more liberal Protestants came forward to support them in their just cause. And this was the beginning of a great political movement which had for its object Radical Reform in Parliamentary Representation, and the enjoyment of the same rights and privileges by all Irishmen, no matter what their religion might be. It was maintained, as a *cardinal principle*, that only by the cordial union of the Irish people could the interests of the nation be safeguarded and advanced. The new association was called the " UNITED IRELAND SOCIETY." Unhappily, in this instance also, the primary end of the organisation was speedily overlooked, and the Roman

[1] *Spicil. Ossor.*

Catholics were again left to their own resources. But they were no longer disheartened, and found occasion to represent their grievances to the King in person; they were graciously received by him and actually succeeded in the year 1793 in having a *comparatively* satisfactory Bill passed in their favour. Historians do not allow much credit to George III. and his Parliament for having granted this long-delayed measure of toleration to the Irish Catholics; apparently it had become a matter of necessity to which the recent Revolution in France had given rise. The sincerely patriotic Protestants among the " United Irishmen " warmly congratulated the Catholics on being thus permitted to exercise some of their rights. They bore the highest testimony to the patient loyalty of the Faithful, although subjected for more than a *century, and solely on account of their religion, to a "persecution equally abhorrent from every maxim of good government, and every principle of genuine Christianity*"![1]

The dreadful state of the French nation occasioned the return of many young Teresian Carmelites to Ireland about this time. A number of the Religious of the Irish Province had been preparing for the priesthood in that country, and were recalled when their sacred profession ceased to be respected there, God Himself having been forgotten by His once faithful people. Neither might postulants be sent, except with very great risk, into Italy or Spain. Hence, in view of the toleration

[1] *Papers of United Irishmen.*

then enjoyed by Catholics in Ireland, the Irish Fathers thought they could safely re-establish their own Novitiate; but in order not to attract the notice of Government they obtained permission from Rome to open it at Loughrea. A new friary and church had been built beside the ruins of the old abbey by Father Joseph of St. Martha in the year 1785, when he was Provincial.[1] It was intended, moreover, that the novices should, after profession, begin their studies in the same place until such time as more favourable circumstances would permit their going abroad to prepare for ordination. We have now (A.D. 1793) arrived at a very interesting epoch in the history of St. Patrick's Province, as will be seen from the events to be recorded in the following chapter.

[1] *MS. in Arch. of St. Teresa's.*

CHAPTER X.

"ST. TERESA'S CHURCH AND FRIARY."

A new church and monastery built in Dublin—The foundation-stone laid by a leader of the "United Irishmen"—Historical list of generous friends—How the permission of the King and Parliament was secured—A lawsuit gained by the Friars—The Irish "Reign of Terror," A.D. 1798—The shock of the Union—"St. Teresa's" completed after many years—The past and the present—Interesting associations.

FROM about the year 1786 the Discalced Carmelites of Dublin had decided not to renew the lease of their house in Stephen's Street, because both the church and friary there were entirely too small, and the rent exorbitant.[1] An effort had been made to afford accommodation to the Faithful by adding new galleries to the little chapel; but the congregation had increased in the meantime, and now the Fathers saw that the only effectual way of providing for the spiritual wants of a great number of Catholic citizens would be to obtain a suitable site and build a much larger church and monastery. Although exceedingly poor at the time, they contrived to set aside every year part of their very limited income for this purpose, and a keen desire to realise the object which they had in view almost

[1] *MS. in Arch. of St. Teresa's.*

caused them to forget the many inconveniences of a rigorous economy, not prescribed by their Rule. On the 1st of August 1793 the long waited for opportunity occurred. A "plot of ground" was for sale in Clarendon Street—so called from the second Earl of Clarendon, who was Lord-Lieutenant of Ireland in 1685—and the Teresian Friars authorised some lay friends to purchase it for them, not wishing to take open part in the transaction themselves, as the law could still prevent them, as Religious, benefiting by the recent repeal of the Penal Statutes (it can, and does so occasionally, *at the present day!*) The foundation-stone of the new church was laid on the 3rd October 1793, by one of the gentlemen who had been instrumental in procuring this site for the community—Mr. John Sweetman, member of an old and highly respectable Catholic family of Dublin. So well known were this gentleman's stanch religious and patriotic principles that Lord Chancellor Clare endeavoured to have him hanged in the course of that very year.[1] But Mr. Sweetman's discretion saved him, for some time at least; he was afterwards arrested because of his connection with the "United Irishmen," as we shall see. Here we may say that the Sweetman family were ever among the most devoted friends and generous benefactors of the Discalced Carmelites of Dublin.[2]

Set in the foundation-stone was a copper plate

---

[1] Madden's *United Irishmen.*
[2] *MS. in Arch. of St. Teresa's.*

bearing the names of the Religious then forming the community at Stephen's Street—Fathers O'Hara, Smith, Ward, Ennis, Fitzpatrick, O'Reilly, and Long. Father O'Hara was the Provincial and resided at Loughrea, but he had come to Dublin to help in forwarding a project which was soon regarded all over Ireland as an event of the utmost importance for the Roman Catholics of this kingdom. The permission of the King and Parliament had to be previously obtained, and, doubtlessly, personal friends of the Friars among both Commons and Peers had done much to ensure the success of their petition, a fact which proves that the fanatical prejudice of the age, when Catholic tradesmen might not so much as aspire to admission into the guilds of their respective crafts, was by no means common to all the Protestants of Ireland. A commemorative slab was placed over the principal entrance to "St. Teresa's" (it is now partially covered by a porch, afterwards added to the body of the church) testifying to the generosity of the Faithful, the goodwill of the Irish Parliament, and to the graciousness of the King.[1]

Every penny subscribed towards the enterprise was carefully recorded by one of the Fathers, who has thus left us, unintentionally, a most interesting document in his "*Book of Expenses and Receipts.*" Each page contains such well-known names as those of "*Emmet,*" "*Sheridan,*" and "*Moore.*" Indeed this "Historical List" is a striking evidence of the popularity of the Discalced Carmelites

[1] *MS. in Arch. of St. Teresa's.*

throughout the country at the end of the eighteenth century: Catholics and Protestants—representatives of every class, those who had the interests of Ireland most dearly at heart, side by side with those who were unable to appreciate the sacred dignity of National Independence—appear in the pleasant character of friendly rivals while assisting the Teresian Friars to build their new church. The Protestant Bishop of Killala, and other dignitaries and clergymen of the Established Religion; many surgeons and physicians; members of the legal profession, and quite a number of officers in the army gladly helped in furthering a project altogether opposed to their own views. And certainly we can discover no sign of "respect of persons" in the entering of benefactors' names. Immediately under the Countess of Ormond's donation of ten guineas is recorded "*a poor old woman's*" offering of thirteenpence.

The several thousand pounds contributed by the public did not defray the expenses incurred even before the community had changed from Stephen's Street; and not for fully twelve years could the building be completed according to the first simple plan. This was mainly on account of a political movement which rendered it almost impossible for the Fathers to proceed with the works, particularly as they themselves had to engage the tradesmen and labourers from day to day.[1]

By this time great numbers of the Irish people were despairing of being ever able to secure full

[1] *MS. in Arch. of St. Teresa's.*

redress of their grievance by constitutional means. There was a growing conviction that only resistance by physical force would put an end to the policy of oppression pursued by the Government. This was precisely the result at which Pitt aimed; he desired to bring about a rebellion in Ireland, so as to execute, all the more easily, his revengeful design on the Nation's Independence. He had a legion of well-paid informers to watch the movements of the "United Ireland" party, who had now formed themselves into a secret society, the majority of their leaders being imbued, unfortunately, with the principles of the French Revolutionists. In fact every association, no matter what its object, fell under suspicion at the time. An unscrupulous attempt was made to connect even the confraternity at the Stephen's Street Friary with a political conspiracy, but failed through the prompt and decisive action of Father Seraphim O'Reilly, the Spiritual Director. He himself had founded a "*Temporal*" or Benevolent Society among the members in the year 1784, so that there might be a fund in reserve to assist those in serious trouble; and for the support of the widows and orphans of the Brother Associates in case of death. It was against this Society the attempt was made; but Father Seraphim himself had dissolved it before the authors of the attack could mature their plans; and re-establishing it under a different name, he was able to render their further efforts futile, the necessary legal formalities to be observed in such an instance having been now fulfilled. A decree of the Court of Chancery was given in his favour, when those anxious to have the management of the Society in their own hands appealed to the law; and by this victory the safety of more then a hundred members of "St. Teresa's Temporal Association" was guaranteed throughout "The Irish Reign of Terror," during the suppression of the Rebellion of 1798.[1]

Roman Catholics were nearly always the principal victims of the outrages then perpetrated by the savage soldiery. The most respectable families were assailed, even when returning peacefully from Mass, by the drunken troopers, and subjected to brutal indignities. Lord Camden himself said in his official report that the people of Ireland were forced to take up arms owing to the "*unutterable horrors*" which were countenanced by the officers who had been appointed *judges* over those against whom they had sworn eternal hatred in their "*Orange Lodges.*" Having been arrested about this time for his sympathy with his afflicted countrymen, Mr. John Sweetman, the friend of the Teresian Carmelites, declared on oath that the "Rebellion" could only be assigned to the wanton crimes openly sanctioned by Government.[2] Mr. Sweetman was detained in prison at Port St. George for several years, where he had to endure terrible privations. However, he was at length released on condition that he would never

[1] *MS. in Arch. of St. Teresa's.*
[2] Madden's *United Irishmen.*

return to Ireland; but in 1820 he got permission to come home—just a few years before his death. Deeply grieved as the Fathers of St. Teresa's had been on hearing of his arrest, they could do nothing to assist him. He was a " Rebel," and the murder of Father Quigley, who had been recently hanged at Maidstone without a tittle of evidence against him, was a warning to all priests that their sacred calling would not shield them should they dare espouse the cause of persons whom Government regarded as "seditiously discontented." On his coming to the country to perfect Pitt's infamous plan, Lord Cornwallis was shocked to find hanging, burning, shooting, and all such atrocities the chief topics of conversation at table, and to witness the inhuman mirth of the company on being informed of the execution of a Roman Catholic priest; and he bitterly complained that he himself had been sent to wage a war of mere plunder and massacre. But his protest was of no avail, a more than usually horrible instance of these excesses being only *praised* in Parliament as *seal* in the utter extermination of the Irish Catholics, for which, the fanatical soldiers were told, the time had now arrived.

Inoffensiveness and loyalty were no guarantee for security, nor was there mercy for those who had been unable to persevere in their heroic struggle of self-defence. Besides, too much reliance had been placed on help promised from abroad ever since Wolfe Tone's mission to America and France. In this instance, as in the foreign support hoped for during the Jacobite war, but a feeble attempt was made by any other nation to assist the insurgent peasantry, and that altogether *too* late. Yet, so determined had the resistance of the people's army been that the tidings of Humbert's arrival at Killala spread consternation among the English everywhere, as the author was once told by an aged gentleman whose memories of "'98" were both clear and thrilling, and whose sympathies had *not* been on the side of the popular party.

The city of Dublin was compared to a "shambles" in those days, because of the many victims of martial law. However, in the month of May 1798 the Teresian Fathers managed to keep a few men employed at the buildings in Clarendon Street. Of course, little progress could be made while every other day some poor fellow whom they had engaged would be identified as a "Rebel," seized, and afterwards done to death in the streets. Contemporary historians occasionally describe the manner of execution in gruesome detail. In such cases it became the duty of the Fathers to help and console the widows and orphans. Several members of the community, too, were unable to bear the strain of their various trials any longer; but as they died, their places were eagerly taken by the fervent young Religious recently ordained, many of whom were well accustomed to similar scenes of cruelty, having been in France at the outbreak of the Revolution, which had at length culminated in a regicide quite as appalling as the murder of Charles I. Nor was it the life of Louis XVI.

only that was sacrificed to the fury then raging; his Queen—Marie Antoinette—the most injured in history since the time of the unhappy mother of the Stuarts, also died upon the guillotine. While devoting themselves to the spiritual welfare of the Faithful of Ireland, these priests had matter for serious thought; on the Continent they had seen to what a state of moral degradation society is quickly reduced when no longer controlled by religious influences; here, in their native land, but among "strangers and degenerate Irishmen," they were witnessing phases of human baseness just as deplorable, springing from an irrational prejudice to the true faith.[1]

The horrors of the year 1798 were followed by the shock of the "Union," the result of an offended statesman's revenge. For sheer callousness to a people's misery, there is not much to choose between this politic measure for the pacification of the country and those means which had been adopted by the soldiers who butchered, without pity, so many of the defenceless peasantry. Pitt succeeded by a system of bribery, which assumed all kinds of forms, to excite the vile passions of ambition and avarice: *twenty-one million pounds sterling* had to be expended in the purchase of the Union. But the indignant opposition which the Act met with, before and after the 1st January 1801, proved that the "people of Ireland" would never consent to forfeit the first of their nation's "inherent rights." And often expression was

[1] *MS. in Arch. of St. Teresa's.*

given to this sentiment by some of the most prudent of patriotic Irishmen—Catholic and Protestant—in the new church at Clarendon Street about the beginning of the present century, when the use of sacred edifices was still permitted in Ireland for meetings convened in the interests of religion and nationality.[1]

The buildings were not considered complete until 1810. We are told that the church was then *even* "ceiled," the walls of the cells "plastered," and all outstanding debts paid. In this finished state, "St. Teresa's" is described as a "splendid chapel" (and the church was an unusually fine one for the times), a hundred and thirty feet long, forty-four in width, and thirty-six feet high to the ceiling. As there had not been sufficient ground to build the monastery according to the plan laid down in the Constitutions, a special dispensation was obtained to provide the offices needful for community-life over the church. There were spacious vaults underneath to be utilised as a place of interment. Parlours, confraternity-rooms, and the porter's lodge were outside the cloister; special mention is made of "a grand porch" over which was a niche for the "town-clock," and of a "pump" in the chapel-yard, to which the Fathers had sole claim! Needless to say that there was not the slightest pretension to architectural effect in the structure, even "the six large windows" of the church being exceedingly plain. (The community were most anxious to add a seventh, but

[1] *MS. in Arch. of St. Teresa's.*

could not afford the "*window-tax.*") Inside, everything was in keeping with the humble appearance of the exterior: the altars were of wood, the high altar standing at the end of the church—which only extended to the entrance of the present sanctuary. An organ had been purchased a few years before the Fathers left Stephen's Street; and a gallery was erected for it in St. Teresa's behind the high altar. There were other galleries all round the interior for the accommodation of a still greater number of the Faithful. A "rent" was paid for the seats, which were reserved by lock and key, as was customary in those days. The floor was earthen, and the walls were whitewashed —and, on the whole, "the splendid new chapel" of the Discalced Carmelites at Clarendon Street was such as to elicit the admiration of the pious Catholics of Dublin over a hundred years ago.[1]

It was fully half a century from the time of its foundation before any "improvements" were made in "St. Teresa's." The church had long since become entirely too small for the congregation; the successive communities having tried in vain to buy the ground which would enable them to enlarge the body and add transepts. But, in the course of time, the perseverance of the Fathers was rewarded; and it would be hard indeed to recognise, in the present truly magnificent church, a transformed chapel of the Penal Days. So well have the several architects succeeded in preserving the symmetry of the whole while making the

[1] *MS. in Arch. of St. Teresa's.*

required alterations, that the building as it now appears seems the realisation of the one same plan. The transepts to the right hand and to the left have been let into the body of the church by lofty arches, springing from massive coupled columns and entablatures of the Ionic order. Handsome brackets support the ceilings—all elliptic groined—most of the windows are of the Decorated style, a beautiful specimen of rose-window being in the transept, to the right of the high altar, which has the principal façade, and opens into Clarendon Street. Above the church, on the Grafton Street side, rises to a height of eighty feet the campanile, which contained for many years the first bell rung in Dublin on the gaining of Catholic Emancipation. Still more recently the interior of the edifice has been enriched by the addition of some rare works of art: there is "Hogan's Dead Christ," beneath a high altar well worthy of this statue, before which the pious sculptor himself used to pray, and which is generally admitted to be the artist's masterpiece;[1] there is a statue of the "Immaculate Conception," hardly less perfect; the designs in the stained-glass windows have been admirably executed; and the sanctuary and the other altars are of the richest marbles. But to the Faithful the chief attraction of "St. Teresa's" consists in its devotional aspect. The "Invisible Presence" can be so fervently realised there! And, then, the present generation of Irish Catholics behold in this church a remark-

[1] *Letter to the Author.*

able evidence of the triumph of their faith. Indeed even in the year 1825 the Fathers of "St. Teresa's" were very glad to be able to commemorate the second centenary of the establishment of their Order in Ireland, by providing a new silver chalice for use at the poor wooden altar, which a Dublin carpenter had made for their humble "*chapel.*" Yet many people were slow to appreciate the "improvements" in "St. Teresa's" at first. They were sorry to see the familiar galleries disappear, and could not understand why the very organ, to which we find frequent allusion made with pardonable pride, should be replaced by another, if finer instrument: the organ which they remembered so well in connection with Father Leo's (Rev. James Oate's) "famous" choir, and which they had heard give forth such wondrous music at the magic touch of Father Augustine of the Blessed Sacrament, the founder of the present church and monastery of the Discalced Carmelites in London, and whom the world will recognise as the renowned pianist and composer, Herman Choen, the converted Jew.[1]

But interesting as these associations are, we may not dwell long on the history of "St. Teresa's" in a digression from more important facts. Neither can we allude to the many Irish "Celebrities" who were the intimate friends of the Fathers early in the present century; nor avail ourselves of the diaries kept by some of the Religious who had to go abroad to receive the brown habit before

[1] *Letter to the Author.*

peace had been restored to Europe by the Battle of Waterloo. Graphic, indeed, would be the account of perils a young Irishman was then called upon to face in order to correspond with the grace of a vocation to Carmel: often we meet with a passing reference to the dangers of sailing from Ireland without a convoy, and to the risk of being "*impressed*" for service in the army or navy if detained at any of the seaports by some unforeseen cause.[1]

However, there are certain other facts which may not well be omitted in this place, being more intimately associated with the history of " St. Teresa's." One of the two side-altars within the present sanctuary was erected by a Teresian Friar in token of his filial love of the Seraphic Virgin; the other has been raised by friends to the memory of a great Irish physician who was interred in the vaults of this church. William Whelan and Joseph Michael O'Ferrall were at school together at Samuel Whyte's Academy in Grafton Street, nearly a hundred years ago. After the death of their learned "Master," also an almost unknown poet, to whom Moore attributes the merits of his own muse,[2] both boys joined a private class which Father Leo of the Clarendon Street Friary had formed, to afford a number of Catholic youths an opportunity of completing their classical education. In the course of time William Whelan became a Discalced Carmelite, and eventually a Bishop; his companion had

[1] *MS. in Arch. of St. Teresa's.*
[2] *Anthologia Hibernica* (A.D. 1794).

to fight a hard battle with the world in the beginning, but in after years he attained to the position of first physician in Ireland.

Dr. O'Ferrall's previous history reveals a still closer bond between himself and the Teresian Friars. His mother had been a Protestant, and on being received into the Church by one of the Fathers at Clarendon Street, was thenceforth disowned by her guardians. The community of "St. Teresa's" provided for her until such time as God raised up a protector for her in the person of a respectable young tradesman, who gave her a very happy, if humble home. Their first son was called Joseph Michael. The father having died in early manhood, Joseph Michael, although a mere boy, undertook the responsibility of supporting his widowed mother and a sister. This prevented him commencing his medical studies until he had reached his twenty-fifth year. But he speedily regained the time sacrificed to filial and fraternal devotion, and was qualified in due course. And now not only did he acquire a great reputation for his skill as a doctor; he was highly esteemed everywhere for his thorough acquaintance with the ancient and modern languages, having availed himself to such advantage of Father Leo's assistance. To the end of his life—he died in 1868—he used to acknowledge publicly the indebtedness of his family to the fathers of "St. Teresa's"; and in turn he himself became one of their most generous benefactors.[1]

[1] *Life of Mary Aikenhead.*

Just as he was becoming better known in Dublin as a successful physician, Dr. O'Ferrall had the happiness of preserving the life of the foundress of the Irish Sisters of Charity. At that time Mrs. Aikenhead—a most devout client of St. Teresa—was endeavouring to open a hospital wherein the sick poor should have the advice of eminent surgeons and physicians, and be cared for by the loving solicitude of the members of the Religious congregation which she herself had recently established. After her recovery from that almost fatal illness, she mentioned the matter which she had at heart to Dr. O'Ferrall, with the result that in a very short time St. Vincent's Hospital, Stephen's Green, was founded, to carry out the charitable project of the zealous Rev. Mother, and, at the same time, to serve as a Catholic School of Medicine for Irish students.[1]

In the annals of another Irish Sisterhood mention is often made of the Teresian Fathers of Clarendon Street.[2] Mother Macauly, the foundress of the Sisters of Mercy, undertook her own great work just as Mrs. Aikenhead had instituted the Congregation of Charity. It appears that the Discalced Carmelites of Dublin had the privilege of showing some little kindness to the Mercy Nuns, while Mother Macauly and her companions were enduring those trials inseparable from the heroic duties in which they were engaged. Gratitude

[1] *Life of Mary Aikenhead.*
[2] *Leaves from the Annals of the Sisters of Mercy.*

has caused the annalists of the Sisters of Mercy to record this attention on the part of the Teresian Fathers as unwonted generosity. Still, it is gratifying to the present generation of Irish Discalced Carmelites to know that their predecessors were instrumental in forwarding an enterprise which has proved so beneficial not only to the Irish Nation, but to so many other countries throughout the entire world. When they had no church of their own, the Sisters of Mercy used to attend Mass at " St. Teresa's." But the Fathers soon got permission for them to have the Holy Sacrifice celebrated daily in a private oratory attached to their convent; and Father Raymond O'Hanlon, one of the community at Clarendon Street, was, also, appointed their Confessor.[1] Another of the Fathers (Rev. William J. Whelan) obtained several special privileges in their favour from Pope Gregory XVI. at a time the Sisters of Mercy most needed encouragement; after this their difficulties began to cease.

There was one request which the Sisters made too frequently, and which, each time, it pained their friends at " St. Teresa's " to be called upon to grant: permission to inter the deceased members of the congregation in the vaults beneath the church. Twelve or thirteen of her nuns died before Mother Macauly herself, although she was still quite young at the time of her death; and yet none of those who went before her attained her age,—several of them were not even twenty,

[1] *Life of Mother Macauly.*

few of them over thirty years. Mother Macauly having been called to her reward, the remains of most of those Sisters who had been interred at St. Teresa's were removed to Baggot Street Convent and laid to rest beside their Mother in the new cemetery there.[1] In 1833 Ireland had the first great public proof of the spirit of self-sacrifice implied in the vocation of Mother Macauly and her nuns. It was during the dread visitation of the cholera. The nations of Europe witnessed, and applauded the same heroism later on when the Irish Sisters of Mercy volunteered to nurse the wounded and plague-stricken soldiers, dying daily by hundreds in the East.

Having alluded to the vaults of "St. Teresa's," it may be said that the *"Book of Obits"* would furnish much interesting material for the further prolongation of this chapter; but we must not forget the object which we have in view. It may be stated, however, that these vaults are no longer used as a place of burial, even for the deceased members of the community of "St. Teresa's." The Fathers recently purchased a splendid site at Glasnevin, and there raised a memorial to their brethren who have died in Dublin since the closing of the vaults. And this seems most befitting, because one òf the Discalced Carmelites of Clarendon Street helped to obtain that magnificent cemetery for Dublin. This was Father L'Estrange, whose own remains rest beneath the church in which he laboured for years. And now that

[1] *Life of Mother Macauly. MS. in Arch. of St Teresa's.*

all the coffins have been placed under earth, in the vaults alone at "St. Teresa's" there is apparently no sign of the marvellous change which has taken place in the original "Chapel and Friary" since the foundation-stone was laid.

CHAPTER XI.

O'CONNELL AND THE FATHERS OF ST. TERESA'S.

O'Connell's protest against the Union—Beginning of his friendship with the Discalced Carmelites—Public meetings held at "St. Teresa's"—"THE VETO"—Ireland's gratitude to the Teresian Friars—The source of O'Connell's power—Foundation of the Catholic Association—The "*Great Meeting*" of 1827—Father L'Estrange and the Ribbonmen—EMANCIPATION—O'Connell and the "*Young Irelanders*"—At "St. Teresa's" for the last time.

AMONG the Irish students who had to leave France at the time of the foundation of "St. Teresa's" was one whose name has become inseparably associated with the Discalced Carmelites of Ireland. Daniel O'Connell was in his eighteenth year in 1793; in 1798 he was called to the Bar, a profession not long open to Roman Catholics; two years later his voice was raised in public, for the first time, to denounce the injustice then about to be done to his country by the passing of the Act of the "Union." A rumour to the effect that Irish Catholics were willing to see their Nation deprived of legislative independence, in the hope of thus forwarding the cause of their own emancipation, had been maliciously circulated. But the young O'Connell, speaking in the name of his co-religionists, indignantly averred that they would rather a thousand times have the Penal Code re-enacted against them in all its former rigour than forfeit so sacred a right. Every effort was made, by lawful means, to ward off the now imminent calamity; the eloquence of the future Liberator, and of other equally patriotic Irishmen, Catholic and Protestant, had revealed the nature of the national degradation implied in Pitt's insidious plan. Curran himself drew up a series of resolutions for adoption at a representative meeting to be held in Dublin; but these were somewhat modified at O'Connell's suggestion, in order to prevent the *possibility* of the motives of the patriotic leaders being misconstrued. In a most logical speech the young Catholic barrister laid down the principles of his own political views, and to these he conformed ever faithfully in after life: that the interests of Ireland should be preferred to those of whatsoever party; and that, forgetting sectarian and other prejudices, the Irish people should unite for the common good of their country. All was in vain; yet on hearing the bells, which the enemies of Ireland set ringing to announce the tidings of the Nation's greatest woe, O'Connell solemnly vowed to devote his own life to the repairing of that shameful wrong.

There is a tradition that O'Connell was of assistance to the Fathers of "St. Teresa's" in raising funds to complete their new church and friary. His friendship for these Religious was most intimate, and dates from the very outset of his public career. It remained the same for over half a century—until his death. In the beginning, the majority of the Irish priests were timid in joining any of those movements for the restoration of national rights, fearing lest such an action on their part might only cause the Government to take still harsher measures with the defenceless people. But O'Connell found his friends at Clarendon Street of an entirely different opinion ; and as there was then no Synodal Decree prohibiting the use of Catholic churches in Ireland for other than purely Religious purposes, the Fathers were able to afford him frequent opportunity of forwarding the twofold ambition of his life : *Catholic Emancipation* and *Repeal of the Union*, and soon "St. Teresa's" became the recognised centre of these great national aspirations. However, it was only in the year 1810 that any appreciable progress was made in Irish affairs.[1] It was then very evident that neither the King nor Parliament were in favour of granting further concessions to Ireland. But the people were now awakening to their own power ; they were beginning to see that Government could be *made* to yield to those constitutional means of agitation so strongly advocated by O'Connell. The ministers of the Crown were not slow to apprehend the efficacy of the moral force which was being quickened into vigorous vitality throughout the country ; so in order to divert attention from the question of "Repeal," they made a pretence of being disposed *to consider* the claims of the Roman Catholics. O'Connell's eagerness in

[1] *Life of O'Connell. MS. in Arch. of St. Teresa's.*

following up this victory was regarded by some as being prejudicial to the cause of National Independence; but he again declared that the Faithful of Ireland would gladly abandon "Emancipation," if their calumniators could show that it was an obstacle to the realisation of the grand object of every true Irishman's most earnest prayer.[1]

At length Government was compelled to meet the wishes of the people, at least in certain respects. The first sign of the fear which O'Connell's agitation had inspired was an offer to concede to the demands of the Roman Catholics, provided the King and Parliament of England should in future be consulted on the appointment of new Bishops for Ireland before submitting the names to Rome. This was required as a guarantee of the loyalty of Irish Catholics, and afterwards became more generally known as "THE VETO." The patriotic Protestants could not understand why serious objection should be made to seemingly so simple a condition; even numbers of the Faithful, of great influence and high position, were eager to accept their freedom with the proposed restriction. But the Irish Bishops and priests indignantly rejected this covert attempt on their independence of action, their views on the subject being adopted and most ardently supported by O'Connell against the opinion of many of his ablest colleagues in the work of national regeneration.[2] Among the latter was the

[1] *Ibid.*
[2] *Papers on the Veto.* Madden's *Unpublished Collection* in the Library at St. Mary's.

veteran statesman and patriot, Henry Grattan. It gave O'Connell intense pain to differ from one whom he had ever regarded as the greatest of Ireland's sons; still he would not suffer his feelings to affect his better judgment, and, foreseeing the dangers of the suggested compromise, he declared at a meeting of the "Catholics of Ireland," held at "St. Teresa's" in 1815, that he believed their interests could be no longer safely entrusted to any one advocating the "*Veto*." As for the document, purporting to be a Papal rescript in favour of the proposal made by the English Government, which had been obtained through Cardinal Quaranttoti while Pope Pius VII. was still a prisoner of Napoleon's, O'Connell, and the Irish Catholics generally, declined to consider it as proceeding from the captive Pontiff in person, especially as it did not bear his signature. O'Connell's conduct was now commented upon most ungenerously by those whom he opposed; but, assured of his own disinterestedness, he merely despised their calumnies, and continued to devote all his energies to the cause of religion and his country. After the Battle of Waterloo the claims of Ireland were disregarded for some time; else, vague promises were held out by Parliament whenever the voice of the people was more loudly raised. This state of things lasted several years, during which O'Connell never ceased to guard the interests of his Catholic countrymen, while gaining renown for himself in the brilliant discharge of the duties of his profession.

Occasionally his method of denouncing injustice had such an unequivocal, personal bearing that he was called upon for satisfaction according to the barbarous code of honour then in vogue. In one well-known instance he weakly yielded through human respect, and he who was destined "*to raise seven millions of people from the debasement of ages to the dignity of freedom without exacting an ounce of gold or wasting the blood of one human heart,*" became responsible to his Creator for the violent death of a fellow-being.[1] Nor could he take credit to himself for having prevented later on a like tragic ending to his "affair of honour" with Sir Robert Peel. Furthermore, at one time (in 1801) he had even been a Freemason; but when told that a practical Catholic might not take the oaths of that organisation, he instantly withdrew his name, preferring the world's reproach to the censures of Holy Church. And in after life, as he knelt before the altar at "St. Teresa's," his soul was stricken with keen remorse for the public scandal which he had given respecting those criminal conventionalities opposed to a spirit of true Christian courage. It was there he took to heart the lessons of humility that convinced him of his own need of guidance and support, though men were proclaiming him the wisest leader of his age. And thus enlightened by the fervour of his faith, Daniel O'Connell did, indeed, become *great.*[2]

On the 8th of July 1817 a meeting of delegates from nearly all the counties of Ireland was

[1] *Last Days of O'Connell.*   [2] *Life of O'Connell.*

held at "St. Teresa's." It is gratifying to find that O'Connell was supported on this occasion by several of his former colleagues who had differed from him with regard to the question of the "*Veto.*" At the close of the proceedings he was asked to propose a resolution, thanking the members of the community, in the name of the Catholics of Ireland, for the generous and patriotic assistance they had lent to the National Cause. Most willingly did O'Connell comply with this grateful duty. He spoke, "*in a long and eloquent speech,*" of the services which the Teresian Friars were rendering to their country in the crisis at hand, and the Protestants present appear to have emulated the enthusiasm of his own affectionate esteem in joining in this tribute to " O'Connell's friends."

By the death of George III. in 1820, one of the obstacles to Catholic Emancipation was removed. That unhappy monarch's furious hostility to a measure of reform, certain to relieve the sufferings of so many of his own subjects, withdraws much of our sympathy from him in the pathetically sad end of his reign. But his inveterate bigotry can be accounted a phase of the dread affliction which should excite pity in all hearts, whether the poor victim frets beneath the regal purple, or writhes on a pallet of straw. His son and successor paid a visit to Ireland the next year. A most loyal welcome was given him by the Irish Catholics, and George IV. made many lavish promises in return. Fearing that the King was *really* sincere, his ministers hurried him from the country; but when tested the royal pledges were found to be of little worth. O'Connell was bitterly reproached for the part which he himself had taken in that demonstration of loyalty. For the present he contented himself with the dignified denial of assertions injurious to his character, and the founding of the "*Catholic Association*" in 1823 was his answer to those who said he had allowed himself to be duped both by Parliament and King.

Again and again Government tried in vain to suppress the now daily growing power of the people. Among the absurd reasons alleged, in 1825, for the further delay of emancipation was a doubt as to whether the allegiance of the Irish priesthood might yet be relied upon; so grievously had the Roman Catholic clergy been wronged in the past, it was thought impossible that they could ever "*forgive*" their persecutors. Then a most extraordinary incident was brought to light—probably at the request of O'Connell—which otherwise the public should not have known, because it redounded to the credit of the principal agent, a Teresian Friar. Fr. Francis Joseph (L'Estrange) had heard quite accidentally of a conspiracy of over five thousand desperate men, which had been recently organised in the counties of Dublin, Wicklow, Carlow, Kildare, and Meath. They were known as "*Ribbonmen*," and were bound by terrible oaths to avenge, according to a code of justice of their own framing, the *legal* crimes perpetrated by Government in Ireland. Realising that all these men had doomed themselves to destruction, Father Francis sought and obtained an interview with the leaders. He declined to say how he had succeeded, but the result was that all the papers of a treasonable nature were destroyed in his presence, and he received the solemn assurance of the "captains" that thenceforth they would abide by the laws of the land, iniquitous as many of those "laws" were, and leave the injuries to which the Nation was subjected to be remedied by constitutional means. Those five thousand Ribbonmen were thus induced to lead loyal and peaceful lives, and a number of them volunteered to give evidence openly, at their own peril, of the serious trouble which had been prevented by Father L'Estrange's timely interference.[1]

Happily, the controversy on the "*Veto*" question was now but a painful episode in the history of the past. The determination of a united people was once more constraining Government to hasten to accede to their claims, although in 1827 a *great* meeting assembled at "St. Teresa's" in consequence of Parliament having rejected a Bill in favour of the Roman Catholics. Most of the leaders of the Catholic movement spoke on that occasion, and so important were the resolutions adopted that the event was regarded as one of historical interest. The church was thronged by representative Catholic Irishmen and their Protestant sympathisers, and in the galleries were a number of ladies of distinction, who seem to have

[1] *Life of O'Connell*, by O'Rourke.

taken a keener interest in the proceedings than in listening to the famous debates of the English Parliament; among them was a daughter of Lucien Bonaparte, the niece of Napoleon I. Sometime afterwards the Duke of Wellington condescendingly advised his Catholic countrymen to desist from "agitation," if they wished to have their cause favourably considered by Government; the people replied by returning O'Connell member of Parliament for Clare. Of course the House of Commons was still closed to those who professed the true faith; but now Emancipation was inevitable, and both Peel and Wellington warmly advocated the Catholic claims from motives of political expediency, although previously they had been very slow to acknowledge the strict justice of the demands made by the Faithful of Ireland. The "Catholic Relief Bill" became law on the 13th April 1829, George IV. having been actually forced to attach his royal signature. O'Connell was, indeed, the "LIBERATOR."

He gained the victory, but not many knew how dearly it had cost him. It was his character to conceal troubles beneath a lightheartedness of manner that deceived all except those from whom he sought encouragement and consolation in the hour of trial. His most intimate friends, those who had often enjoyed his hospitality and remembered those flashes of wit, which could become so terribly caustic when directed against bigotry or deceit, would hardly have recognised him as the same man, while assisting among the poor at early

Mass in Clarendon Street. Neither was he timid or ashamed in admitting his dependence for spiritual support upon the priests of his religion if more severely tried by the wearying strain of public life. He never seemed so happy as when there was one of them by his side ; and his familiar intimacy with them only increased his reverence for their sacred profession. Once he was accused of having spoken disparagingly of the Spanish clergy, but he denied the imputation as indignantly as if he had been charged with the commission of some heinous crime. He wondered how any one could deem him guilty of so grievous a fault, knowing that the mere sight of a priest inspired him with secret sentiments of veneration ; and he believed that it was impossible to prosper even in this world without paying to God's ministers the respect they might claim as their due. Likely O'Connell felt that accusation all the more keenly because a member of the community at " St. Teresa's " was a Spanish priest, Father Christopher Nogueras. As a further beautiful proof of his filial confidence in the " Lord's Anointed," it may be said that O'Connell—the recognised " Hero of Christendom," whom the Sovereign Pontiff would have clasped to his breast—selected as his own Spiritual Director one of the youngest Confessors in Clarendon Street, Father Joseph Francis of St. Teresa, already spoken of as " Father L'Estrange." [1] This Religious was

---

[1] *Life and Last Days. MS. in Arch. of St. Teresa's.* (*Note:*—The documents in this and the other *Archives* quoted by the author were written before the year 1835.)

regarded as the "*Liberator's*" lieutenant, and as such shared the sneers so freely bestowed upon his friend and penitent.

O'Connell always wished to have Father Francis with him on those occasions which he was wont to consider most eventful for Ireland ; but he took care not to trespass inconsiderately on the time which had to be devoted to the discharge of monastic duties. Father L'Estrange was, moreover, an indefatigable student of mystical theology, a branch of the sacred science in which O'Connell himself was well versed. Although there was a private oratory attached to the "*Liberator's*" city residence, in which Father Francis had permission to offer the Holy Sacrifice from time to time, O'Connell himself, when in Dublin, preferred to walk over to "St. Teresa's" in the mornings ; and occasionally, after he had approached the altar, he liked to surprise the Fathers by asking them to invite him to breakfast.

His Confessor did not long survive the triumph of Emancipation: Father Francis died in 1833, his death causing a great shock of grief to his devoted spiritual son.[1] All the other Fathers were equally dear to him ; but O'Connell retained a touchingly grateful remembrance of Father Francis Joseph to the end. And in the year 1838, when overwhelmed by sorrow for the death of his wife, he sadly missed the sympathy which that true friend would have given him, if only as a member of the community at "St. Teresa's"; for Mrs.

[1] *Life of O'Connell*, and *Letters to the Author*.

O'Connell's attachment to Clarendon Street was hardly less devoted than the "*Liberator's*" own.

The granting of Emancipation was, after all, only part payment of the debt which England owed to the Irish people. There were yet many injuries to be remedied in accordance with strict justice; of these the tithe extortion was most intolerable to the Faithful. Having waited patiently for some time to see whether the Government would take the initiative in the matter of needful reform, O'Connell at length resolved to bring the question before Parliament, now in dread of the great moral force over which it was known he had absolute control. Meanwhile (A.D. 1830) William IV. had succeeded his insincere and profligate brother, and a crisis having occurred in English politics at the beginning of this reign, of such a nature as to afford the "*Emancipator*" an opportunity of forwarding the great project which he had now at heart, O'Connell would allow no other Irish interest to clash with that of " Repeal." But in order to test the good faith of Government regarding Ireland, he held up to the English nation the gross injustice of calling upon the Catholics of this country to pay those obnoxious tithes. No redress having been granted before the year 1840, the Repeal Association was founded, another King of England having, in the interval (A.D. 1837), passed away. The new organisation made rapid progress, O'Connell himself being in a position to render the cause more valuable assistance than ever. For by a recent Act of Parliament he, as a Roman Catholic, was qualified to become Lord Mayor of that Corporation which a few years previously would not suffer itself to be "*contaminated*," to use the expression of the Dublin Protestant papers, by the mere enfranchisement of Catholic citizens.

Government grew alarmed at the latent possibilities of the "Repeal" movement, and actually instituted a prosecution against its leaders for conspiracy. An unjust verdict was quite easily procured, but an appeal was made, and the sentence of the Courts *had* to be reversed by the House of Lords; and O'Connell and his fellow-"Conspirators" were free again to teach the Irish people how their National Independence could be "*legally*" regained. Meetings of the Association were convened all over the country, as many as a million "*Repealers*" having come together on occasion to listen to the exhortations of their "Emancipator." Seeing him still in the vigour of health, although advanced in years, they were convinced that he himself should behold the realisation of his second grand ambition. And even while thus engaged in the pressing duties of his political career, he found time to compose "A MEMOIR OF IRELAND," which he respectfully dedicated to the young Queen, and which proved a startling revelation of the misgovernment of this kingdom; for his assertions were based, for the most part, on the evidence of English Protestant writers.

Still O'Connell's method of agitation appeared entirely too *slow* to some over-ardent spirits, who *did* sincerely long to see their country resume its lost prestige among the nations. It was an open secret that the brilliant "YOUNG IRELANDERS" were but biding their time to have recourse to the sword. The "*Liberator*" foresaw the result of this rashness; and grief and concern for his brave countrymen were causing his heart to break. Just now it was a truly pathetic sight—that is for those who *knew*—to see him "enveloped in a very ample cloak which he usually wore," as he prayed in "St. Teresa's" for the welfare of Ireland. Only from his friends there might he seek comfort in such sorrow: to the world he was ever the "*Liberator*," whose greatness became all the more manifest as the difficulties of his undertaking continued to increase.[1]

In the beginning of the year 1847, O'Connell, unconsciously and yet with a certain presentiment, paid his last visit to his favourite church, and to those Fathers whom he loved so well. Of late years his relations with them had become hallowed by the memory of many Religious who had died in the course of his long unchanging friendship with the Friars of "St. Teresa's." He was now leaving home for London on urgent public business. Some said he was doing so at the positive risk of his life; because latterly his health had become seriously impaired owing to his extraordinary mental exertions. But famine was imminent—in fact its fatal hold was already tightening on Ireland — and Government alone could prevent the worst results of this awful

[1] *Life of O'Connell* (O'Rourke).

visitation. The much-needed help was not forthcoming, so O'Connell believed it to be his duty to remind those responsible, that the lives of *hundreds of thousands* of the Irish people were dependent on the prompt fulfilment of England's most solemn obligations. It was the day of the great man's humiliation; his soul had to be thus chastened before the close of his marvellous career. For all his wonted light-heartedness in bidding his friends at "St. Teresa's" good-bye, they saw how keenly he realised the true nature of his mission: he had taken upon himself the painful task of telling the Parliament of England that the dauntless Irish people, of whose power he had so often spoken with pride, were about to perish; and that he had come to *crave* for them pity and relief. This was his last speech in the House of Commons; it was listened to with profoundest sympathy; every one regretting the marked alteration in the "*Liberator's*" appearance and bearing. Nevertheless his warning was not heeded, and his prophetic words were verified in a truly terrible way.

The physicians insisted on his retiring immediately to the south of England. They said the sole hope of restoring him to the service of his country rested on an entire change of climate and occupation. Sorely disappointed at being unable to continue his labours, O'Connell availed himself of this opportunity to carry out a desire which he had cherished for many years: to visit Rome, in order that he might obtain the Holy

Father's blessing. As soon as he felt sufficiently strong to undertake the journey, he proceeded to France, his tour through that country being more like a triumphal march. But the enthusiasm of the French people became mournfully subdued when informed that the doctors had still grave apprehensions concerning the "*Liberator's*" state of health. At Paris he was presented with an address by Count de Montalembert in the name of Catholic France. That noble son of a regenerated nation — the first of his race to do by the *pen* what his ancestors had accomplished by the *sword*—claimed O'Connell as the "Model and glorious Preceptor" of all true French patriots: "The man of the age who had done most for the dignity and liberty of mankind, and especially for the political instruction of Catholic nations.[1] Montalembert attributed his own splendid victories in the cause of religion to the wise counsels which he had received from the "*Liberator*" in Ireland. "Illness and emotion" prevented O'Connell replying to so generous an expression of grateful admiration ; notwithstanding the reassuring messages sent home to the Irish people, their "*Emancipator*" was dying. He could only bequeath his heart to Rome ; for he died a most holy death at Genoa on the 15th of May 1847.

By the command of the Pope, the obsequies were performed at the public expense in the Eternal City, with a regal magnificence greater than what is recorded of the funeral of Charlemagne, or

[1] *Last Days of O'Connell.*

even than that of Constantine the Great. The whole Catholic world was represented in the vast assembly that had gathered to witness the arrival of the "PILGRIMAGE OF THE HEART." Pius IX. *privileged* all the altars in Rome for the occasion, and *thousands* of masses were offered upon them according to the rites of both Churches, Latin and Oriental, for the repose of O'Connell's soul. Bitterly did the august Pontiff himself deplore the favour denied him by the "*Liberator's*" death; but O'Connell's youngest son received the Apostolic embrace of the Father of Christendom in the "*Emancipator's*" stead.

At first the people of Ireland would not credit the woeful news: they said *he* had often told them that they might count upon him until he had reached his ninetieth year! And among the millions made sorrowful by the sad tidings, the Fathers of "St. Teresa's" were, after their "*Friend's*" near relatives, most painfully shocked; but now they had to conceal their own deep grief in order to comfort the broken-hearted members of O'Connell's family. One of them, "than whom," said the papers, "the Emancipator had no dearer friend," had just returned from India; heretofore, he had been known in Dublin as "Father John Francis of St. Teresa." It was he who accompanied O'Connell's children on the steamer to be present with them during the harrowing ordeal of meeting the vessel "with the mortuary chapel," when it came in view off the Irish coast. That Friar now wore the Bishop's ring; but sympathy was just as welcome and as soothing from Dr. Whelan, as it would have been from "Father John."[1]

The demonstration at the "*Liberator's*" funeral was "*unprecedented in any country or at any age.*" A Frenchman who had witnessed the reception given to the remains of Napoleon I., on their being removed to Paris, was heard to say that it could not be compared with what he saw in Dublin on the arrival of O'Connell's coffin. The solemn Requiem Mass was chanted in the cathedral, Dr. Whelan having been chosen from among the assembled Bishops to officiate on the occasion. And as if it had been providentially ordained that the Discalced Carmelites should be nearest to their "*Friend*" in this last sad scene, another Teresian Friar came forward, by right of precedence, with the other senior prelates, Drs. Murray, M'Hale, and Keating, to give the final Absolution. This was Dr. Nicholson, Archbishop of Corfu, whom O'Connell knew best as "*Father Joseph of the Annunciation.*" Among those whom the reporters classed as "the intimate friends," were seveial members of the communities of "St. Teresa's" and of the Abbey, Loughrea. Only two of the Prelates then present survived to take part in the celebration of the centenary of O'Connell's birth in 1875 ; and these were Drs. Whelan and M'Hale.

When speaking some years ago of the victory of Catholic Emancipation, the Archbishop of Dublin— the Most Rev. Dr. Walsh—referred to the way in

[1] *Last Days of O'Connell.*

which the Teresian Friars of St. Patrick's Province helped to second the efforts of the "*Liberator.*" So that a friendship, based on mutual affection and esteem, has been likewise the means of associating names deeply revered in Ireland; and which are to be found inscribed, either on that grand memorial raised in Glasnevin Cemetery, to perpetuate the Nation's gratitude to O'Connell, or on the humble monument of the Discalced Carmelites, to be seen there also, not far away.

CHAPTER XII.

REOPENING OF THE NOVITIATE.

The Abbey of Loughrea : past and present—Formal reopening of the Novitiate there—Numerous Vocations to Carmel—A General Visitation : Cardinal Gotti—The "REGULAR LIFE" at the Abbey—After Profession : the first trial.

THE Discalced Carmelites built a church and friary at Loughrea the very year Emancipation was granted to the Faithful. A little chapel and dwelling-house had been already there since 1785, and these were enlarged considerably on the Novitiate being canonically opened at "The Abbey," when the difficulty of sending postulants abroad arose by reason of the Revolution that raged throughout the Continent. The new monastery, first placed under the Invocation of "Our Lady of Mount Carmel," was re-dedicated to "ST. JOSEPH" later on, because the Convent of the Carmelite Sisters at Loughrea bore the former title.

The references made to this Foundation show how interesting the "Annals of the Abbey" would have been if transmitted to us from the beginning. We have seen that the remains of the original friary, founded A.D. 1300, passed into the possession of the Teresian Carmelites, with the sanction of the

Pope, in 1640, a *Catholic* Earl of Clanricarde having allowed the Discalced Fathers to inhabit the ruins about the time he himself had to take the field against the Parliamentarian President of Connaught, the notorious Sir Charles Coote. The fate of the first community was similar to that which had befallen the Friars of "The Abbey" at its suppression under Henry VIII. If anything, Cromwell's "*System of thoroughness*" was more barbarous in detail than that of the arch-persecutor of the Monks. And since the Protector's Commissioners made Loughrea the centre of their operations, while tediously deliberating over the settlement of the miserable "*Transplanters*," perhaps it is a merciful dispensation that there are no contemporary "Records" left us by an "*Outlawed*" Friar of the historic monastery to increase the horror of that terrible account of the people's sufferings given by Father Agapitus of the Holy Ghost.

The modern church occupies a site only a few paces distant from the ruins; in fact, the tower of the "Old Abbey" still serves as a belfry. The house, built in 1829, once stood a little further apart; but of recent years it has been connected with the sacred edifice by a spacious building—the Novitiate proper—so that "*St. Joseph's*" (or "THE ABBEY," as it is more familiarly called) now presents quite an imposing monastic appearance. The situation is admirable for the purpose to which this monastery has been devoted, being sufficiently secluded to ensure a desirable retirement for those dwelling within the cloister. Year after year improvements have been made in the various buildings and in the grounds adjoining; a transept has also been added to the church, and many alterations made in the interior of the friary to render the "Offices" more convenient for the practice of the "*Regular Life.*" "The Abbey," like "St. Teresa's," is an evidence of the triumph of the faith, particularly if contrasted with those venerable ruins which remind one unceasingly of the sufferings and constancy of the priests and people of Ireland.

Among the Religious received into the Order at Loughrea as soon as the Novitiate had been opened there, long *before* the time of Catholic Emancipation, were many who distinguished themselves in after life, at home and abroad, in the discharge of the duties of their holy vocation. From "The Abbey" came forth divines, philosophers, and Prelates who gained renown for their Order and for the Irish Province; some of the first novices became the pioneer missioners of Christianity to the most distant parts of the earth, and not a few of them had the happy lot of labouring to the end among the Faithful of their native land, and are still affectionately spoken of by the children of those who experienced the unwearying devotion of that bygone generation of Teresian Friars. The Catholic families of the county seem to have always held the "Fathers of the Abbey" in great esteem. In a corner of the ancient ruins, now reserved for the burial of deceased members of the community, there is a mural tablet which shows that the sons of several of these families were wont to aspire to the dignity of priesthood in the Order of Carmel, dying at Loughrea after having spent their lives on the Irish Mission. The names of a number of the Fathers who were called to their reward there during the present century will be mentioned in another place, when we come to speak of the efforts made to preserve the "*Obituary*" of St. Patrick's Province.[1]

The Religious at "The Abbey" have invariably taken part in the missionary duties of the diocese, the most cordial relations existing between them and the secular clergy. The warm welcome which their predecessors had received from the Bishop of Clonfert—"Robert of Canterbury"—on coming to Loughrea at the beginning of the fourteenth century, was, in the seventeenth, equally accorded to the Discalced Carmelites by Dr. John Burke. And the successors of both these Prelates in the See of St. Brendan have often acknowledged, most gratefully, their indebtedness to the Teresian Friars.

Having been recalled from France at the outbreak of the war with Germany, in 1870, the Discalced Carmelite students of the Irish Province were sent to Loughrea to continue their scholastic course at "St. Joseph's." For some years past postulants had not been received there; the monastery at London being then under the jurisdiction of the Irish Provincial, it was found more convenient to have the young Religious pass their

[1] *MS. in Arch. at Loughrea.*

noviceship in that place. This arrangement ceased in time, and Irish subjects were thenceforth educated in France, until the expulsion of the Religious Orders in 1881. Vocations to Carmel becoming more numerous in St. Patrick's Province, it was now found expedient to reopen the Novitiate at "The Abbey," and accordingly a prior was canonically elected there the following year; hitherto, because of the changes which had taken place in the Province about the middle of this century, " St. Joseph's " only ranked as a vicariate for some years. All necessary permissions were gladly granted by the Superiors-General at Rome; and a new epoch in the history of the Irish Discalced Carmelites thus dates from the auspicious year 1882, while the Tercentenary of St. Teresa's death was being solemnly celebrated throughout the entire Order. It is an interesting fact that the gold medal offered, as a prize, by the University of Salamanca for the best Commemorative Ode in honour of the Seraphic Virgin was won by an Irish poetess on that occasion. St. Teresa herself obtained a far greater reward for that tribute of homage to her memory : some years afterwards the successful competitor received the vocation-grace, and took the veil in a community of Carmelite Sisters.

The postulants who had entered "The Abbey" immediately after the reopening of the Novitiate, enjoyed the special privilege of being clothed in the brown habit by the Father-General himself. He was making the usual canonical Visitation of the Irish Province, and being at "St. Joseph's" in the month of September 1882, gladly officiated at the ceremony. Father Jerome Mary of the Immaculate Conception—the General's name—was then accompanied from Rome by a Lay-brother for whom the present Holy Father, Pope Leo XIII., has had an affectionate regard for a great number of years, having known this Religious from his own early manhood. The Father-General, also, was himself highly esteemed by the Sovereign Pontiff, who has since required him to undertake certain responsibilities from which ecclesiastical dignity is inseparable. When elected to the supreme government of the Discalced Carmelites at the General Chapter of 1881, "Father Jerome" had been professed thirty years, during many of which he had taught at "St. Anne's" in Genoa, his native place, with remarkable success. He had assisted at the Vatican Council as Theologian; being Procurator-General of his Order about the same time. He was re-elected General in 1889, having been in the meantime connected with various Roman congregations; either as member of the Congregation of Bishops and Regulars, or Consultor of the Propaganda and Holy Office; and he was, also, Doctor of the Theological College of St. Thomas Aquinas. In 1892 he was consecrated Archbishop of Petra, and appointed Apostolic Internuncio and Legate Extraordinary to Brazil. Three years later he was recalled to Rome, on his elevation to the Cardinalate. And now the whole Catholic world rejoices in having a prince of the Church in the person of CARDINAL GOTTI, who still desires to be remembered among his brethren, the Discalced Carmelites, as "*Fra Jerome* of the Immaculate Conception." In a farewell letter addressed to all the Religious of the Order, on his resigning the office of General, he spoke in a touching manner of what it cost him to be constrained, by obedience, to leave the cloister wherein he had passed over forty happy years, and which should remain his home in spirit until death. Cardinal Gotti continues to be as deeply interested in the welfare of St. Patrick's Province, and, indeed, of the Irish Nation, as he was on the occasion of his visit to this country in 1882.[1]

In less than six months after that General Visitation, several Choir-postulants entered the Novitiate, and when these young Religious had completed the term of probation, there was not a vacant "cell" in "The Abbey."

"THE REGULAR LIFE" was now practised at "St. Joseph's," just as it had been led in "*the Friary of Our Lady of Mount Carmel*," Cook Street, Dublin, before the Puritan persecution. The "spirit" of the novices was being formed according to the self-same principles of asceticism, contained in the works of writers of the Order— who were among the very first to embrace the Teresian Reform in the beginning. One of the highest of these authorities is the Venerable John of Jesus Mary, who joined the Order the year St. Teresa died, and soon became remarkable for the great sanctity and learning which have since

[1] Daily papers, official documents, and letters to the Author.

helped innumerable souls to make wondrous progress in the spiritual way. He assisted in drawing up the "Constitutions" of the Italian Congregation of Discalced Carmelites, and is the author of many profound treatises on divers subjects, his *"Instructions for Novices,"* and *"Directions"* for those responsible for the guidance of young Religious, being constantly in the hands of the "Father Master" and his novices during the year's probation. Nor did the writing of these books prevent the Venerable John of Jesus Mary exercising great zeal for the salvation of souls. One of the Definitors-General of the Order at the time the Teresian Friars came to Ireland was the VENERABLE THOMAS OF JESUS, whose works are also much consulted by the Master of Novices in forming the spirit of those under his charge. There is a treatise by this author in explanation of the *"Primitive Rule,"* which the Discalced Carmelites value next to the writings of St. Teresa herself, and those of St. John of the Cross.[1]

During the noviceship, the young Religious are kept apart from the professed members of the community, in conformity to the Apostolic Constitutions; the Father Master alone being held primarily responsible for their spiritual training; he must see that they become thoroughly conversant with all the obligations of their new state of life. However, it rests with the Fathers of the Conventual Chapter to determine whether the novices really possess a vocation to Carmel, and

[1] *Ménologe.*

may prudently be permitted to take the Holy Vows in due course. Naturally, this is deemed a duty of gravest importance, the life-long happiness of others being at stake. But the Fathers can discern, almost by instinct, what postulants shall probably persevere; and very seldom a candidate is admitted into the Novitiate to be found wanting afterwards in the qualifications considered necessary in aspirants to the Order. In the case of the Choir-brothers, the twelve months' probation merely affords opportunity for the development of the virtues accompanying the vocation-grace. So that the community have a moral certainty of the young Religious having been supernaturally called, when the time for simple Profession draws near; but the Solemn Vows, by a Decree of Pope Pius IX., are not taken for a further period of three years. The majority of the postulants seek admission when in their eighteenth year, having completed their classical studies, in which they must pass a preliminary examination before the community. Many apply at a much earlier age, just as they begin to understand that the world is more to be feared than are the austerities of Carmel. However, the Fathers may not yield to the earnest entreaties of these young men, until the conditions presupposed by the Canons are all fulfilled; having satisfied themselves, moreover, that such eagerness is really a sign of the religious vocation.

While at Loughrea, the chief occupation of the brother-novices is to acquire a practical knowledge of the "Science of the Saints." The "Primitive Rule" is to be their guide in this respect, the Church having pronounced it a most efficient means in attaining to holiness. They have even to commit it to memory; but, as confirmed by Pope Innocent IV., at the prayer of St. Simon Stock, the Carmelite Rule is brief, and usually prefixed to the "Constitutions," which have been drawn up by the first Superiors-General of the Teresian Reform, and approved of by the Church. In studying these latter, the young Religious grow familiar with their monastic duties, which are all obligatory without binding (in every instance), under pain of sin. Then there are the "*Ordinary,*" containing "*Instructions*" relative to conventual offices; the "*Ceremonial,*" chiefly pertaining to the choir; and the "*Manual,*" having more particular reference to the functions exercised in the Church; with each of which the novices must become quite conversant, in order to conform fervently and exactly to "*The Regular Life.*" Besides, from their very entrance to the Novitiate, they are taught how to recite the Divine Office; and unceasing application to this branch of the Sacred Liturgy causes the comparatively short time of probation to pass more rapidly still. All these manuals being in Latin, a happy necessity removes the obstacle which often impedes the progress of even advanced students applying themselves to scholastic philosophy.

With regard to the austerities of the Discalced Carmelite's mode of life, about which those outside the cloister sometimes think and speak so hardly, the novices take them quite as a matter of course, knowing that by them they are enabled to correspond to their vocation—impossible unless accompanied by a spirit of self-denial; just as the beautiful brown habit of their Order would not seem complete if worn without the tonsure and sandals. In fact, long before the end of the noviceship, these austerities become second nature to the young Religious; the midnight office and the early rising being all the more attractive instead of producing that wearisomeness which we are wont to associate with unvarying routine. And, since the happiness of the *interior life* is usually experienced for the first time in the Novitiate, the brother-novices grow very attached to "The Abbey." Even those dearest to them on earth—their parents—with whom they part for ever on the day of profession, appear to realise this joy of contentment of soul, and are grateful to God for their children's choice; nor would they wish them to change their state for the highest honours which the world has power to give.

The Father Master may use his own discretion in selecting books suitable for spiritual reading. But, as the novices are always anxious to learn everything relating to *their* glorious Order, he affords them frequent opportunity of perusing the works of Teresian writers, whether treating of the "Reform of Carmel," or of the lives of those who have sanctified themselves by the observance of the Primitive Rule; or of "Mental Prayer," to the very sublimest forms of which he encourages them to aspire. He teaches them, moreover, how to form a "taste" for the serious study of subjects not generally supposed to have much attraction for the young. And after a little while he can see for himself the solid advantages which his novices are deriving, from what they believe to be merely an act of kind indulgence on his part; not the least of these desirable results being the acquisition of a sound sense of discernment, that will prove of the utmost utility to them, as priests, in future life.

On being received into the Order, the Lay-postulants must pass three years as Tertiaries, during which time it is not necessary that they should reside at "The Abbey." The Father-Provincial may send them to either of the other monasteries; but having persevered thus far in their vocation they return to Loughrea and enter the Novitiate; and after a further period of two years' probation, they are allowed to make their simple profession. Their spiritual training is as carefully attended to as that of the Choir-novices; but in such wise as to prepare them for the duties of their particular state. They observe the same Rule; and, consequently, have the same facilities for advancing in the way of perfection.

The lapse of time is marked in the Novitiate by the recurrence of the greater festivals; and almost before the young Religious themselves have begun to hope for it, the Fathers determine by secret vote whether their novices may safely take the vows. Indeed, during the past twelve months all the *anxiety* was on the part of the Conventual Fathers, the novices having had but *one* thought to trouble them,—to moderate the happiness of which a daily increasing brightness of disposition was the manifest sign,—the fear of being found deficient in the qualities indispensable to all who would serve God within the cloisters of Carmel: *goodwill* is not the only proof of a true vocation. Eventually the Chapter has decided in their favour; and now, before entering on their career as students, they are required to devote another full year to the further perfecting of their "*spirit*" by exercises similar to those which they had practised in the Novitiate previous to their Religious profession.

The Constitutions provide for a monastery for "The newly professed"; but here in Ireland the Choir-brothers remain at "The Abbey" until their Superiors wish them to begin their scholastic course. In the interval they are required to revise their classical studies, and, in fact, all other subjects hitherto acquired and likely to be useful to them in after life. Their spiritual progress, however, is still the principal concern of their Superiors, who would have the novices so grounded in the monastic virtues as to ensure perseverance in their first fervour when preoccupied, later on, with the trying duties of the Collegiate. The pious practices of the Order, and the traditional customs of the Province are now regarded by the young Religious as the highest standard for the regulation of their conduct outwardly, as their dispositions are being formed by their more mature appreciation of the principles of the interior life. Thus, they naturally assume that monastic simplicity of manner which the Teresian Friar finds as serviceable as modern etiquette in his necessary relations with those outside the cloister. But, although detached from the world, by the very dread of it, and from everything the world holds dear, the novice begins to think, with sadness, of the many sacrifices which he shall be called upon to make when pressed by Christian charity to labour for the salvation of souls. . . .

Soon after the Feast of St. Teresa, in the year 1884, the three Choir-brothers, professed in "The Abbey" after the reopening of the Novitiate at Loughrea, were told that a new Foundation was about to be made in St. Patrick's Province, and that they themselves were to proceed thither in a few days. For this friary was to be the "*House of Studies*": the first canonically re-established in Ireland since the suppression of the Teresian College at Drogheda in Cromwell's time. So a great victory was at length achieved by the Discalced Carmelites in reward of their patient struggle of many years; it was the evident success of the Novitiate at Loughrea—the increasing prosperity of the Irish Province. The new monastery was to be founded in one of the suburbs of Dublin, its first community being formed of Religious both from "The Abbey" and from "St. Teresa's," Clarendon Street. Accordingly, towards the end of October that year (1884), three Choir-brothers, accompanied by three other Religious—a Conventual Father and two Lay-brothers—left the home to which they had become so attached during their noviceship. Nor is it the recently professed only who find it hard to be changed from Loughrea. Although in "The Abbey" there is ample scope for the missionary zeal of the Fathers, always very popular with the people both of the town and of the surrounding districts; yet it possesses, in a remarkable way, that air of retirement so well suited to the spirit of the Discalced Carmelite, and which is hardly more soothing in the Teresian " Deserts "—especially intended for Religious of the Order who are permitted, at the discretion of their Superiors, to apply themselves solely to a life of prayer.

The leaving the Novitiate is the first *serious* trial which the young Friars have to bear. Probably, never once had the sweet peace of that happy retreat been interrupted during their residence at Loughrea; still so full in itself had each day been, every hour agreeably occupied by the performance of duties of which the novices could never tire, that the *reality* of their life was forcibly impressed upon them, making them most content with the state to which they had been called by God. And now they could only console themselves by thinking of their certain return to "St. Joseph's" as "*Conventuals*" at some future time. The same hope caused them to grow yet fonder of "The Abbey" when they remembered that within the ruins of the ancient Church their own predecessors, for centuries back, have found "The *last* Home," surrounded by many a generation of the Faithful among whom they had laboured and died.

CHAPTER XIII.

"THE HOUSE OF STUDIES."

The foundation of "St. Mary's"—Gayfield House—The "*Regular Life*" during the Scholastic Course—Blessing of the new college at Gayfield—The Discalced Carmelite schools of Philosophy and Theology—"The Studies"—Some scholastic exercises—The Science of the Saints.

"GAYFIELD," on the Morehampton Road, Dublin, is an ideal situation for the College of the Irish Discalced Carmelites. Being for sale in the Landed Estates Court some twenty years ago, the residence and adjoining grounds (about seven acres) were secured by the community of "St. Teresa's" under favourable circumstances, a large sum of money having been already bequeathed for the purpose by a generous benefactor.

First built in the eighteenth century as a suburban residence for a member of the Yelverton family, "Gayfield House" was afterwards rented out annually until the Teresian Fathers obtained the fee-simple; a private Catholic school opened by a clergyman there having been recently closed. The mansion itself has been altered beyond recognition, losing, it must be said, much of that old-world grandeur of appearance characteristic of the homes of the Irish aristocracy when Parliament was held in College Green. But the grounds remain almost unchanged. Indeed the original owner would only miss a number of the fine elms that lined the avenue on either side when he and his guests passed through, discussing Grattan's fearless policy, or commenting on the merits of Curran's latest speech. Neither was Gayfield then surrounded by those terraces, containing the private dwellings of citizens who wish to live removed from the bustle of town life, and ensuring for "St. Mary's" (as the new friary is called) an air of retirement hardly less impressive than the monastic quiet of the Abbey of Loughrea.

The diocesan authorities were glad to sanction another Foundation for the Discalced Carmelites in Dublin, although it is unusual for a Religious Order to have more than one monastery in the same city, Gayfield not being even quite a mile distant from "St. Teresa's." In granting the necessary permission, the late Cardinal Archbishop (M'Cabe) heartily congratulated the Fathers on what he considered a certain presage of the future prosperity of "St. Patrick's Province." The secular clergy of the district were equally pleased; the parish priest being most anxious to have a community established in Gayfield at once, if possible. But many obstacles prevented the Fathers carrying out their project for nearly ten years; then each monastery must be self-supporting, as prescribed by Canon Law, a condition which could not be complied with in the case of a foundation at Gayfield, because the Fathers had not yet the means of opening a public church there. However, as soon as the first Choir-novices were ready to leave the Abbey, the Superiors-General at Rome allowed the community of "St. Teresa's" to undertake the grave responsibility of providing an income for the new friary until such time as the source of revenue, ordained by the Constitutions of the Order, and granted, as a special privilege, by various Sovereign Pontiffs to the Discalced Carmelites, should become available for the support of the college. This arrangement caused (and does still cause) serious inconvenience to the Religious at Clarendon Street; but they did not mind, so long as they saw their Province restored to the position which it had held in the Order before the Penal Days. And, happily, they were able to bear the burden a little more easily, as they incurred no debt by the purchase of the Gayfield property.

All canonical ordinances having been now fulfilled, immediate preparations were made for the reception of the first community at "St. Mary's." These were not of an elaborate kind: simply to put the old mansion in a much-needed state of repair, and to supply such furniture as was absolutely indispensable. The latter part of this task was not very hard of accomplishment, the "cells" for the Religious requiring not much more attention than that bestowed on "the little chamber" which the Sunamite woman made ready for the Carmelite Prophet Eliseus, putting in it for him "*a bed, and a table, and a stool, and a candlestick.*"[1]

[1] 4 Kings iv. 10.

Still on their arrival at Gayfield, the 28th of October 1884, the students were rather disappointed to find that they would not have to experience any of the privations suffered by their predecessors at Drogheda early in the seventeenth century on opening a "House of Studies" amid the ruins of the ancient abbey. The inconveniences of the new Foundation did not prevent them, for a single day, conforming to "*The Regular Life*," just as they had practised it during their noviceship in Loughrea. On the very first evening the house was privately blessed, and placed under the invocation of Mary's Holy Name. The largest room was converted into what proved a very pretty oratory; and the Holy Sacrifice was offered there the following morning. Once the Blessed Sacrament was preserved in the humble tabernacle, formal possession had been taken of the new Foundation—at least in St. Teresa's own opinion. The recitation of the Divine Office was also begun in an apartment adjoining the little chapel, which served as a tolerable choir; all other conventual exercises following as a matter of course. So that a casual visitor to "St. Mary's" on the 29th October that year would have thought that the practice of "*The Regular Life*" had been long inaugurated there.

For the present the college was established as a vicariate, because the number of Fathers necessary for the erection of a priory could not be spared from the other monasteries. Three priests, three students, and two Lay-brothers formed the first community of the "House of Studies."

The scholastic course was, likewise, formally entered upon without delay; two Professors having been elected by the Superiors-General at Rome, as "St. Patrick's" was then a semi-Province. One was appointed to teach Mental Philosophy, the other to read Sacred Scripture with the collegians. They held their respective classes daily, either in the morning or afternoon, for each of which the students had to prepare in their "cells" by several hours' private study. Such close application, day after day, did not prevent the young Religious spending some portion of their short recreation in the pleasant task of giving "St. Mary's" a more monastic appearance. They succeeded marvellously, remembering the purpose for which Gayfield House had been originally designed. They called the various rooms, utilised for conventual purposes, by the names of the "*Offices*" in a friary proper; and the familiar titles caused the members of the little community to feel just as much at home in Gayfield as they would have been in the Abbey, or at "St. Teresa's," Clarendon Street.

In the college time passes with almost terrifying rapidity; so much has to be done in the comparatively brief space of *eight* short years. During the first twelve months of its foundation some important changes took place at "St. Mary's" owing to the triennial election held in 1885; not that the new appointments could interfere with the discharge of the duties of the scholasticate in any way. For the method of teaching must be always the same, it being a most serious matter of conscience to raise to the professorship only those known to be thoroughly competent to undertake the responsibility. Other novices·had been professed in the meantime, and sent to "St. Mary's," wherein there was now a fairly large community.

Three years after their Simple Profession, the first students took the Solemn Vows, and completed their philosophical studies some months later on. They were already advanced in Theology, preparing for Holy Orders, when a great event occurred at Gayfield—the laying of the foundation-stone of the "House of Studies," for the building of which a large sum of money had been laid aside. In the beginning the Fathers thought the entire plan of the new monastery could not be carried out with the funds at their disposal; but during the progress of the works they were unexpectedly enabled to finish the several sections, the building of the church alone being still deferred, pending more favourable circumstances.

Early in the year 1889, the new college was opened and blessed by the present Archbishop of Dublin. A great number of distinguished guests had assembled from all parts of the country to witness the ceremony, thus wishing to express their deep interest in the welfare of the Discalced Carmelites in Ireland : a manifestation of the Irish people's affectionate esteem, very gratifying to the Religious themselves. The venerable Bishop of

Clonfert, the late Most Rev. Dr. Duggan, accompanied by several of the dignitaries of his diocese, came in person to prove his own warm regard for the Teresian Fathers; many of the secular clergy of Dublin, and of even the most remote dioceses, also attended; while conspicuous among the members of the Religious Orders were the Calced Carmelites, who rejoiced in the success of their brethren of the "Reform." The city was represented by the Lord Mayor and gentlemen of the Municipal Council. And there were numerous representatives of Catholic families with whom, like that of O'Connell, reverence for the Discalced Carmelites has been traditionary for generations.

In fact, this event was looked upon as one of national importance, the proceedings being afterwards fully reported by all the leading papers in England and America as well as in Ireland. Even the Protestant press had long comments on the subject, and these were far from being either ungenerous or bigoted. The felicitations conveyed to the Fathers were of the most enthusiastic kind; every one seemed to take a personal pride in the beautiful new building intended for the education of Teresian students. Frequent mention was then made of the services rendered to the country by the Religious of St. Patrick's Province, which we may not repeat; and his Grace the Archbishop availed himself of that occasion to congratulate the Irish Church on the fact of Gayfield having passed into the hands of the Carmelite Fathers. Dr. Walsh had first known "St. Mary's" when it was a private school, where several renowned Irish Prelates received their primary education. The Archbishop also spoke of the inconsistency of the British Legislature, which, with its much-vaunted spirit of religious toleration, is still disgraced by some of the most shameful statutes of the Penal Code.[1]

Outwardly, "St. Mary's" is a strikingly handsome building. Completed by the addition of a church, it will form a quadrangle enclosing a cloister somewhat similar to those in the Carmelite Monasteries on the Continent. The Gothic style of architecture prevails throughout, the material used being red brick with limestone courses in all the storeys except the basement, which is of granite. The interior has been well adapted to the requirements of a "House of Studies." Long and lofty, the corridors have a fine appearance; the refectory is on the ground floor, with the library overhead, extending nearly the whole length of this section, in which the dormitory is, also, containing the cells of the students; and the parlours, class-rooms, and cells for the other members of the community, occupy the section with the façade.

A splendid collection of books, including the best edition of the works of the Fathers of the Church, fill the shelves of the library. The departments of Philosophy and the Sciences; of Theology and Holy Scripture; of Hagiology, Liturgy, and Canon Law; of the Classics, Literature, and History, have been gradually well

[1] Daily papers.

supplied with the writings of standard authors. A special place is allotted to Irish history, and, of course, to the writers of the Order, whose works are sufficiently numerous to be quite conspicuous among the many thousand volumes in the library, although *few* relatively to the fruits of the labours of those Teresian Carmelites who, from the time of the Seraphic Virgin herself, have tried to advance God's glory by the *pen*.[1] It may be said that it is exceedingly difficult to procure those works of the Discalced Carmelite authors, and only by keeping in constant communication with continental booksellers has the present valuable collection been obtained for "St. Mary's." Of all the books in the library, precious as numbers of them are — and not excluding a work, in the original boards, of a Carmelite who wrote in the fifteenth century — the one most prized by the Religious is that quaint little volume, bound in age-seared vellum, which had been in the Teresian Monastery at Ardee (A.D. 1640).

A few months after the blessing of the new college, another event of special interest is to be found recorded in the *"Annals of St. Mary's"*: one of the students was ordained priest; and, in all probability, he was the first Discalced Carmelite to have been professed, and to make his entire course of studies in Ireland, since before the Cromwellian persecution. This was in April of the year 1889.

Henceforth, scholastic life might be led all the more easily at Gayfield, and in greater conformity

[1] *Collect. Script. Carmel. Excalceat*, vols. i. ii.

to the traditions handed down among Teresian students from the establishment of the famous Theological College of their Order at Salamanca, during the lifetime of St. Teresa, and from the foundation of an equally renowned School of Philosophy. It was not for their own pupils alone, or merely for their own age and country, the Professors known as the "*Complutenses*" and the "*Salmanticenses*" laboured. Their works are still read throughout the Catholic world. The Philosophical Course, or "*Complutenses*," is the result of the joint efforts of Father Anthony of the Mother of God (A.D. 1587), who composed three of the four volumes containing the various treatises, and of Father Michael of the Holy Trinity (A.D. 1588), who wrote the logic. This "*Course*" soon became very popular all over Spain, France, Italy, Belgium, and Germany, being adopted by the Catholic colleges and universities of these countries. At a General Chapter of the Oratorians, held in 1675, it was decreed that Philosophy should be taught in the congregation according to the Doctrine of St. Thomas of Aquin, as explained by the Angelical's most reliable exponents—the "*Complutenses*."[1] Seeing how universally appreciated their "Philosophy" was, the Discalced Carmelites decided on publishing a Theological Course after the method of their college in Salamanca. The fame of this school was already wide-spread; so much so, that the Doctors of the great University in that city had the MS. lectures

[1] *Collect. Scrip. Ord. Carmel. Excal.*, vols. i. ii.

of those Fathers transcribed at great expense for their own instruction, and for the benefit of their students. And when within the brief space of six months, over *fifty* of their own most distinguished graduates doffed the academical gown for the brown habit of the Teresian Reform, their former masters were the first to congratulate them on having chosen such a career.[1] The grand task of writing the "Theology" was undertaken by Father Anthony of the Mother of God, one of the "*Complutenses.*" It was his intention simply to comment, clearly and concisely, on St. Thomas's "*Summary,*" which the Discalced Carmelite Professors are strictly bound to follow in Philosophy and the Sacred Science. But Father Anthony had only had time to compose the explanatory Treatises on the "*First Part*" when he died. The work was then continued by Father Dominic of St. Teresa, whose commentaries were chiefly on the "*First of the Second Part*"; the remainder of the "Course"—with exception of the Treatise on Penance by Fathers Anthony of St. John Baptist and Alphonsus of the Angels — being completed by Father John of the Annunciation, whose death took place at Salamanca in 1701. Among the numerous editions of the "*Salmanticenses,*" perhaps the one at present most in favour is that brought out in Paris some years ago (twenty-two vols. 8vo) by the well-known firm of VIVES. Needless to say that this is the "*Dogmatic Course,*" quite distinct from the other

[1] *Ibid.*

great work by the Fathers of Salamanca on *Moral Theology*, so frequently quoted by St. Alphonsus Liguori, and which the late Cardinal Newman was wont to refer to as a favourite standard authority on Casuistry. The latter "*Course*" was prepared by Fathers Francis of Jesus Mary, Andrew of the Mother of God, Sebastian of St. Joachim, and Alphonsus of the Angels. It was published in six full-sized tomes, between the years 1717 and 1724; various Summaries being immediately prepared for use as "Text-Books" in ecclesiastical colleges.

The "*Salmanticenses*" commends itself principally for a directness of style in argument and explanation, together with an unassuming elegance of Latin diction; features, also, characteristic of the "*Complutenses*." No matter how profound the subject, and subtle the distinction needful for the understanding of the question at issue, the student is never left at a loss for principles on which the easy solution of the difficulty depends. But in thus speaking of the merits of works that have, for centuries, been receiving praise from the learned of all nations—the highest coming from the members of the Order of St. Dominic—we would not have our readers think that the Teresian Philosophers and Theologians are bound to confine themselves to, or even to *use* as their class-books, either the "*Salmanticenses*" or "*Complutenses*." So long as the doctrine of St. Thomas is taught, the Constitutions leave it to the discretion of the Superiors of each Province to select suitable Commentaries for the assistance of the students. The Theologians, however, are required to read the "*Summary*" of the Angelic Doctor in class; but they are permitted to study some standard Thomastic author at the same time. The Professors must be familiar with practically all the greater authorities on the particular subject of their own lectures; and, it may be said, if they *do* give any preference to the writers of their Order, the partiality is excusable for more reasons than one, considering how fair the Teresian method of argument is—literal and full quotation of adverse opinions being invariably introduced. . . .

The Scholastic Course, as followed at "St. Mary's," lasts eight years, three of which are devoted to Mental Philosophy, Holy Scripture, and Church History, the remaining five to Divinity, Sacred Liturgy, and Canon Law. An "Academical year" extends from the 15th of September to the 23rd of June, leaving about twelve weeks for the "Long Vacation," during which the collegians study privately. Two classes are held daily —either Professor lecturing on the subject-matter which he has been elected to teach—except on Thursdays, when the students only attend in the morning; and on Sundays, usually devoted to the "Weekly Disputations," Philosophical or Theological, alternately. In a Province, having the canonical number of Foundations, there are two separate colleges; but in Ireland this ordination has been dispensed with for the present, in order that the young Religious may be educated at home. The students are now very rarely sent abroad, and merely that some of them may have an opportunity of seeing how "*The Regular Life*" is the same in practice all over the world ; or, perhaps, to prolong their course of studies at the International College of the Order lately re-established in Rome.

At "St. Mary's" the morning class is either in Philosophy or Theology, other subjects requiring less preparation being reserved for evening lecture. Latin is the only language spoken in the class-room, but practice soon makes the students quite at their ease in this respect. Part of the prescribed time is set apart by the Professor for the explanation of the next day's lesson, the collegians being allowed and encouraged to take notes and ask questions, especially with regard to the more difficult treatises. They are then examined in the matter which they have already prepared ; afterwards objections are proposed from every conceivable standpoint, so that the students may learn how to refute them by the application of the principles upon which the doctrine of the "Angel of the Schools" is based. This system of instruction accustoms the young Religious from the very beginning to a most effective method of detecting error and defending the truth. It enables them, moreover, to derive the utmost profit from their reading, since they are thus taught to discover and retain the substance of each article ; for they see how those scholastic principles must necessarily affect the issue of every argument, remote as the conclusion itself may seem.

The weekly "*Disputations*" are so many interesting episodes in college life, the source of great pleasure, as well as of much instruction, to the Fathers of the community in whose presence they are held. "*A Theologian*" or "*a Philosopher*" undertakes to "*defend*" a "*Thesis*," either an Article of Faith or a received theological opinion, or some philosophical truth. The other students (of the respective "Courses") make it *their* serious duty to advance plausible reasons for opposing the assertion which he has made. Their efforts are warmly seconded by the Conventual Fathers present, whom the Professors invite to take part in the discussion. On these occasions, modern errors may be, and are frequently introduced, by way of objection. Naturally the expertness then acquired in exposing *fallacies*, often very ingeniously concealed, proves of great practical utility in after life; while these scholastic exercises always afford an agreeable mental relaxation during the time of arduous study.

A further satisfactory proof of the proficiency made in the course of the year is to be had by annual examination. The duty of the Fathers-Examiners in this respect is of serious obligation; they may only give their votes in favour of the collegians whom they find undoubtedly qualified. Still their office is neither burdensome nor unpleasant; study is too grave a responsibility with the young Religious themselves to be looked upon in any other light than that of *their* sacred duty; hence do they succeed, because they have conscientiously done their best.

Without a Dispensation from the Holy See, candidates for the priesthood must now spend three years in the study of Theology before they may present themselves for ordination. Preparing for this, the greatest event of their lives, causes time to pass more rapidly still at "St. Mary's." But the "*Instructions for the House of Studies*" do not leave much leisure at the free disposal of the students. However, there is a little time which each one may employ, with the permission of the Father-Master, in acquiring or perfecting the knowledge of any subject or art for which he may have a particular inclination; such as the natural sciences, painting, music, literature, and the languages. Only care must be taken that the development of the *special* taste does not interfere with the all-important obligation of the "Studies." Sacred eloquence is also attended to during the Scholastic Course; the principles of this art most insisted upon being those so beautifully inculcated by St. John of the Cross: "The better the life of the preacher, the greater the fruit, though his style may be homely, his eloquence scanty, and his teaching common; for warmth proceeds from the living spirit within." Not that the Saint, no more than the Apostle of the Gentiles, "who came not in loftiness of speech," condemns a good style of preaching, for, "as a noble expression elevates and restores what is low and mean, so, on the other hand, a poor style debases and ruins even that which is noble."[1]

"*Mystical Theology*," as taught by the ascetical writers of their own Order especially, can never be neglected by Teresian students. The most popular manual on this profound subject is by Father Philip of the Blessed Trinity; a recent edition of which has been published at Brussels, receiving the highest praise from the Doctors of Louvain.[2] Father Philip was the twenty-first Superior-General of the Italian Congregation, and died in the year 1671. He had taken the deepest interest in the welfare of St. Patrick's Province, and when writing his "*History of the Order*," he included much information relative to the Mission of the Fathers in this country, and to the heroic perseverance of the Faithful of Ireland during the Cromwellian persecution. He also composed a complete course of Philosophy, and afterwards one of Theology; but of all his works, Father Philip considered his treatise on "Mysticism" the most important. His treatment throughout is methodical and simple; and he has been the means of popularising the study of this "Science," even outside the cloisters of Carmel.

While fervently observing "*The Regular Life*," the students are actually putting into daily practice their acquired knowledge of the Science of the Saints, and so advancing in holiness. They try to sanctify themselves by study, for no matter how

---

[1] *Life and Works of St. John of the Cross*, vol. i.
[2] *Theol. Mystica. By Phil. a SS. Trinitate.*

preoccupied they may be, they can always make progress in the spiritual way. Speaking of the duties of the Teresian Professors, Cardinal Gotti, himself one of the first exponents of the "Art of Teaching," alludes to the impossibility of ever becoming truly learned, if knowledge does not lead one nearer to God.[1] Together with the two hours' Meditation every day, and the time passed in the Choir for the recitation of the Divine Office, there are various other conventual exercises, which help to preserve the students' spirit of fervour. Then there is the yearly retreat of ten days, made separately by each Religious, when he is exempt from all duties, save those connected with Choir, that he may have more leisure for prayer. Indeed, all through his college course, the Teresian Carmelite spends most of his time in the retirement of his "cell," according to one of the ordinances of the "Primitive Rule"; and nowhere else, except before the Tabernacle, can he find the peace and contentment which he experiences there.

Having finished their Theological Course, the newly ordained priests pass a last examination as students, after which they become Conventual Fathers. They may now be changed from "St. Mary's," should their Superiors require their services elsewhere. But they have yet to prepare for their missionary labours; and in all Discalced Carmelite Monasteries, Theological as well as Spiritual Conferences are given once a week; so that "study" becomes a matter of necessity

[1] Letter to the Author.

throughout life. And, as it does not rest with any of the Fathers to determine how they can best forward the interests of their Province, there is always a likelihood of their being recalled to "St. Mary's" to perpetuate as Professors those pious traditions of the Order which imply the secret of success in a Teresian student's career.

CHAPTER XIV.

A FRAGMENT OF THE "OBITUARY."

Loss of the "Obituary" of the Irish Province—Why the "Names of our Dead" are preserved—Father Serapion's task—Some Religious of St. Patrick's Province whose death occurred before that of Father Seraphim Power.

SEEING what efforts the Irish Discalced Carmelites have made to perpetuate the traditions of the "*Teresian Reform*" in St. Patrick's Province, from their first coming to Ireland early in the seventeenth century until the close of the nineteenth, we now consider it our duty to pay a humble tribute of gratitude to their memory by associating their names with the victory which we have seen them achieve. But, for the most part, the Teresian Friars of past generations are unknown to us; and we may only speak of the Religious who are *dead*. We have already stated why the Fathers of the Irish Province have to deplore the loss of so interesting a document as the "Obituary," notwithstanding the "General Necrology" of the Order preserved in the Archives at Rome; and the "Book of Obits" kept in each monastery; and "The Mortuary Charts," which are hung round the cloister to remind the living to pray for the repose of the souls of those gone to their eternal rest.

At the beginning of the present century one of the Fathers of Clarendon Street—Father Serapion of St. Francis—made a most praiseworthy attempt to repair, even partially, the effects of Puritan vandalism. And although he succeeded in discovering a good many of the names of the Teresian Carmelites who had died in Ireland during the Penal Days, we find that the fruits of his long research hardly repaid the arduous labour of so toilsome a task; for comparatively few entries are made in the "*List of Obits*" which he had begun carefully to prepare.[1] However, we are thankful to be able to submit this "List" to the reader, having altered the form, and supplemented it from sources not within Father Serapion's reach.

I. Irish Discalced Carmelites of the Seventeenth Century.

Father Edward of the Kings. The first Teresian Friar to devote himself to the duties of the mission in Ireland, Father Edward was called to his reward before any of his fellow-labourers; he died at Dublin in the year 1627. Having spoken of his successful career in a previous chapter, we need not revert again to the life and virtues of this holy Religious.

Father Paul of St. Ubaldus: Father Edward's companion, and, like him, most fervent in fulfilling the obligations of his sacred profession.[2] The annalists do not record either the time or place of his death.

[1] *MS. in Arch. of St. Teresa's.*   [2] *Ibid.*

Father James Bricklane, a native of the north of Ireland, was one of the first allowed to return from France, where he had been professed and ordained, in order that he might share the labours of Fathers Edward and Paul. As already stated, he died in England (1636) while discharging the office of Visitator-General, which had been delegated to him on his being appointed Vicar-Provincial of the Irish Province.[1]

Father Thomas Aquinas of St. Teresa died for the faith in Ireland during the Puritan persecution of 1641.

Fra Angelus of St. Joseph merited a like glorious crown the following year; and

Brother Peter of the Mother of God received the Martyr's Palm on the scaffold, in Dublin, on the Feast of the Annunciation, 1643.[2]

Father Bede was, also, one of the Teresian Confessors put to death by the heretics; this fact alone being mentioned by the annalists.[3]

Father Patrick met the same fate; but neither in this instance are any details of the martyrdom given.

Father Lawrence of St. Thomas died in the year 1667 from the effects of a long, harsh imprisonment, suffered for the faith in Ireland.[4]

Father Kieran of St. Patrick laboured on the Irish Mission about the same time as Father Lawrence. Captured, likewise, in the exercise of his priestly functions, he was kept in close confine-

[1] *MS. in Arch. of St. Teresa's.* [2] *Enchyr.*
[3] *Annales du Carmel.* [4] *MS. in Arch. of Lond. Monast.*

ment for several years; but at length made good his escape, after having converted several of his jailers to the faith. Probably he died on the Continent.

Father Patrick Donovan. Mention is made of this Discalced Carmelite by De Burgo and others, who speak of him as holding office in the Province soon after the foundation of the first house of the Order in Ireland.

Father Simon of St. Teresa succeeded Father Bricklane as Provincial. The year of his death is not known.

Father Malachy of Jesus was present with Fathers Simon and Patrick at the General Chapter of 1641; we are not told when he died.

Father John Rowe. Very likely Father Rowe spent the last few years of his life in Italy, devoting his time to study and prayer.

Father Victor of St. Michael. No further account is given of the career of this zealous priest, who had entrusted to him the foundation of the Teresian Friary at Ardee.

Father Columbanus had been sent to assist Father Victor in carrying out that project, although only a student at the time; we are told that he became most distinguished in after years, but the annalists furnish no details.

Father Cyril of St. Joseph. This was the Friar who had escaped out of the hands of the Puritans when arrested on his way to the General Chapter in 1646. Ten years later he was Provincial of the Irish Province, all his subjects being then among the "*Outlawed.*" The year of Father Cyril's death is not recorded; the annalists merely alluding to his devotion to the persecuted Faithful of Ireland during those trying times.

Father Agapitus of the Holy Ghost. To him we are indebted for much of the information concerning Ireland, and the Province of St. Patrick, to be found in the chapters that treat of the Cromwellian persecution. He wrote his "*Statement*" in the monastery of "Santa Maria della Vittoria," Rome; probably it was there, also, he died, towards the close of the seventeenth century.

Father Lawrence of St. Teresa was "the Theologian" to whom lengthy reference has been made in another place. He died at Rome in the fortieth year of his age (1670); his name being still revered throughout the Continent on account of the "Treasure" he has bequeathed to posterity in his theological works.

Father Joseph M'Carthy. Born somewhere in the south of Ireland, Father Joseph had joined the Order in France a short time before Fathers Edward and Paul left Louvain. He was ordained in 1628; and was allowed to return to his native country in 1631. Having passed fully thirty-nine years on the Irish Mission, experiencing all the trials which a Teresian Friar of St. Patrick's Province had to undergo during that terrible epoch, he was summoned to his eternal reward in 1670— the year his death occurred at Dublin.

Father Patrick of St. Brigid.[1] When about to

[1] Or, "*of St. James.*"

be hanged by the Puritans, Father Patrick's life was miraculously preserved that he might still labour in the interests of his Order on the Continent. In Italy, especially, his reputation is, even at the present day, only second to the fame of those Friars who first embraced the Teresian Reform. He died in that country towards the end of the seventeenth century.

Father James Smith was a native of Ulster. Having joined the Teresian Carmelites in France, he was ordained there in due course for the Irish Mission.

Father Anthony Dogherty was also a Northern. On his return from France he proceeded to Drogheda, and became "Prior" of the monastery there, but we are not told in what year, nor is the date of his death assigned.

II. SOME "OBITS" OF THE EIGHTEENTH CENTURY.

Father Joseph Power was born in Meath. On joining the Order he was sent to Italy for his studies, and died at Rome in 1725. Nothing is known of his missionary career in Ireland.

Brother John Lynch. His entire Religious life seems to have been passed in the friary at Loughrea. His death occurred at the same place, and his remains were interred amid the ruins of the old abbey.

Father Joseph Halfpenny belonged to a Dublin family of that name. He became a Discalced Carmelite in France, and after his ordination returned to the labours of the Irish Mission, dying eventually in his native city.[1]

Father George Hidderton. One of the Friars of St. Patrick's Province, this Religious died at Rome in the year 1726.

Father Felim Kennedy came from Munster. He studied and was ordained at Paris. On his return to Ireland he was appointed Conventual of the Teresian Friary in Dublin, his missionary career having been passed among the Faithful of that city.

Father Patrick Burke belonged to "an ancient and noble Irish family." He was born in the Co. Dublin, and having joined the Discalced Carmelites at an early age, was sent to France for his studies. After ordination he was recalled to his native country, and devoted the remainder of his life to the work of the Mission in Dublin, where he also died.

Father Columbanus Coleman was from Galway. Although ordained in France for the Irish Mission, he appears to have exercised his zeal in England also, for it was there his death occurred.

Father John Dolphin. A member of one of the Catholic families of the Co. Galway. He joined the Teresian Friars in Italy, where he was duly ordained. On returning home, he was appointed Conventual at Loughrea, and became Prior of that monastery in the course of time, and it was there he died.

Father John Ward held the same office at the

[1] *MS. in Arch. of St. Teresa's.*

Abbey. He, too, had made his studies in Italy, whence he returned to the Teresian Friary in his native county.

Father Henry Brady was also Prior at Loughrea, where his death occurred. He had been received into the Order in one of the French Monasteries.

Father Nicholas M'Hugo, of a well-known Galway family, became a Discalced Carmelite in Italy, and was ordained there for the Irish Mission.

Father Jeffrey M'Hugo, a member of the same family, was also received into the Order in Italy. In after life he became Prior of the Abbey, where he died.

Father James Monahan. This Religious was born in Galway. Having made his studies for the priesthood in France, he was ordained in Italy. He was Prior at Loughrea some years before his death, which took place in that monastery.

Father Paul Kenny was "clothed" in the brown habit, and ordained in France. A native of the Co. Galway, he died at Dublin, having devoted his life to the duties of the Teresian Mission in Ireland.

Father James of St. Bernard. Although most painstaking in his efforts to furnish a complete "List of Obits," Father Serapion does not mention the name of this Religious, who was one of the Irish Provincials (A.D. 1719—25). Reference has been made to Father James's great zeal. He took a particular interest in the welfare of the Sister-Tertiaries of the Order in Dublin, translating their Rule and Instructions into English, and being most anxious to assist them in the difficulties with which they had to contend, while persevering in their good resolutions. In all probability he died at Dublin.[1]

Father Dominic of Jesus Mary, whose name in the world was Dowling (some say Loughlin), made his noviceship at Sienna, but studied and was raised to the priesthood in France. He died at Dublin, having been Provincial in Ireland for a number of years.[2]

Father Joseph Renatus (Ralph Kilkenny) was born at Dublin. He studied in France and Italy, being ordained in the latter country. Having spent his life on the Irish Mission, he died in his native city.

Father Raymund M'Hugo. This Religious was born in Galway, ordained in Italy, and died at Loughrea.

Father Patrick Dodd was professed and received Holy Orders in France: he died in Dublin, his natal place.

Father Patrick Hart, of Longford, was sent abroad for his studies, and ordained in France. His death occurred at the Dublin Monastery, of which he had been Prior for some time.

Brother John Sheehan. Having entered at Loughrea as a Lay-brother, he dwelt in the Abbey until his death.

Father Marcellus of St. Teresa (Cullen was his family name) joined the Order in France. After his return to Ireland he was stationed at Loughrea. Having filled the office of Prior in that friary, he

[1] *MS. in Arch. of St. Teresa's.*   [2] *Ibid.*

died there, and was interred within the ruins of the ancient monastery.

Father John of the Cross was a native of Dublin, his parents' name being Mullaly. He was ordained in Italy for the Irish Mission, but died there before he had an opportunity of realising the object of his holy ambition.

Father Denis Farrell was another of the Discalced Carmelites of St. Patrick's Province, who did not return to Ireland, having died in Italy some time after his ordination.

Father Columbanus of St. Paul belonged to a Dublin family named Boylan. He studied for the priesthood in France. During the course of his missionary career he became Superior of the Dublin Friary, where his death took place.

Father Edward of St. Thomas (Savage was his name in the world) was born in Dublin, and joined the Teresian Friars in France. On his return to Ireland he was elected Prior of the Monastery in his native city.

Father Anthony of St. John Baptist (called Conelan in the world) was from the Co. Galway. Professed and ordained in France, he became Prior at Loughrea, where he died, July 1741, in the seventy-fourth year of his age.

Father Peter Cullen also came from the same county. He entered the Order at Marseilles, and was ordained there. His entire missionary life was passed in Ireland, and he died somewhere in Clare, July 1745.

Brother John Hynes, a Lay-brother, whose death

took place at Dublin on the 11th of January 1746, when he was fifty-six years old.

Father Nicholas of St. Angelus was one of the Colemans of Galway. He became a Discalced Carmelite in Italy, and studied there for his ordination. He was in his eightieth year at the time of his death, which occurred at Loughrea in the December of 1746. He held the office of Prior in the Abbey for some years.

Father Francis of the Blessed Sacrament, of the same family, being a nephew of Father Nicholas, was born in 1698. He, too, was educated in Italy; and only survived Father Nicholas a few weeks, having died at the Abbey on the 5th of January 1747.

Father Patrick of St. Gerard, known as Delahoyde before entering the cloister, was born at Dublin in 1711. He received his conventuality in the same city immediately after his return from France, and was Prior there a short time previous to his early death, May 1747.

Father Patrick of St. John Baptist, of a Kildare family named Fitzsimons, was ordained at Charenton, France. Having taught Philosophy and Theology, and filled the office of Provincial for a number of years, he died at Paris 1748.

Father Angelus Anthony of the Immaculate Conception. (The Teresian theologians always maintained what is now a Dogma of Faith in the Church.)[1] Educated and ordained in France, Father Angelus died at Dublin in the fiftieth year of his

[1] *Salmanticenses.*

age, having been born in the same place about the year 1703.

Father Urban of St. Teresa (Corry being his secular name), having completed the usual course in one of the Italian monasteries, was recalled to Ireland and appointed Superior of the residence which the Discalced Carmelites then had at Ardbreccan, Co. Meath. His death occurred there in the year 1752, before he had attained the age of fifty.

Father Robert of Jesus Mary. This Religious was very popular in Dublin during the earlier half of the last century. He was best known as Father Fitzgerald. His ordination took place at Malta, after which he taught Philosophy and Divinity for some years on the Continent before entering upon his missionary career in Ireland. While Provincial he re-established the "*Brother-Tertiaries*" at the Stephen's Street Friary, his signature being attached to the various reports of the "Council-Meetings" from the 19th of March 1747. We have also noticed his name among the subscribers to the first edition of De Burgo's "*Hibernia Dominicana*," published the year before Father Robert's death, which occurred at Dublin on the 21st March 1763, when he was in the sixty-third year of his age.

Father Patrick Fitzsimons. This is one of several names which we should be inclined to identify with others repeated by Father Serapion in his "*List*." But we find in such instances circumstances whereby Religious bearing the same name can be distinguished from each other. In the present case, although Father Fitzsimons was educated, ordained, and died in France, and filled the offices of Provincial and Professor of Philosophy and Theology, like his namesake Father Patrick of St. John Baptist, while the former is said to have been a native of Meath, we are told that the latter was born in the Co. Kildare.

Father Nicholas Coleman belonged to a Galway family to which reference has been made more than once in this chapter. Ordained at Malta, he devoted many years of his life to the teaching of Philosophy and Theology, dying at length in the place where he had been raised to the priesthood.

Father Joseph of St. Martha, known as Father Dowling outside the cloister, was from the Co. Longford. He was Professor of Theology, which he taught in the Teresian College of Sienna, where he himself had been ordained, his death occurring in the same place.

Father Thomas Savage was born in Dublin. He received the priesthood at Charenton, and died in that monastery, having never returned to Ireland.

Father Stephen of the Child Jesus. Born in Meath, he was "clothed" in the brown habit at Rome, afterwards studying and being ordained in Viterbo. He was Provincial in Ireland for some years, but died at Dunkirk, in the north of France, where the Teresian Carmelites had a friary with which the Irish Fathers seem to have been in frequent communication.

Father Seraphim Power. We have already alluded to the extraordinary holiness of this Religious. And now Father Serapion assures us he himself had such evidence of his sanctity as to feel convinced that, were it not for the French Revolution, the cause of Father Power's canonisation would have been introduced at Rome before the close of the last century. A native of Limerick, Father Seraphim became a Discalced Carmelite at an early age. He made his noviceship and Religious profession at Toulouse, where there was then a monastery of the Order. Having been sent to Bordeaux for his studies, he was ordained in that city, being immediately affiliated to the Province of Aquitaine, and thus prevented returning to Ireland. In after years he was called upon to hold various offices, while his humility still shrank from what brought him into prominence before his brethren and the world outside the cloister. He was Provincial of Aquitaine, and also taught in the Teresian schools of Philosophy and Theology for thirty-six years. The several Sovereign Pontiffs repeatedly offered him highest ecclesiastical dignities, but he implored them not to lay upon him so heavy a burden, and the Popes graciously respected his beautiful spirit of humility. He died at Bordeaux in the year 1776, with a wide-spread fame for virtue. His tomb was sealed by the Archbishop himself, in view of having the necessary steps taken for Father Seraphim's beatification, and in order that the Faithful, who already regarded the dead priest as a Saint, and persisted in keeping candles lighted at the grave, might not remove portions of the remains. But the dread Revolution prevented the Discalced Carmelites of France carrying out their predecessors' intention with regard to the holiness of that Irish Teresian Friar, whose memory has been preserved almost by miracle after the troubles of those eventful years.[1]

[1] *MS. in Arch. of St. Teresa's.*

CHAPTER XV.

"THE LIST OF OBITS" (*continued*).

MANY of the Fathers ordained abroad for the Irish Mission died before Father Power, although their names do not precede his on the "List" drawn up by Father Serapion, who probably recorded the fruits of his patient industry in the order of discovery. With rare exception we follow the same order, Father Serapion being our principal authority for even assigning the "*Obits*" to the seventeenth century, rather than to the eighteenth.[1]

Father Paul Lacy's name is to be found mentioned towards the end of Father Serapion's "List"; yet we are told that he died on sea in the year 1746. Beyond this we only know that he was from the south of Ireland, and was professed and ordained in Italy.

Father Hilarion of St. Teresa was the Religious who, as "The Rev. James M'Kenna," obtained, after death, such favourable notice in the *London Gazette* (Oct. 1756). He received Holy Orders in Malta, where he had made his studies; and died in 1754, at Dublin, the place of his birth.

Father Stephen of the Blessed Virgin, member of

[1] *MS. in Arch. of St. Teresa's.*

a family named Lawlor, was born in Kildare. He joined the Order in France, but after his profession was sent to Florence for his studies, returning to the former country for ordination. He did not labour on the Irish Mission, having died at Dunkirk on the 13th of October 1756.

Father Urban of St. Hilarion, one of the Barnewalls of Navan, was received and professed in Rome, and ordained at Viterbo. His death took place in the Eternal City.

Father Antony Conelan, of the Queen's Co., was professed, ordained, and died in the Discalced Carmelite Monastery at Marseilles.

Father Ignatius Heverin was born in Roscommon. He entered the Order at Rome, and was ordained in Viterbo. He died at Rome, having passed his life in Italy, although professed for the Irish Province.

Father Francis of the Blessed Sacrament was another Teresian Friar whose ambition to return to Ireland could not be realised. Born in Galway, he received the brown habit at Marseilles, and died there some years after his ordination.

Father John M'Donagh, of a Kildare family of that name, took his Vows and was ordained in one of the monasteries in Italy, but died at Marseilles.

Father James M'Hugo died at Naples. He was a member of a Galway family which gave quite a number of Teresian Friars to the Church since the time one of his ancestors (probably) caused that silver chalice, of which we have spoken in another chapter, to be made for the Discalced Carmelites of Loughrea (A.D. 1641). On being received into the Order, he was sent, after profession, to prepare for the priesthood in the place where God willed he should also die.

Father Joseph Daverin's death occurred likewise at Naples, where he had been professed and ordained.

Father Francis Tumulty was from Munster. Having made his noviceship in Rome, he went to Viterbo for the usual course of studies. On returning to Ireland he was called to assist his brethren in Dublin; and there he died in the monastery of his Order.

Father John Hearns, whose death took place in Dublin about the year 1763, was a native of Co. Meath. On becoming a Discalced Carmelite, he was sent to Italy to study for the priesthood. He was ordained at Viterbo (having made his Religious profession in Rome), and after his return home he was elected Prior of the Friary at Dublin.

Father James of the Resurrection received the holy habit at Malta. He was ordained in the same place, and died at Genoa in 1770. His parents' name was Hickey, Galway being their place of residence.

Father John Baptist Hogan was also from Galway. He went through his entire preparatory course at Abbeville in Picardy (now Somme), where his ordination took place. He was sometime Prior of the Abbey, Loughrea, where he died eventually.

Father John Lennon was born in the same town. He received Holy Orders at Naples; became Conventual at the Abbey; and had completed his missionary career there when called to the reward of his labours.

Father Isidore of St. Paul was one of the Lacys of Dublin. He studied for the priesthood in Italy. After his return to Ireland he was elected Prior at Dublin, his death occurring in the same place.

Father Peter of the Assumption (Callanan was his secular name) became a priest at Marseilles, where he had been educated. Born in Galway, he died at the Abbey, Loughrea, having held the office of Prior there for some time.

Father John Glennan was from Roscommon. He died at Marseilles, where he had been received into the Order and ordained for the Irish Province.

Father Michael Creagh died at the Abbey of Loughrea, in his native county. He had been elected Prior of that monastery soon after his return from Italy.

Father Albert of St. Lawrence. This Religious, a native of Galway, was professed at Loughrea in the latter half of the eighteenth century. He was afterwards sent to Italy to complete his theological course; and when ordained, he was recalled to his own Province, being Conventual at the Abbey, for the most part, until his death.

Father Thomas of the Sacred Stigmata belonged to a Galway family named Nugent. Having returned from Italy, where he had been professed and ordained, he was sent to the House at Loughrea, of which he became Prior. There also he died.

Father Joseph of St. Francis (one of the Barretts of Galway). He studied for the Order in Italy. Having devoted his life to the duties of the cloister and of the mission in Ireland, he died at Loughrea.

Father Joseph of St. Martha (Rev. John Robertson-Dowling), was one of the Provincials of the Irish Province in the last century. A native of Galway, he made his studies on the Continent, and was ordained at Sienna. While in office he built a small chapel and friary at Loughrea; but, as has been seen, these were afterwards replaced by the present church and monastery. He was Conventual in Dublin at the time of his death.

Father Thomas Mannion was educated as a Discalced Carmelite, and raised to the priesthood at Sienna. His parents belonged to Galway. Having passed his career on the Irish Mission, during which he had to bear the burden of Priorship at Loughrea, he died in the Abbey.

Father Isidore of St. Alexius was well known in Dublin as Father Callaghan over a hundred years ago. He was born in Meath. Having been received into our Lady's Order at Toulouse, he was sent to Bordeaux to prepare for the priesthood. He taught Philosophy and Theology for several years before his appointment as Vicar-Provincial in Ireland. At the same time the Superior-General, Father Michael of St. Philip, deputed him "*Visitator*"; and Father Eusebius of St. Anne, Father

Michael's successor, re-nominated him to both these offices. In July 1764, Father Isidore held a Visitation of the "Tertiaries" connected with the little chapel in Stephen's Street. He exercised the same function among the Religious of the Province during the October of 1770.[1] His death occurred in July of the following year, and he was interred in the "Family Vault" at Meath, as the Teresian community of Dublin had then no burial-place of their own.

Father Joseph Francis of Jesus Mary (Rev. John Friend or M'Cann) was from Dublin. He was professed in Naples, and while making his studies there gained a high reputation for learning, being known to his contemporaries as a "*Great Mathematician*." He was one of the Conventual Fathers at Dublin in 1780, and died in the same place before the close of that year.

Father James Mooney's death is also said to have occurred at Dublin about this time (A.D. 1780). Born in Galway, he was ordained at Marseilles, and held the office of Prior in the Dublin Monastery.

Father Michael Heffernan was another Galway man who became a Teresian Friar in Italy. He passed a good many years on the mission in Cork, where the Discalced Carmelites seem to have had a temporary "*Residence*" towards the end of the last century. Having died in that city, in 1780, his remains were interred in one of the cemeteries there.

Father Robert of St. Patrick (Rev. Stephen

[1] *MS. in Arch. of St. Teresa's.*

Dowdall), who had been born in Dublin, was professed and ordained at Bordeaux. He became very popular among his fellow-citizens, of all creeds and classes, on his return to Ireland. He was soon made Provincial; and, like many of his predecessors, while holding office received a command from the Holy See to discharge important Apostolic functions in this kingdom. His death took place at Dublin in July of the year 1782.

Father Patrick of St. Justin (called Hanigan in the world) was from Kildare. He joined the Order at Toulouse in 1773, and was also ordained on the Continent—at Bordeaux. He died at Loughrea, July 1795, having been Vicar of the Abbey for some time.

Father Mark of St. John Baptist (Rev. Edward Walsh), was born at "Fingal," Co. Dublin. Professed and ordained in Florence, he was appointed Vicar at Loughrea on his return to Ireland. His death occurred at Dublin in 1794, but his remains were interred in "Fingal."

Father John Whearty, of Dublin, died at Genoa on his way home to Ireland from Florence, where he had been ordained.

Father Eliseus of St. Patrick (Rev. Joseph Smith) died at Dublin, which was his birthplace, in the year 1795. He joined the Order in Rome, where he remained until after his ordination. Having become Provincial in Ireland, he took a deep interest, like Father Dowdall and several other of his more immediate predecessors, in all that concerned the welfare of the "Tertiaries," and he was one of those instrumental in securing the site for the new church and friary at Clarendon Street.

Father Thomas of Jesus Mary, member of a family named Ennis, was born at Kilcock, Co. Kildare. He also was indefatigable in forwarding the building of "St. Teresa's." He was professed in Genoa, and returned thither for ordination when he had completed his studies at Bordeaux. He discharged the duty of Visitator-General in Ireland, and was Prior of the Dublin Monastery when his death occurred there, 30th November 1796.[1]

III. "Obits" of the Irish Province during the Nineteenth Century.

Father Patrick Mary of St. Joseph, whose secular name was King, became a Religious and a priest in Florence. He died at Dublin, his native place, in the year 1802.

Father Thomas Mary of St. Elias (Rev. Andrew O'Hara) was Vicar-Provincial in Ireland at the founding of "St. Teresa's." He had been born near Sagart, Co. Dublin, and went to Florence to join the Discalced Carmelites, making his studies and being ordained there. He held the office of Provincial several times; also the Priorship, both in Dublin and at Loughrea, for many terms. In the year 1800 he was busily engaged trying to complete the new church at Clarendon Street, where he died in 1806 (probably).

[1] *MS. in Arch. of St. Teresa's.*

Father Isidore of St. Michael (Rev. Michael Long) was born at Loughrea in the year 1755. He made his studies in Bordeaux, and died at the Abbey on the 12th of April 1808.

Father Simon O'Brien (he received the name of Christopher in baptism) was also a native of Loughrea. He entered the Order and was professed at the Abbey, and was sent to one of the monasteries in Holland to prepare for the priesthood. He died at Loughrea on the 17th of June 1801, when in the forty-fifth year of his age.[1] . . . The following names are not included in Father Serapion's "List," but they are to be found in documents preserved in the monastic archives either at "St. Teresa's" or in the Abbey, Loughrea. It should also be mentioned that that "List" is in *tabulated* form, which we could not very well adopt, and at the same time give certain items of information evidently not possessed by Father Serapion.

Father Paul of St. Patrick (Rev. Ralph Fitzpatrick) was professed at Genoa in the twenty-third year of his age, having been born in Dublin in 1750. He studied at Bordeaux, and was in due time recalled to Genoa for ordination. Having passed a number of years on the Irish Mission, he received permission to go to America, and died at Philadelphia, in the United States, before the time appointed for his return to Ireland.

Father John of the Cross (Rev. John O'Reilly) was born in Meath on the 2nd of February 1777

[1] *MS. in Arch. of St. Teresa's.*

Having become a Teresian Friar, he was sent to Barcelona, Spain, 26th October 1807, to complete his studies. He returned in August of the year 1810, and was made Conventual at Loughrea. He became Prior of the Abbey later on, and died there in 1833.

Father John of St. Teresa, a convert, was member of a Protestant family named Carter, dwelling in Galway at the time of his birth, 1795. He was received into the Church in 1815; four years afterwards he became a postulant in the Abbey, where he took the Vows the following year. He was then sent to Paris for his studies, but came back to Loughrea for ordination. His death occurred in the same place, A.D. 1840.

Father Angelus of the Holy Ghost was the name taken in religion by Walter Hughes from Co. Galway, on entering the Novitiate at Loughrea. He went to Portugal soon after his profession, and returned a priest in 1810. He was in the fortieth year of his age—having been born in 1770—when elected Prior of the Abbey. He seems to have died at "*Ballinakill*," a locality not far from Loughrea.

Father John Roache's birth took place at Drogheda in the year 1776. He was sent to Cadiz, Spain, for his studies, 27th April 1800. On his return to Ireland, 27th December 1806, he became Conventual at Clarendon Street, where he died on the 17th December 1841.

Father James Mackan. Born in Dublin, he was educated and ordained in Italy for St. Patrick's Province.

Father Leo of the Blessed Virgin Mary (Rev. James Oates) died at Dublin on the 24th January 1846, in the seventy-fourth year of his age. He had been very popular in this city during the earlier part of the present century, as may be inferred from the allusion already made to his name. He had studied for the priesthood on the Continent.[1]

Father James Mangan was born in Galway, ordained on the Continent, and died at Dublin.

Father Christopher Nogueras, a Spaniard, was born in the year 1789. Ordained in his native country, he was many years Conventual in the Irish Province; and died at Clarendon Street on the 7th October 1849.

Father Francis Joseph of St. Teresa (Rev. James Finnigan) was ordained abroad, and died at Dublin, 18th July 1862, in the fifty-second year of his age.

Father John of Jesus Mary (Rev. John Maher), whose birth took place at Kilkenny in the year 1770, was ordained at Cadiz, and returned to Ireland on the 27th December 1806. For some years he was Prior at Dublin, where he died on the 13th October 1850.

Father Christopher Flynn was Conventual of "St. Teresa's" in the year 1800. He was one of the Religious responsible for the foundation of that monastery.

Father Patrick Whelan, born at Dublin in 1779, was sent to Lisbon for his studies in the November

[1] Letter to the Author.

of 1805, and was ordained there for the Teresian Mission in Ireland.

Father Bernard of the Blessed Virgin (Rev. Martin Kelly) was born near Ennis, Co. Clare, in 1820, and joined the Discalced Carmelites in Belgium. He was Provincial in Ireland at the time of his death, which occurred at Dublin on the 18th of February 1863, in the seventeenth year of his Religious profession.

Father John Walsh, from the town of Kildare, was born in the year 1782. He was ordained at Figuéras in 1810, whence he returned immediately to the Irish Province.

Father Joseph of the Annunciation (the Most Rev. Francis Nicholson, D.D.) was born at Dublin in the year 1803. He studied both in Ireland and on the Continent. After ordination he became Conventual at the Abbey, and subsequently at "St. Teresa's." While a member of the latter community he made O'Connell's acquaintance, and was ever regarded by him as one of his dearest friends. Not being of robust health, Father Joseph was allowed to change to a monastery in Italy for some years. And so highly esteemed was he by his brethren on the Continent, that they unanimously elected him Procurator-General of the whole Order. But he declined this great honour; and only on receiving a formal precept of Holy Obedience did he consent to take the Doctor's Diploma granted him by the Pope in acknowledgment of his learning and service to the Church. He seems to have been especially devoted to liturgical studies. In his own "*Autobiography*" Dr. Ullathorne speaks in terms of highest praise of Father Joseph's abilities. The Teresian Friar and the Benedictine Monk had frequently met on the Continent; and, like the Bishop of Birmingham, Dr. Nicholson was required, although earnestly desiring to remain in the cloister, to submit to the burden of the Episcopate. He was consecrated Archbishop of Corfu, and appointed Vicar-Apostolic of Verapoly. Having discharged the onerous duties of his office for some years, he was compelled, through ill-health, to return to England, where he died in the June of 1855, when only in the fifty-second year of his age.

Father Raymond of Our Blessed Lady of Mount Carmel (Rev. Redmond O'Hanlon) was a Leinster man. Born in 1786, he was ordained on the Continent for the Irish Province, of which he afterwards became Provincial. He died at Dublin on the 7th of February 1864, having been professed nearly sixty years.

Father Nicholas French, one of the Frenches of Castle French, Co. Galway, returned from Spain in 1834. He had been sent to a monastery there to prepare for the priesthood, sometime after his profession at the Abbey. He died at "Ascragh" in his native county.

Father John Joseph of the Immaculate Conception (Rev. Peter O'Reilly), who belonged to the Co. Longford, joined the Order at Loughrea. He was ordained in Spain in 1835, and on returning to Ireland the same year was appointed Conventual at the Abbey, where he spent most of his life until 1853, when he died.

Father John Francis of St. Brigid (Rev. Patrick Ward) was born in Dublin in 1748, and died there in the sixty-sixth year of his age. He was Prior in 1791 when summoned, as Theologian, to the famous Conference on the Oath of Allegiance; he had already taught Philosophy and Divinity, and was afterwards appointed Provincial in Ireland.

Father Nicholas Murray, a native of Dublin, was professed and ordained on the Continent, and returned to St. Patrick's Province in 1804.

Father Serapion of St. Francis (Rev. Edward Gregory O'Reilly), the Religious to whose labours we owe great part of the information relating to the "*Obituary*," was born at Loughrea. He was ordained abroad, and afterwards laboured with much success for the welfare of the Irish Province, over which he presided for many years. He was also a most zealous missioner, as may be inferred from what has been said about him in another place. Nearly his whole life was passed in the Dublin Monastery, of which he was Prior several times. The precise date of his death is not known; probably it occurred at St. Teresa's early in the present century.

Father Aloysius of St. Joseph (Rev. William Fahy) was born in Loughrea; and having become a Discalced Carmelite, made his profession at the Abbey. He was ordained in Spain, whence he returned to Ireland in 1833. Having fulfilled the duties of Prior at Loughrea, he was changed to Dublin and died there in 1853.

Father Francis Joseph of St. Teresa was Father L'Estrange's name in religion; he who was the "*Liberator's*" friend. Born in Dublin, he was educated and ordained on the Continent; and was Provincial of the Irish Province when Father Aloysius was studying in Spain. He died at "St. Teresa's" the year Father Fahy returned to Ireland (September 6, 1833).[1]

Father Joseph of St. Teresa (Rev. John O'Reilly). This Religious was born in Loughrea and died at the Abbey, having spent his life in the labours of the Irish Mission.

Father John of St. Joseph (Rev. Myles Gannon) was from the Co. Galway, where he was born in the March of 1781. On becoming a Discalced Carmelite he was sent to Figuéras, Spain, 15th May 1806, and recalled to Ireland on 6th of August 1810, soon after his ordination. He was Prior of the Abbey for a number of years, and built the present church and friary while in office. He died there in 1864, having completed the eighty-sixth year of his age, and fifty-seventh of his Religious profession.

Father Theodore of the Mother of God (Rev. Peter O'Loughlin) was born in Loughrea in 1815, and studied on the Continent for the priesthood. Having passed many years on the Irish Mission, both at "St. Teresa's" and in the Abbey, he was affiliated to one of the Italian Provinces, and did not return to Ireland.

---

[1] *MS. in Arch. of St. Teresa's.*

Father Bonaventure of St. Simon Stock (Rev. David O'Brien) was ordained in Belgium for St. Patrick's Province. He was Vicar-Provincial in Ireland, and died at "St. Teresa's" on the 2nd of May 1855, at the early age of forty years; during fourteen of which he had dwelt in the cloisters of Carmel.

Father Joseph of St. Mary (Rev. Michael Mahon) was born in the Co. Galway in 1820. He entered Religion in Belgium, and was ordained there after he had gone through the usual course of studies. He was Superior at the Abbey for some time, and died in that monastery on the 13th March 1870— the twenty-fifth year of his profession.

Father Joseph of St. Francis Xavier is still remembered in Dublin as "Father Edward Hyland of Clarendon Street." Born in the Co. Kildare on the 3rd of July 1783, he joined the Order at an early age, and "sailed for Figuéras" on the 15th May 1806. Four years later he returned to Ireland to pass nearly the whole of his long and successful career at "St. Teresa's." His death occurred on the 12th November 1871, when he was in the ninety-first year of his age, and over sixty-four years a professed Religious.

Father John Francis of St. Teresa (the Most Rev. Dr. William Whelan) was born in Dublin on the 12th July 1798. He joined the Discalced Carmelites in his eighteenth year, and was professed on the 4th of October 1817. Having made his studies in Italy, he was ordained in Florence, and soon afterwards returned to Ireland. He was appointed Vicar-Provincial in 1832, and was required on various other occasions to undertake the same responsibility. In 1842 he was called to Rome to be consecrated Titular Bishop of Aureliopolis, and then sent as Vicar-Apostolic to Bombay. Having discharged the duties of that very difficult mission for a number of years, the honours bestowed upon him and many congratulatory addresses proving his success, he was at length permitted to resign and return to Ireland. Although still one of the community at Clarendon Street, the late Cardinal Cullen wished him to continue to exercise his episcopal functions in the Archdiocese of Dublin; and Dr. Whelan did so until his death in December of the year 1876. His remains were interred in the vaults of "St. Teresa's," beneath the altar which he himself had erected to the Seraphic Virgin.

Father Gregory of St. Mary (Rev. Bernard Verdon) was from Galway, where he had been born in 1822. He joined the Order and was ordained in Belgium. Many times Prior at "St. Teresa's," and in Loughrea, he also held the office of Vicar-Provincial. He died in Clarendon Street on the 25th March 1887, in the forty-first year of his profession, and was the last Religious to be interred at "St. Teresa's."

Father Malachy of St. Teresa (Rev. William Timothy) was born in Roscommon in 1845. He made his profession in Belgium, studied both in the south of France and at Loughrea, and was ordained in England. He was the first Professor of Mental Philosophy at St. Mary's. Like Father Paul

Lacy, he died on sea, in 1890, when returning to Ireland.

Brother Joseph Mary of the Sacred Heart. Born at Glengariff, Co. Cork, in the year 1840, he was known in the world as Mortimor O'Shea. He entered the Order as a Lay-brother, and was professed at London in 1867. Three years later he was recalled to Ireland, and passed the greater part of the remainder of his Religious life at the Abbey, where he died on the 17th of May 1891.

Father Angelus of St. Mary (Rev. Daniel Fogarty) was from the Co. Tipperary. Having first graduated at Trinity College, Dublin, he was received into the Order in Belgium, and ordained there on the completion of his studies. He was frequently Prior of "St. Teresa's," and also Provincial. His death occurred on the 30th of November 1889, in the seventieth year of his age, and the forty-fourth of his Religious profession. His remains were interred in the new burial-place of the Teresian Friars at Glasnevin.

Father Joachim of the Holy Family (Rev. Edward Russell) was born in Dublin in 1838. He was received into the Order and ordained in Belgium. Most of his life was passed at "St. Teresa's," where he held the office of Prior. He had been thirty-six years professed at the time of his death, which took place at Clarendon Street on the 31st of July 1893. His remains were also interred in Glasnevin.

Father Albert of St. Patrick (Rev. Patrick Callanan) died the same year, at "St. Mary's," on 15th September. He was born in the Co. Galway in 1850, and made his profession in London in the year 1872. He studied for the priesthood in the south of France. He was Vicar at St. Mary's for some time, and taught Moral Theology there. He was only in the forty-third year of his age when he died; at his own express wish, his remains were taken to Loughrea for interment in the "Old Abbey."

Father Columbanus of St. Patrick (Rev. John O'Brien), who was from the north of Ireland, spent some years at Maynooth in preparation for the secular mission. But finding himself called to the cloister, he became a Discalced Carmelite in Belgium in 1857, and after the required course of studies was ordained there for St. Patrick's Province. On his return to Ireland he was appointed Conventual, first at the Abbey, and subsequently at "St. Teresa's," where he dwelt many years. He died in the former monastery on the 25th February 1896, having been forty years a professed Religious, and in the sixty-sixth year of his age.

Father Patrick of the Cross (Rev. Henry Kelly) also died last year (1896). He was in the fifty-first year of his age, having been born at Athy, Co. Kildare, in 1845. He studied and was ordained at Ghent in Belgium, and had only attained the twenty-fourth year of his age when recalled to the Irish Province. He was Conventual at the Abbey (he did much to forward the building of that part of the friary which is now used as the

Novitiate), and at "St. Teresa's"; but the latter years of his life were spent in England, where he died. . . .

Perhaps the record of these names—comparatively so few, when we think of the great number of Teresian Friars of St. Patrick's Province who must have died since the year *1625*—may not seem to form a chapter of sufficient interest to attract the reader's special attention. Yet each and every one of them suggests what is admittedly the dominant strain throughout our entire narrative: the *pressing reality* of the Religious Life. Hence the name *should* suffice to recall the struggles and the triumphs of the individual career —even when least is known of that particular life-history, with its secondary *unimportant* details. Not one of those Religious could have received the brown habit, and failed to appreciate the object of his holy vocation; for all were duly permitted to undertake the dread responsibility of the Solemn Vows. Before entering the Novitiate each had made his final choice between the world and the cloister; between the hidden reward—waited for in the patience of faith and hope—of labour in God's service only, and such fame as one's success may sometimes elicit from men. It was their highest, their grand ambition to tread in the way marked out for them by the fervour of their predecessors, and thus perpetuate in St. Patrick's Province the Teresian traditions of Carmelite prayer and zeal; and in so doing to become the loyal guardians of Ireland's treasure of the faith.

Because this was their ambition when embracing the "Teresian Reform," we would now associate their names with the prosperity of the Irish Province, and if we have not lingered over their memory, it certainly was not for dearth of evidence of "virtues practised and good works done,"[1] but rather in conformity to that spirit of the Order —so strikingly illustrated by the example of St. John of the Cross—which would have caused them, while still on earth, to shrink from the thought of being thus spoken of in praise, whether during life or even after death.

[1] *MS. in Arch. of St. Teresa's.*

CHAPTER XVI.

THE TERESIAN NUNS IN IRELAND: THEIR VOCATION.

Canonical establishment of a Carmelite Sisterhood—The blessed John Soreth—Irishwomen embrace the Teresian Reform abroad—A convent founded at Loughrea—How the Sisters lived during the Penal Times: evidences of their fervour—Vocations in Ireland at the present day—Influence of the Spirit formed according to the original "Constitutions."

THERE were "DAUGHTERS OF CARMEL" from the earliest ages of Christianity: countless pious women who devoted themselves to their Divine Master's service by emulating the spirit of the holy hermits on that "Sacred Mount." And the tradition of the sanctity of these "Virgins and Widows," who frequently formed themselves into large communities, is still preserved in the East. The Church accepts the facts thus transmitted, allowing the Carmelites to claim as children of their Order such glorious Saints as the Virgins Euphrasia and Euphrosyne, whose holiness edified the world about the time St. Brigid's extraordinary virtues were the wonder of Ireland.[1]

However, not until the year 1453 was a Carmelite Sisterhood canonically established, the

[1] *Ménologe.*

BLESSED JOHN SORETH, Prior-General of the Order, being the founder. This zealous son of Elias was born at Caen, Normandy, in 1394.[1] Having entered Religion when very young, he soon became distinguished for his talents and great virtue, and was entrusted with some of the most important offices. Henry VI. of England was suzerain of that part of France when the fame of Soreth began to attract people's attention to Caen; and having established a university in that city, he prevailed on the humble Carmelite to teach there. In compliance with the King's request, the blessed Soreth occupied the first professorial chair for many years. At length, when called to the supreme government of his own Order, he resolved to ensure the integrity of the Holy Rule by exhorting his subjects *not* to avail themselves of the *entire* Mitigation granted by Pope Eugene, and by organising a Sisterhood, whose members should sanctify themselves, away from the world, in the practice of the Carmelite spirit of Penance and Prayer. Having this end in view, he gave the same Rule, with certain necessary modifications, to the pious women who had placed themselves under his spiritual direction.

The Holy See readily approved of the project, and the first convent of Carmelite Nuns was formally opened in Guelderland, Holland, about the year 1453.[2] After a little while the *new* Sisterhood became very popular all over Europe, many devout ladies of exalted rank embracing the austerities of the Carmelite mode of life. The Duchess

[1] *Ménol.* [2] *Ibid.*

of Brittany lent invaluable help to the enterprise in the beginning; she was clothed in the brown habit herself in the course of time; and has, within recent years, been raised to our Altars as the "Blessed Frances Ambosia." The holy Soreth visited the English Province in person while Superior-General; but it is impossible to ascertain whether he came to Ireland also on that occasion. Neither is any allusion made to the introduction of Carmelite Nuns into this country before his death in 1471, nor, in fact, previous to the Teresian Reform, nearly a hundred years later on.

When saying, in another place, that numbers of the "*children*" of Irish exiles on the Continent found an irresistible charm in the cloisters of Carmel from the time of the Seraphic Virgin herself, of course their *daughters* were then included, although we referred directly to the vocation of their sons. However, as for reliable information concerning the actual establishment of a community of Teresian Nuns in Ireland, the foundation of a convent at Loughrea, towards the close of the reign of Charles II. (A.D. 1680), is the earliest we have been able to verify.[1] *De Burgo*[2] tells us that this house owed its origin to an aunt of his own —Mother Eleanor Bourke—who was herself the first to receive the holy habit there. But Father Serapion, who has also succeeded in discovering the names of a number of the deceased Sisters of the Irish Province, does not mention this fact when recording the dates of the "*Professions and Obits*"

[1] *Vide* Lewis's *Topogr. Dict. of Ireland.*   [2] *Hiber. Domin.*

of those Teresian Nuns. A Mother Margaret Lynch, who took her vows at Loughrea in 1692, is the first spoken of by him; and the last Religious on his list (of twenty-five names)[1] is a Sister Catherine Rourke, who died at Ranelagh, Dublin, on the 22nd of March 1807. . In a letter from the Mother Prioress of the Carmelite Convent at Bordeaux, dated the 12th of May 1726, and addressed to Mrs. Teresa Bourke at Loughrea, there are circumstances which lead us to infer that "*Mother Teresa*" was De Burgo's relative's name in Religion. This letter is (or *was* in 1880) preserved among the "Parliamentary Papers" in the Four Courts, Dublin. It is a most interesting document, and important inasmuch as it gives us a fair idea of the efforts made by the Teresian Sisters to observe their Rule in Ireland during the Penal Times. Mother Teresa, then in charge of the little community at Loughrea, had written to the Prioress of "the *great Convent*

[1] *Mothers Margaret, Teresa, Mary*, and *Magdalen Lynch* (professed at Loughrea); *Eleanor Bourke, Cecilia M'Hugo* (*ibid*. A.D. 1728); *Agnes Bellew* (Dublin, 1731); *Mary Moran* (Dublin, 1740); *Brigid Daly* (Loughrea, 1729–78); and *Anne Bourke* (Loughrea, 1785). Sisters *Mary Sanns* (professed at Loughrea, 1724—she died in Limerick); *Margaret Neillan* (Dublin, 1730); *Jane Daly* (*ibid*. 1731); *Agnes Curtis* (*ibid*. 1731); *Mable Kelly* (Loughrea, 1734); *Mary Cotter* (Dublin, 1734—she died in Cork); *Lucy Bellew* (Dublin, 1735); *Brigid Daly* (Loughrea, 1736); *Catherine Bourke* (*ibid*. 1738); *Sister — Ivers* (Dublin, 1742); *Brigid Costello* (Loughrea, 1786); *Jane Bourke* (Loughrea, 1806); and *Catherine Rourke*. There was also a *Sister Jane Coleman*, professed at Loughrea on the 15th January 1785, who died there on the 24th of July following, in the twenty-fourth year of her age. And in the same convent there was a Sister (name not given) who lived until the year 1775, having taken her vows in 1692.—*From Father Serapion's MS.*

of Bordeaux," asking to be instructed on certain points in the Constitutions and Ceremonial, in order that the other Religious might know how "*The Regular Life*" was being practised on the Continent. In reply, Mother Mary Anne of Jesus (Anne Jayneon), the Superioress of Bordeaux, gave the required information. It seems that Mother Teresa had invited her over to Ireland; but Mother Mary Anne could not come, because she should have to live "*as a secular*," a necessary precaution to which neither she herself nor her Superiors would ever *submit*. As the nuns in Loughrea had, likewise, some doubt concerning the precise form of the habit worn by the Sisters of the Teresian Reform abroad, the Mother Prioress, with admirable forethought, sent them a "doll" dressed, in every respect, like one of the Carmelites of the convent at Bordeaux. The box, containing this and several other little presents, was forwarded to a Galway merchant named White, and reached its destination in safety; but evidently the authorities considered the letter "*treasonable*"; and thus it came to be placed with similar documents in the Record Office at the Four Courts.

De Burgo further states that at the time of his writing the "*Hibernia Dominicana*" (A.D. 1760–62), the Teresian Nuns had a house in Dublin, also, founded by three Sisters named Bellew. From Father Serapion's MS. and other sources we learn, moreover, that there were convents at Limerick and Cork early in the eighteenth century. On the renewal of the persecution of Irish Catholics under

William and Mary, the Carmelite Sisters were compelled to remain concealed in the homes of their friends, if they did not wish to accept the only alternative and try to escape to convents of the Order on the Continent. A good many of them must have risked every peril to cling to their own country, for in her letter Mother Mary Anne alludes to the heroic constancy of the Irish Sisters; and Father Serapion gives us to understand that the nuns professed both in Dublin and at Loughrea always remained in Ireland. Long before the year 1726 the Religious had formed themselves into little communities again, dwelling in private houses; and although they dared not wear the beloved habit of their Order, they received novices, and educated them according to the traditions of Carmel, just as fervently as if they were enjoying most perfect security within the canonical cloister. In the year 1757 the Holy Rule and Constitutions were translated into English for their benefit, but there were certain clauses which the circumstances of their state did not permit them to observe. Thus, they had to support themselves by teaching, while the spirit of their vocation required them to devote themselves solely to a life of *penance* and *prayer*. In the course of time the struggle ceased to be so wearisome, and we find them comparatively prosperous about the year 1804. They had then already made several new Foundations, in conformity to Our Lord's express command to their Holy Mother St. Teresa: "*Hasten, daughter, to build monasteries, wherein I shall find souls in whom I can delight*"; that year also the Fathers of Clarendon Street made another translation of the "*Rule*," "*Constitutions,*" and "*Ceremonial*" from the original Latin for greater convenience of the Sisters.

The community of Teresian Nuns at Dublin resided for many years in a house on Arran Quay. While there they suffered much from the frequent inundations of the Liffey; and on one occasion the waters destroyed part of the building, ruining, among other things, certain valuable documents which had escaped the agents of Government.[1] In the course of time possession was obtained of an old suburban mansion, which, like Gayfield, passed through strange vicissitudes before it became a Carmelite convent : once the property of a Protestant Archbishop, "St. Joseph's," Ranelagh, was even utilised as a place for public entertainments.[2] From the Foundation made there in the year 1807 nearly all the other Irish houses were established. This community was originally a branch from the Loughrea Convent, which has always been regarded as the mother-house of the Teresian Nuns in Ireland. In the beginning Ranelagh was, as the Constitutions presuppose, subject to the jurisdiction of the Father-Provincial, and through him to the Superior-General of the Discalced Carmelite Order. But early in the present century the obedience of the Sisters was transferred, owing to motives of expediency approved of by the Sacred Congregation, to the Archbishop of Dublin ; and, for very obvious reasons, the

[1] Let. to Author. [2] Dalt. *Hist. of Dublin.*

Holy See does not easily revoke a dispensation of this kind when once granted. Consequently the Ranelagh Convent, and all Foundations since made from it, continue under Episcopal jurisdiction. Of course this fact cannot offer the slightest obstacle to the perfect observance of the Holy Rule and Constitutions, whereby the Religious perpetuate the traditions which they have received unchanged from St. Teresa. Only two Convents are now subject to the Order in Ireland: that of "The Incarnation" at *Tranquilla*, Dublin, and "Mount Carmel" in Loughrea.

Besides these two convents, and the one at Ranelagh, there are nine other Irish houses of Teresian Sisters, seven in the Archdiocese of Dublin: *Roebuck, Kilmacud, Blackrock, Hampton, Firhouse, Delgany,* and *Mount Tallant.* In the Diocese of Ferns, there is one at *New-Ross;* another at *Tallow, Co. Waterford.* It does not come within the scope of our task to give, even in outline, a sketch of the history of these communities separately; each has its own interesting annals, which doubtlessly contain numerous details quite similar to those so graphically recounted by the Seraphic Virgin herself when speaking of the progress of her wondrous undertaking. The Irish Carmelite Sisters had to encounter trials which were so disheartening that they could only be borne by the spirit of patient zeal characteristic of St. Teresa and her first companions. Indeed the efforts made to conform to the Primitive Observance were often truly heroic. On the other hand, the

Sisters would never dream of claiming merit for the needful self-sacrifice, knowing that the prosperity of the particular community is entirely dependent on fervour in the practice of "*The Regular Life*," to which all difficulties, sooner or later, yield.

However, special mention, no matter how brief, must be made of the Convent of "*Our Lady of Mount Carmel*," Loughrea, since the Teresian community established there over two hundred years ago has always been under the jurisdiction of the Fathers of St. Patrick's Province. The site of the original house, founded by Mother Teresa Bourke, is not known. From the violation of the "Treaty of Limerick" to the end of the eighteenth century, the Sisters at Loughrea had to live in concealment, and endure privations of every kind, while waiting a favourable change in political affairs. Not until the year 1829 did a long-prayed-for opportunity occur, and then they built the present church and nunnery, having received generous assistance from their friends.[1] Although plain in design, the new convent was well adapted for the practice of "*The Regular Life*," and is situated in view of the old abbey. About the same time they also ventured to resume wearing the brown habit; hitherto, like the Teresian Fathers of St. Patrick's Province, they had to disguise their sacred profession beneath secular apparel. From the beginning there was a numerous community at "*Mount Carmel*," but

[1] *Vide* Lewis's *Topog. Dict. of Irel.*, and *MS. in Arch. of Abbey*.

of recent years vocations became so frequent that postulants have had to wait, in many instances, for a considerable time before they could be received into the Order there.

As in all the other Teresian convents of Ireland, the Sisters at Loughrea cherish the names of deceased members whose sanctity is not altogether unknown to the world—influenced by the virtues practised within the cloister, which ward off evils threatening it in every age. Great, indeed, must have been the holiness of those nuns if their sisters in Religion deem it extraordinary; for the every-day life of the Saints is being led behind the grating in those *homes* of Penance and Prayer. It was easy to have foreseen that such should be the effect of the Carmelite Rule and Constitutions when fervently observed by women. The Constitutions for the Nuns of the Order are, like those for the Friars, the safeguard of the Holy Rule. They embody what St. Teresa had learned from experience to be most necessary for the preservation of the true spirit of Carmel. Drawn up by the Seraphic Virgin herself, they were approved of in the General Chapter of 1581; and, with some slight alterations, received the Papal sanction in the course of time.[1]

St. Teresa's spiritual daughters are indebted to the Venerable Mother Anne of Jesus for the Constitutions in their original form. This Religious, known in the world as Anna de Lobera, entered Carmel about eight years after the foundation of

[1] *Ménologe.*

the first Teresian convent. Her previous career had been strikingly marvellous. A deaf-mute until her seventh year (A.D. 1552), she had been miraculously restored to the use of hearing and speech; and from that early age made wonderful progress in virtue. In Religion, she was regarded as a model of prudence and fervour; she became St. Teresa's most zealous helper in the work of the Reform; and had even the grand privilege of founding convents during the lifetime of her mother and friend—the Seraphic Virgin. After the latter's death, St. John of the Cross was heard to say that in sending the children of Carmel so heavy a trial, it pleased God to console them by giving them Mother Anne of Jesus.[1] Having seen the "Reform" flourish in Spain, she obtained the permission of her Superiors to introduce it into France, Belgium, Germany, and Holland. During her own lifetime, she founded, in person, as many as *sixty* houses; and, like St. Teresa herself, she had to confront difficulties that developed into a violent persecution; because there were some who did not appreciate the Saint's method of forming the Carmelite spirit; and Anne of Jesus was determined that the Constitutions should be published just as they came from the pen of her Seraphic Mother (with the modifications made by the Superiors in General Chapter). She succeeded; and the approval of Popes Sixtus V., Gregory XIV., and Urban VIII. bears testimony to the wisdom of her action. She also ensured the preservation of those

[1] *Ménol.*

writings which have obtained for St. Teresa the glory of being ranked among the Doctors of the Church; and which, even in our own times, are accounted of such value as to have obtained the unique distinction of being reproduced in a "*Facsimile MS. Edition of the Seraphic Virgin's Works.*" While Fathers Edward and Paul were still in Louvain, preparing for their mission to Ireland, Mother Anne of Jesus died at Brussels (A.D. 1621), with a reputation for holiness which has since been confirmed by the Church.

The Constitutions, whose every page manifests the prudence of their holy Mother, enable the Carmelite Nuns to conform, as St. Teresa herself would have desired, to "*The Regular Life.*" There are explicit instructions regarding the fulfilment of the various duties, choral or domestic, from which none of the Sisters may be dispensed without sufficient, serious cause. The Religious rise early and retire late, still hardly having time to perform the usual conventual exercises. Besides several hours of mental prayer, made in common, they are obliged to recite the Divine Office in Choir, according to the Ceremonial of the Discalced Carmelite Fathers. And far from growing weary of the daily routine, which seems so monotonous to those in the world, they find happiness in each hour, having so many means afforded them of advancing the glory of God. This may not appear evident to people without the cloister; but any one can understand it who grasps the object of a Carmelite Nun's vocation, and has the conviction of faith for the efficacy of prayer. The austerities of claustral discipline not being such as to appeal to hearts only moved by human sentiment, perhaps the generosity of the sacrifice implied by this vocation is not so apparent as in that of Sisterhoods which society considers more meritorious from a utilitarian point of view. The purely contemplative mode of life, as led by the Teresian Nuns, may even seem to deprive those grand works of Christian charity of the services of so many zealous women who would otherwise have tried to sanctify themselves by becoming messengers of mercy to the suffering poor. But to think so convicts one of forgetfulness of the world's unceasing, urgent need of intercessory prayer. However, the vocation-grace is one of God's all-wise ways of providing for His own glory and for the welfare of men ; while the peopling of the cloisters of Carmel remains a mystery, because the world *will* not understand, nor admit its own indebtedness to those Carmelite Nuns. Only practical Christians feel that St. Teresa's labours have borne lasting fruit ; that her spiritual daughters are a *power* in the Church to the end of time. Neither are *they* incredulous when told that nations owe faith, honour, and security to the prayers of the Teresian Sisters; they do not deem it impossible or strange that Antwerp should have been saved from Maurice of Nassau, at the intercession of a dying woman— the Venerable Mother Anne of St. Bartholomew, whom the Seraphic Virgin had dearly loved ;[1] and

---

[1] A. D. 1622 (*Ménol.*).

they acknowledge the prudence of Napoleon I. in bringing back to France, in triumph, the companions of those Carmelite Nuns recently put to death upon the guillotine. . . .

Being strictly cloistered, each community of Teresian Carmelites has its own Novitiate. But the Canons make provision for the founding of houses, so that a little colony of Religious may be sent by any community to open a convent elsewhere. A few years ago such an event did happen in Dublin; and already the new Foundation (at Kilmacud) has the number of Sisters allowed by the Constitutions; a proof of the popularity of the Carmelite Vocation in Ireland. Indeed the prescribed "*Limit*" is the sole reason why several of the Irish communities have frequently to decline applications for admission. Not more than twenty Religious, including three Lay-sisters, may dwell in each convent; the only exception to this rule being in favour of some *one* postulant of "extraordinary merit," should she receive the *unanimous* suffrage of the Conventual Chapter. But when the revenue of a particular house is insufficient for the maintenance of so many Sisters, the number has to be further limited to fourteen —at least until the source of income permits others being received.[1] The fact of these convents being the homes of the daughters of the Irish people is another motive for the very deep interest taken in each Teresian community by the Faithful of Ireland year by year. Although

[1] *Const. of Discal. Carmel. Sisters.*

the Constitutions insist on the greatest discretion being used in determining the vocation of candidates, even after their entrance to the Novitiate, still very few postulants fail to persevere, numerous as are the aspirants to the Teresian habit; those who do return to their friends being generally obliged to leave the cloister on account of ill-health. For determination of will alone does not suffice for the practice of the austerities prescribed by the Rule, which, nevertheless, may be freely embraced without grave inconvenience by those who have been most tenderly cared for in the world. Speaking on this subject to his daughter, Louis XV. of France was naïvely informed that the keenest mortification she had experienced since receiving the brown habit was to find herself so useless in the kitchen.[1] Her only comfort (derived chiefly from her beloved companion, friend, and guide—the Holy Mother *Juliana Julia Mac-Mahon*, an Irishwoman)[2] was that with a good spirit she *might* improve in time. And we know how true a daughter of Carmel that princess became, the Catholic world being edified to this day by the life of Mother Teresa of St. Augustine— Madame Louise of France.[3] Like her, the Carmelite Nuns delight in what the world regards with such disfavour, being so opposed to its own spirit of self-indulgence and ease; but the Sisters have absolute reliance on the wise ordinances of those " Constitutions " in which St. Teresa's

---

[1] *Ménologe.* [2] Who died A.D. 1785 (*Ménologe*).
[3] *Ibid.*

characteristic "common-sense" has provided for their life-long peace.

Postulants apply, more frequently, to be received before they have attained their twentieth year, although many enter the Order at a much earlier age. They begin to lead "*The Regular Life*" at once, attending the Acts of Community with the Novices and Professed Sisters. Six months after admission they commence their term of probation under guidance of the "Mother-Mistress," a nun who must take upon herself the responsibility of directing them in the way of perfection, that is, so far as to teach them how to acquire the true spirit of the "Teresians." Several years are assigned for this purpose, the vows being taken at the end of the second; but the time seems to pass all too quickly to the young Religious, when, at length, they are taken from the Novitiate; in order that, thenceforth, as professed members of the community, they may apply themselves unceasingly to the task of preserving their first fervour, by which they ensure the success of their grand vocation; and enjoy that contentment of soul nowhere so soothing as in the cloisters of Carmel.

CHAPTER XVII.

OTHER CLIENTS OF CARMEL IN IRELAND.

The brown scapular—Zeal of the Irish Teresian Friars in preaching this devotion—The Tertiaries—Foundation of "*St. Joseph's Monastery*," Clondalkin—Interesting historical associations—Drumcondra and its memories—The vocation of the Tertiaries.

THE "Influences" affecting the world from the cloisters of the Teresian Sisters are not the only means whereby the clients of Carmel are advancing the welfare of nations. It is well known that, no matter what troubles may afflict a people loyal to the faith, the prosperity and peace of their country become, as Christian historians prove, merely a question of time; until God raises His chastening hand. Now, Irish annalists consider the "*Brown Scapular*" of Carmel one of the simplest explanations of their forefathers' devotion to the Catholic religion during the "*Penal Days.*" And this assertion is often to be found made as confidently as if the subject were beyond dispute; as if even those outside the Church could not fail to be convinced of a fact so evident to the Faithful of Ireland. It may seem strange that we ourselves have left mention of the great privilege of the Carmelites almost to the close of our narrative. But this is due to a certain order of priority which had to be observed.

So wonderful are the favours promised to those wearing the *"Brown Scapular"* that their authenticity has, like the antiquity of the Order of Carmel, given rise to various controversies. Here, however, we merely state the facts received by the Church,[1] who would have her children fervently cultivate a devotion preached by the Carmelites from the time of St. Simon Stock, to whose prayers we owe the "Scapular."

When a very young boy, St. Simon had been called by God to make reparation for the sins of the world by a penitential life; and he fled from his parents' home. In England, his native country, the days were then most evil; the blood of the Blessed à Becket had been shed quite recently at Canterbury. Impressed by the necessity of voluntary self-sacrifice to appease the Divine wrath for the crimes of men, the holy youth knew that this virtue could be best practised in some solitary retreat away from his kindred, who were noble and wealthy. Accordingly, he retired into a desert place and dwelt there in the hollow trunk of a great oak tree, whence his surname "*Stock.*" He had been leading this austere mode of life for about twenty years, when the Carmelites, not very long established in England at the time, founded a monastery in the neighbourhood of his lonely abode (A.D. 1212). Simon was at once attracted by the spirit of these Religious, and soon became

[1] *Brev. Rom. Carmel.*

a member of their Order. After profession he was sent to the University of Oxford to study for the priesthood. (The more lasting fame of that ancient seat of learning has been secured by the Monks.) On being ordained, he had to accept various offices of importance, which he filled with remarkable success. At a most critical epoch in the history of Carmel we find him Prior-General of the Order, now placed, through his persevering efforts, under the immediate special protection of the Holy See (A.D. 1251). He himself attributed all his victories to the patronage and intercession of the Queen of Carmel. He implored Her aid in every difficulty; and never once did he appeal to Her in vain. As a further proof of Her loving protection, he even asked for a visible sign of Her favour: the "*Brown Scapular*" was Our Lady's gracious answer to his prayer. She appeared to him in a vision, holding this sacred badge in Her hands, and told him that she had obtained from Her Divine Son that all who died wearing the same, for Her sake, should not be lost for ever! . . .

The whole world knows that Simon Stock died a Saint in the year 1265. One of the chapels in the Cathedral of Bordeaux is dedicated to him; and his remains may still be seen beneath the altar; for they were interred there soon after the Saint's death, while that city was yet an English possession. The promise thus made to the clients of Carmel has been accepted by the Church in its *literal* interpretation; and the Blessed Virgin Herself, as if to confirm Her devout children in their pious belief, secured for them another great privilege, which is known to the Faithful as the "*Sabbatine Indulgence.*" In this instance She appeared to Pope John XXII. and promised, under conditions very easy of fulfilment, to release from Purgatory, on the first Saturday after their demise, the souls of those who had died clothed in Her sacred livery. These facts are stated in the *Roman Breviary* without comment or explanation of any kind ; and far from thinking the sinner could look upon them as a way of escaping the temporal and eternal punishment merited by his crimes, the Church has ever encouraged devotion to the scapular, as a most efficacious means of ensuring her erring children's return to the path of virtue. And generation after generation—not unfrequently year after year—Her Spiritual Treasury has been opened with truly lavish generosity to the Carmelites, including all who have become affiliated to the Order as wearers of the scapular. For all clients of Carmel have the extraordinary *right* of participating in the meritorious works of the professed Religious ; in every austerity practised ; in every prayer said ; in every vigil kept by thousands of Friars and Nuns throughout the entire world. An organisation, known as the "*Sodality of the Brown Scapular,*" has been established, and may strictly be said to date back to the time of St. Simon Stock ; because the mere receiving (from a priest duly authorised) and wearing of the holy symbol, together with having one's name enrolled on the authentic Register, and by saying the prayers prescribed, embrace the essential conditions of membership—at least for the enjoyment of the favours and privileges of the Order.

Once the *Doctrine* of Our Lady's great bounty to the children of Carmel had been promulgated in the Church, people of every rank and condition hastened to avail themselves of such loving, maternal solicitude. It was to manifest their gratitude that the clients of the Queen of Carmel began to practise, in common, various exercises of piety in Her honour, with the final result of the Confraternity of the Brown Scapular, as it is now known to the Faithful, being formally inaugurated. Branches were established in all churches of the Carmelite Order. The Bishops and the secular clergy became just as zealous as the Religious themselves in publishing the efficacy of Mary's solemn pledge; since they had ample evidence of Her watchfulness over the Associates, men and women, who daily continued to receive much assistance, temporal as well as spiritual, from Her in return for their fidelity in observing the few simple rules. For it was not as a mere object of devotion that the members regarded the Scapular in which they had themselves invested. They believed it to be significative of an invisible shield guarding them against the dangers of their life's struggle; a guarantee of the unceasing patronage of One whose word is all-powerful before the Throne of Mercy and Grace. Wearing it, they grew more confident, more determined in the hour of trial. And when persecuted for their faith, the children of Carmel were ever found ready and happy to bear testimony to the truth, even by the shedding of their blood. It would seem that in Ireland especially, those promises of the Blessed Virgin were hailed with joyous praise. Having first received the brown scapular from the White Friars, who came among them not long after the death of St. Simon Stock, the people thenceforth regarded it as a certain safeguard against all perils; later on, when pressed hardly to renounce the faith, they beheld in their scapular a *visible* pledge of the reward awaiting those who should persevere; and the fury of fanaticism, which raged fiercely for centuries, never once prevailed.

The Teresian Carmelites of St. Patrick's Province—who, of course, possessed all the privileges of their brethren of the Mitigation, together with many Apostolic favours granted to the Discalced Fathers[1]—emulated the zeal of their predecessors in preaching devotion to the brown scapular as a special channel of grace. Wherever a Foundation was made by them, there a branch of the confraternity soon flourished, its members proving themselves true "Carmelites" in spirit during those troublous times. Not only did they endeavour to sanctify themselves by obedience to the rules of the Sodality; in their zeal they desired to lead others to the practice of virtue. And thus for several hundred years, in secret when they might not openly, the Teresian

[1] *Privilegia Carmelit. Excalceat.*

Clients of Carmel have exercised an influence for great good all over Ireland down to the present day.

More recently the Church of the Discalced Carmelites, Clarendon Street, may be said to have become the centre of this "*influence*," which, nevertheless, extends to the remotest part of the country. The members of the confraternity at " St. Teresa's " take a holy pride in their traditions, earnest in transmitting them by the fervour of their piety. Indeed, it is a sight to move the most indifferent, to see that spacious Church crowded now with men, who assemble every "third Friday" evening for spiritual instruction in preparation for their approach to the altar on the following Sunday; now with women, who meet for a like purpose on the Friday preceding the first Sunday of each month. Those not Catholics who visit Clarendon Street on such occasions are struck by the simple devotion of the thousands they behold relying so confidingly on the promises of the Blessed Virgin. But this absolute trust is based on faith, since Mary's Clients *know* She has the power to keep Her word. Often, too, the air of quiet determination of so many men and women, of every station in life, serves as a striking argument in favour of the truths in which Roman Catholics believe.

The members of the Sodality, both men and women, have always taken the deepest interest in the welfare of " St. Teresa's "; most eager to assist in any good work inaugurated by the Fathers.

To their persevering efforts is largely due the success of such enterprises as the "*Total Abstinence and Temperance Association*," the "*Christian Doctrine Classes*," the "*Children's Mass*," and of other most beneficial and charitable projects now identified with the name of this Church. And while thus hoping to advance God's glory in a humble way, they ensure for themselves a happy contentment of spirit—inseparable from the edifying lives which they lead.

And just as those devout Clients of Carmel would prove their gratitude to their Queen, showing themselves worthy of Her livery by their fervour as members of the Sodality of the Brown Scapular, there are others affiliated to the Order who aspire to still higher perfection, and who are equally devoted to "St. Teresa's." These are the "*Tertiaries.*" They ambition to lead the life of *Religious* amid the fret and worry of temporal affairs; even binding themselves by Vow to acquire the object which they have in view. Like the nuns, they owe their origin to the Blessed John Soreth, who obtained the necessary Papal sanction for the founding of the "*Third Order of Carmel.*"[1] This mode of life became very popular among the Faithful, many of whom had been longing for this means of closer union with God, but had been prevented embracing the monastic state by their domestic ties. The obligations of the "*Tertiaries*" are not incompatible with the perfect discharge of the duties of each one's particular sphere of duty;

[1] *Ménologe.*

and dispensations are freely granted should circumstances prevent the members being able to conform in every respect to their Rule; as, for example, difficulties with regard to the disposal of time, the "*Brothers*" being required to assemble in their oratories, evening after evening, for the recital of the Office of the Blessed Virgin. Still the most self-sacrificing efforts are invariably made to carry out all the pious practices enjoined.

We have related how the "*Teresian Tertiaries*" were reorganised in Ireland a century and a half ago, their zeal producing many admirable effects within the city of Dublin particularly. After the community had changed from Stephen's Street to "St. Teresa's," an oratory was provided for the "*Brothers*" in the new monastery, and there nightly, throughout the year, they came to pray, notwithstanding the fatigue of the labours of a hard-spent day.[1] They, likewise, had their own traditions, and lived up to them conscientiously. They were proud of their beautiful brown habit, which they are allowed to wear when assisting at devotions in the church. The "*Sister-Tertiaries*," too, have an oratory in " St. Teresa's," and are quite as eager to sanctify themselves and assist others by their prayers and good works as their fervent predecessors, for whom Father James of St. Bernard had translated (A.D. 1719) the Rule and Instructions which they are privileged to observe.

About the beginning of the present century a number of the "*Brother-Tertiaries*," connected with

[1] *MS. in Arch. of St. Teresa's.*

Clarendon Street, expressed to the Fathers there an earnest wish to withdraw themselves from the world altogether, in order to devote the remainder of their lives to God's service more perfectly. This was the fruit of their having realised the efficacy of a spirit of prayer. As soon as possible, arrangements were made to comply with their edifying request, the ecclesiastical authorities also approving of the project, since these zealous men were not bound by other obligations. A small house, which the "*Brothers*" called their monastery, was secured in the outskirts of the city. They opened a poor-school there (in face of all the penalties threatened by the law), so that the children of the poorer Catholics of Dublin might have an opportunity of being instructed in the principles of their religion at least. The undertaking was a marvellous success in every way. The "School" prospered beyond the hopes of the most sanguine, and many young Irishmen were called to follow the mode of life led by that first community of the "*Tertiaries*" of St. Patrick's Province. In the year 1813 another much larger house was founded at Clondalkin, Co. Dublin, and in the course of time a very pretty church, also, was opened there. While thus mindful of the education of the children of the poor, the Brothers were now convinced of the pressing need of Catholic colleges in Ireland, and invoking the patronage of St. Joseph for their enterprise, they established the well-known "*Carmelite Seminary*" of Clondalkin. It is impossible to exaggerate the services rendered to the country by this school during a very critical epoch in the history of the nation. One result of the efforts then made was that a great number of Irish Catholic youths obtained a higher education in their own country, the learned professions throughout the world being, as a matter of fact, indebted to "St. Joseph's" for not a few of their most distinguished members. In order to form an efficient teaching staff, several of the "*Tertiaries*," already thoroughly educated themselves, were required to devote themselves almost exclusively to the study of the languages and sciences, and to undergo a special course of training in preparation for their duties in the class-room. The assistance of eminent secular Professors was procured, when needful, in order that the students might enjoy every advantage in their college career. It may be said that many of those who had been educated there were afterwards called to the cloisters of Carmel. And in more recent years Clondalkin has given subjects quite frequently to the Irish Province. Being under the immediate jurisdiction of the Father-Provincial, with one of the Teresian Fathers for their spiritual Director, naturally the "*Brother-Tertiaries*" have the welfare of St..Patrick's Province very dearly at heart. But this fact would never have ensured vocations to the Order were not those under their charge first drawn to the Religious Life by the virtues which they had admired in their *Carmelite* teachers at "St. Joseph's." Hence, year after year, while this college retains its prestige among the Catholic schools of Ireland, young men who have come thither to prepare for the duties of life—thinking of their future, with every ambition of eager youth — suddenly and unaccountably find themselves called to embrace a career which, as yet, they can hardly understand. Praying for guidance from on High, the vocation-grace is given them, and the glamour of this world's attractions vanishes before the "Glory of Carmel," which seems to them resplendent in the Teresian Novitiate at Loughrea.

The historical memories of "St. Jóseph's" are many and most interesting; a number of notable names being associated with this seminary, and members of the community have gained fame for learning, among them Brother Luke Cullen, an indefatigable student of the history of his country, who has a special claim to the gratitude of posterity. He spent much labour and time in collecting material for a work on the Irish Rebellion of 1798, and had just completed his MS. when he died. His papers, however, were placed at the disposal of the late Mr. W. J. FitzPatrick, who freely utilised them, duly acknowledging his indebtedness to Brother Luke.[1] Near this "*Teresian Tertiary's*" grave, in the little cemetery at St. Joseph's, a mural tablet has been erected by Henry Grattan to the memory of a very dear friend interred within that sacred enclosure. Numbering the veteran Irish statesman among their sincerest well-wishers, the Brothers were happy to grant him the favour

[1] *Secret Service under Pitt.*

which he sought on a certain sad occasion. Other names hardly less revered in Ireland occur in the annals of Clondalkin Seminary. Father Henry Young was chaplain there for many years; Gerald Griffin would have gladly ended his days in that calm retreat; and one who had a life-long enthusiastic admiration for the brown habit of Carmel used often to conduct the annual retreat of the Brothers—" Father Bourke," the great Dominican preacher. Often, too, the students heard a venerable Prelate recall his own grateful recollections of "St. Joseph's." The Most Rev. Dr. Lynch, Archbishop of Toronto, loved to speak before them of the goodness of the "Brothers" to him when he was a schoolboy in Clondalkin, and of how helpful their advice and encouragement had been at the outset of his eventful career.

The zeal of the "*Tertiaries*" received still wider scope when they undertook to instruct and provide for the most helpless of their fellow-creatures, the blind. At first they devoted themselves to this great work of charity at Glasnevin, where a small community opened an institution for destitute boys and men so afflicted. This project also proved successful beyond all expectation. Large temporary work-rooms were constructed until such time as the Brothers, assisted by the generosity of the Irish people, could secure a more favourable site for a "*Great National Asylum.*"

After some years, the historic mansion known as "*Drumcondra Castle*," with the adjoining grounds, was purchased for this purpose. At present the community resides in the "House" itself, which has, however, been completely rebuilt from the first storey during the course of time. But on the ground floor may still be seen various apartments of the ancient castle, erected in 1560 (as a mural slab records) by a gentleman named Bath, a great favourite in Queen Elizabeth's court by reason of his musical abilities. His after life was spent in the Society of Jesus, of which he became a distinguished member, his wife—a daughter of Lord Gormanstown's—having died while he was yet in his early manhood. It is now almost certain that this was the castle in which Hugh O'Neill found refuge and hospitality after his romantic elopement with the sister of Sir Henry Bagnal, thenceforth the most relentless enemy of the Earl of Tyrone. There also the marriage was celebrated.[1]

In a remarkably short time, taking into account the large sum of money required for such an undertaking, the foundation of the present magnificent building was laid at Drumcondra. The church and work-rooms appeared later on, all within the past decade of years, and by the voluntary contributions of the Irish people at home and abroad. Still the Brothers have not yet realised the object of their ambition for the welfare of the blind. Their work is not to be considered complete until they have carried out a plan whereby the Drumcondra Asylum will be rendered, perhaps, the most perfect of its kind in Europe.

[1] *Hist. of Ireland,* and *Dist. Irishmen of Sixteenth Century.*

Nor is it Ireland only that has profited by the labours of the "*Tertiaries.*" Little colonies have been sent to America and to Asia, assisting everywhere, according to their vocation, in the salvation of souls. And thus all the Irish Clients of Carmel, Teresian Friars and Nuns, Tertiaries and members of the confraternity, are animated by the self-same spirit that enables them to co-operate in the one grand work of charity, implying their own sanctification, and the saving of countless souls.

CHAPTER XVIII.

CONCLUSION : RETROSPECT.

The "difficulties" of the work—Present state of the Irish Province—Its "Restoration"—The General Visitation of 1896—Ireland, Carmel, and Rome—The world and monasticism in these latter times—THE END.

AND now our task is done: the reader has had an authenticated historical account of St. Patrick's Province, and can judge whether the author has collected a sufficient number of important facts to show how closely the Discalced Carmelites have been related to Ireland for nearly *three hundred years*. Of course "*difficulties*" presented themselves while this effort was being made; the obvious necessity of knowing, for certain, what related to the Fathers of the Mitigation, what to the Religious of the Teresian Reform—not by any means the least. However, in many instances, where diligence in research may have been wanting to throw light on the subject, happy chance has given a useful clue. And remembering Father Serapion's almost disheartening attempt in a similar direction over a century ago, maybe still more favourable circumstances will encourage some other Discalced Carmelite to improve upon this very incomplete notice of the Order in Ireland. By merest accident the Author has discovered several original documents of much interest and importance; doubtlessly, unknown to him, equally valuable papers may exist; but not in any of the archives or libraries to which he has had access. In Rome and Genoa there are various MSS. pertaining to the history of the Irish Mission; for the most part, these had been already utilised by the Teresian annalists, and do not assist one farther than the period of the Cromwellian persecution. But if the aim of our work admitted of it, they might still have furnished us with numerous unpublished details.

With regard to the method of narrative, we may seem to have been negligent in making more particular reference to the sources of our information, and to have overlooked the utility of explanatory notes. As the authorisation of the Superiors-General is only given when they have satisfied themselves of the authenticity of the statements made, we have assumed that their permission will be considered a sufficient guarantee of trustworthiness by those who may not have leisure to test the merits of the work from a historical point of view, according to the canons of criticism: then, items of information relegated to footnotes are not always an argument for care having been bestowed upon the text. For the rest, it was not St. Teresa's intention to give her spiritual children an occasion of profitless controversy when she desired that the annals of each Province should be kept with scrupulous exactitude. By such a record of facts she would exhort succeeding generations of Discalced Carmelites to emulate the fervour of their predecessors, adopting the means ordained by Divine Providence for the perpetuation of the Reform of Carmel to the end of time. Hence, in the preceding chapters no assertions have been made which we were unable to verify by conscientious research, even the most manifest inferences being, very often, left to the reader's own discretion. Now, as to the intrinsic worth, the importance, of the facts thus chronicled, there may well be a diversity of opinion. But the Author cannot sincerely offer an apology for having tried to obtain for them special recognition, by submitting them outlined against a familiar background of Irish history. More than once it has been expressly stated that, while the object of this work was to trace the influence of the Teresian Carmelite's vocation in Ireland during those several centuries, an attempt would be made to show how every record of St. Patrick's Province must needs find a place in the annals of the nation.

Still, on reviewing the results of our pleasant labour, we can see that the subject-matter might have been made much more attractive by the introduction of some of those charming historical episodes, for the sake of graphic effect, as the opportunity occurred, and when it was not in our power to supply information in *requisite* detail; our excuse is, brevity had to be consulted in what claims to be simply a popular account of the Irish Province. It is for the future *Historian* to accomplish what we have left undone, and to remove the faults herein so apparent to the critical eye.

Since our task furthermore implied that we should give an insight into the manner in which the Irish Teresian Carmelites strove to attain the object of their vocation, either in time of peace or during persecution, frequent reference had to be made to their success from the beginning in overcoming obstacles that hindered them in the discharge of their sacred duties. In doing so, with a feeling of pardonable pride in the victories achieved by our predecessors, we have taken care to insist, like other writers of this Province in the seventeenth and following centuries, on the zeal of all priests in Ireland, whether belonging to the regular or secular clergy. It was sufficient for us to find that our Irish Fathers were ever loyal to the traditions of Carmel, worthy of the fame of the Teresian Reform.

And, perhaps, the most certain proof of their self-sacrifice and devotedness in former ages is the present prosperity of the Irish Province. Not since the year 1638 were its prospects brighter; for after all the struggles and trials of so lengthy a period, it was restored to its full canonical prestige at the last General Chapter held in Genoa in 1895. This may seem a *very long time*, indeed, for the repairing of injuries inflicted upon the Discalced Carmelites of Ireland by the Penal Laws. Yet, shall we be surprised, remembering those statutes that still *disgrace* the Legislature, notwithstanding the progress of civilisation, which is supposed to include a *high respect* for *every* form of religious belief? As a matter of fact, neither the Teresian Friars nor any other body of regular priests may consider themselves at all exempt from those petty legal annoyances which have the baneful effect of recalling bitter memories of those terrible Penal Days. Thus the welfare of the Irish Province depends now, as in the past, on the persevering fervour that will forward the object of the Teresian Carmelite's vocation under such a difficulty as active hostility on the part of the State.

Another, and still easier way of accounting for the success which we have recorded, would be to attribute it to the necessity of the Carmelite's mode of life in the Church : a divinely appointed means for the greater sanctification of souls. Nevertheless, had the Fathers of St. Patrick's Province hitherto failed to transmit those traditions of their Order, the "*Glory of Carmel*" in Ireland could never have been so reflected as to attract postulants to aspire to "*The Regular Life.*" Whereas, now the "Rule and the Constitutions," embodying all that is needful for the attainment of holiness, are becoming daily better understood among the Irish Faithful, the severe corporal austerities being looked upon merely as a matter of course.

A very practical test of the feeling of the people in this respect was the enthusiastic welcome given by all classes to the Superior-General, *Father Bernardine of St. Teresa*, on the occasion of the

Canonical Visitation during the autumn of last year (1896). It was a touching proof of Ireland's love for the Order of the Blessed Virgin. Addresses and testimonials were presented by the Tertiaries and the members of the Sodality, both men and women, taking part in these tributes of filial regard. Repeated allusion was made to the bond of affection that exists between the Faithful and the Teresian Fathers; nor was an expression of sincere gratitude wanting in this manifestation of the people's devotedness to Carmel. There was special graceful mention of the peril which many of Father Bernardine's predecessors had risked in coming to Ireland to discharge the duties of their office in other days. And when at "St. Teresa's" he was shown the two Monstrances that recall the trials and triumphs of the Irish Fathers as related in the annals of the Order: the one a poor *souvenir* of the first centenary of the advent of the Religious to this country; the other, a magnificent memorial of the hundredth anniversary of the foundation of the friary in Clarendon Street, an event celebrated with great solemnity in 1893, a year after the grand commemoration of the tercentenary of the death of St. John of the Cross. . . .

But the limits assigned to our work may not be further exceeded; although, nowadays, what relates to monasticism—even to the *very* particular account of "*The Regular Life*" in a modern friary—appears to be well received; as if people were amazed to find the ascetical spirit quite as vigorous in these latter times as they are told it had been in the "*Ages of Faith*." They wonder how its "influence" is brought to bear on the world in the so-called "advancement" of this nineteenth century. Their surprise becomes all the greater when popular "leaders of thought" quote from the writings of those who had lived and died in the cloister; for it is not the Discalced Carmelites only who have published St. Teresa's fame. But much of the curiosity thus manifested has its origin rather in some fanciful sentiment than in a genuine desire to know the truth, and merits little consideration from one merely anxious to establish a series of facts, from history or tradition, proving the usefulness of "*The Religious Life*" by the good it actually effects. This we shall have done if the reader is convinced of the success of the Teresian Friars in perpetuating the spirit of their Order in Ireland.

Hence, in preserving this incomplete record of St. Patrick's Province, it is to be borne in mind that St. Teresa would have nothing committed to writing which does not directly, or at least indirectly, serve as a motive to edification. For thus only can the history of the past inspire others to follow in the footsteps of those who have left an example of the good that may be accomplished under the guidance of grace. And if the perusal of this narrative should be the means of helping in any way another generation of Irish Teresian Friars to realise more clearly still the aim of their Institution, and their privilege in being called to labour among the Faithful of their native land, the Author's task has been *well done* indeed; and were he ambitious for highest appreciation of his humble efforts, then, without his ever knowing it, he shall have received the most desirable of all praise.

The good opinion of those outside the cloister will depend, no doubt, on what *they* may be pleased to consider the merit of the work. They may not be inclined to allow for a Friar's loving esteem of his Order, and disregard his enthusiasm for the monastic traditions of his Province; yet we can say that anything which we have written reads disparagingly when compared with what others relate of the Discalced Carmelites, not to speak of the affectionate regard entertained for them by the Irish people. When recently a deputation of the "Confraternity of the Brown Scapular" waited upon the Superior-General, it was to assure him that the "Fathers" and themselves were *one*, that they knew their own welfare was the Teresian Friar's care, and that it was the ambition of their lives to participate in the spirit of Carmelite zeal.

So have we deemed ourselves justified in identifying those annals of the Irish Province with the Nation's history, especially since the Faithful of Ireland seem so eager to acknowledge the Order's claim. And as many writers assert that the Discalced Carmelites were once more popularly known throughout the country by the name of the great Saint whom God has raised up to restore the

"*Glory of Carmel*" under the Primitive Rule, only the unworthiness of our work has prevented us giving to this unassuming historical account of St. Patrick's Province another, and still more appropriate title: "HIBERNIA TERESIANA."

INDEX.

ABBEYS, Carmelite—
  Ardee, 30, 33
  Ardnacranna, 34
  Athboy, 31
  Ballingall, 35
  Ballinismale, 36
  Ballynahinch, 36
  Ballywilliam, 35
  Borniscarra, 29
  Castlelyons, 36
  Cloncurry, 33
  Cork, 35
  Crevebane, 36
  Drogheda, 31
  Dublin, 32
  Frankford, 34
  Kildare, 25, 33
  Kinsale, 36
  Knockmore, 37
  Knocktopher, 34
  Leighlin Bridge, 35
  Little-Horton, 34
  Loughrea, 37, 198 *sqs.*
  Pallice, 36
  Rathmullen, 29
  Thurles, 36
Abbeys, List of, 29
Act of Settlement, 124
Act, the Black, 125
Adeodatus, Father, 111
"Adventurers," the, 117
Agapitus, Father, 109, 123, 236
—— Official report of, on state of Ireland, 109
Aikenhead, Mrs., 174
Alan, Blessed, 4

Albert of St. Lawrence, Father, 250
—— of St. Patrick, 264
Aloysius, Father, 260
Alphonsus, Father, 224
Andrew, Father, 224
Angelus of St. Mary, Father, 264
—— of St. Joseph, Brother, Life and Martyrdom, 96-100, 234
—— of the Holy Ghost, Father, 256
Anne, of Jesus, the Venerable Mother, 277 *sqs.*
—— of St. Bartholomew, Mother, 280
—— Queen, 139 *sqs.*
—— St., Monastery of, 21
Anthony, Angelus, Father, 242
—— of St. John the Baptist, Father, 223, 241
—— of the Mother of God, Father, 222, 223
Association, the Catholic, 185
—— the Repeal, 190
Athlone, Siege of, 132
Aughrim, Battle of, 132
Aungier, Sir Francis, 33

BAGGOT, Sir Robert, 32
Balrayne, Robert Fitzrichard, 36
Barnewall, Patrick, 35
Barry, De, 36
Beck, John, 32
Bede, Father, 104, 234
Bermingham, 36

310 INDEX.

Bernard of the B.V., Father, 258
Bernardine of St. Teresa, Father, 303
Berthold, St., 5
Bill, Catholic Relief, 187
Bonaventure, Father, 262
Book of Expenses and Receipts, 161
—— of Obits, 176
Bouillon, Godfrey de, 5
Boulter, Archbishop, 148
Bourke, Father, 296
—— Mother Eleanor, 270
Boxam, John, 32
Boyne, Battle of, 131
Bracken, Father Edward, 34
Brady, John, Father, 239
Bricklane, Father James, 52, 234
Brigid, St., 268
Brittany, Duchess of, 270
Brocard, St., 4
"Brothers of the Blessed Virgin," 2, 3
Brown, Father Henry, 34
Bruce, Robert, 30
Bulkeley, Lancelot, Archbishop of Dublin, 49
Burgos, De, 36, 68, 270
Burke, Patrick, Father, 238
Butler, 36

CAMDEN, Lord, 104
"Carmel, Daughters of," 268
Carmel, third order of. *See* Tertiaries
Carmelites—
  Abbeys of. *See* Abbeys
  cells of, 28
  come to Rome, 21; Ireland, 20, 23, *seq.*
  Mitigated, 5, 6
  Primitive Rule restored by St. Teresa, 6 *seq.*; and St. John of the Cross, 15 *seq.*
  reform of Blessed John Soreth, 6
  retain the "Ancient Rite," 18
  Rule of, 3, 4
  sisterhood of, 268

Carmelites—*continued*—
  why called "Calced," 17
Carmelites, Discalced, the—
  arrive in Ireland, 45
  first Foundation of, 15
  Province of, 17
  Vicar-General, 17
  persecution of. *See* Persecutions
  the Teresian Reform, 15
  why so called, 17
  zeal for Missions, 18
  Irish, constituted as a Province, 55
  ancient abbeys transferred to, 58
  archives burnt, 60
  building of Clarendon Street Friary, 161-169
  conference of, 156
  connection with O'Connell. *See* O'Connell
  Constitutions of, 207
  Convents of. *See* Convents
  Foundations of. *See* Foundations
  General Chapter of, 55, 61, 86, 235, 302
  General Visitation of, 69, 76, 121, 146, 154, 304
  lay their grievances before the Pope, 65
  Mystical Theology, 229
  National Synod, 80
  Provincial Synod, 79
  Re-establishment of Novitiate, 158
  Seminary of, 293
  Sisterhood, 268 *sqs.*
  strained relations with Papal Nuncio, 64
  the House of Studies, 213 *sq.*
  the newly Professed, 210
  the Novitiate, duties of, 205 *sq.*
  the "Regular Life," 71-74, 83
  the Scholastic Course, 216 *sq.*, 220, 225

INDEX.

Casey, Thomas, 31
Catholics, Persecution of. *See* Persecution
Celestine, Pope, 21
Centenary of Teresian Friars, 145
Cepeda, Don Alfonso Sanchez de, 7
Charles I., 43, 53, 71, 76, 81, 87
—— II., 122, 124
Charter Schools, 148
Charts, Mortuary, 232
Chesterfield, Lord, 147
Cholera in Ireland, 176
Clanricarde, Earl of, 37, 67, 199
Clement VI., Pope, 25
—— X., Pope, 42
Clonfert, Bishop of, 201
Coleman, Columbanus, Father, 237
—— Father Anthony, 150
—— Nicholas, Father, 244
Columbanus, Father, 63, 73, 235
—— of St. Patrick, Father, 265
—— of St. Paul, 241
"Complutenses," the, 222
Conelan, Anthony, Father, 248
Confederation of the Catholics of Ireland, 80
Convents of Discalced Carmelites, 270, 272, 275
—— at Loughrea, 270, 276, *sq.*
—— of Dublin, 274
Coote, Sir Charles, 199
Cornwallis, Lord, 165
Covenant of the Puritans, 81
Creagh, Michael, Father, 250
Croly, Philip, Father, 120
Cromwell, Oliver, 68, 88, 107, *sqs.*
—— Richard, 122
Cullen, Brother Luke, 295
—— Peter, Father, 241
Curran, 129
Curry, John, Dr., 151
Cyril, Father, 235

DAVERIN, Joseph, Father, 249
Davis, Sir John, 34
Declaration of Indulgence, 130

Dempsey, James, Vicar-Apostolic, 119
Dickson, William, 34
Dillon, Robert, 34
Dodd, Patrick, Father, 240
Dogherty, Anthony, Father, 237
Dolphin, John, Father, 238
Dominic, Father, 223, 240
—— St., 19
Donovan, Father Patrick, 68, 69, 234
Drumcondra Castle, 297
Duggan, Dr., Bishop of Clonfert, 219
Duruelo, Settlement of Carmelites at, 15, 46

EDMUND, Father, 33,
Edward, III., 25, 32
—— of St. Thomas, Father, 240
—— of the Kings, Father, 43
  character of, 51
  elected Prior, 48
  death, 51, 233
Elias, St., the Prophet, Founder of the Carmelites, 2
—— Italian Congregation of, 18
Eliseus, Father, 154, 253
Elucidarium Thomisticum, 112
Emancipation, Catholic, the, 180
Eugene IV., Pope, 5, 18, 269
Euphrasia, St., 268
Euphrosyne, St., 268

FALLON, James, 136
Famine, Irish, 146, 193
Fénelon, Archbishop of Cambrai, 128
Ferdinand of St. Mary, 18
Fineach, Father James, 121
Fitzsimons, Patrick, Father, 243
"Flight of the Earls, the," 30
Foundations of the Discalced Carmelites—
  Ardbreccan, 69, 154
  Ardee, 62

Foundations—*continued*—
Athboy, 62
Dublin, 61, 137, 142, 154, 156, 214
Galway, 64
Kilkenny, 65
Limerick, 66
Loughrea, 67, 142, 154, 158, 198
Youghal, 68
Flynn, Christopher, Father, 257
Francis, Father, 224
—— of the Blessed Sacrament, Father, 248
—— of Jesus Mary, Father, 252
—— Joseph, Father, 261
—— Joseph of St. Teresa, Father, 257
—— of St. Brigid, Father, 260
French, Nicholas, Father, 259
Friars in Ireland, 39 *ff.*
—— of the Reform, 17, 18
—— Praise of, 35
—— Teresian, first Foundation of, 15
—— the White, 20

GAYFIELD House, 213
Geoghegan, Antony, Bishop, 119, 125
George I., 143
—— II., 145
—— III., 151
—— IV., 184
Glennan, John, Father, 250
Gotti, Cardinal, 203, 230
"Graine-ni-Mhaile," 28
Gratian, Father Jerome, 1
Grattan, Henry, 153, 182
Gregory of St. Mary, Father, 263
—— XIII., Pope, 17
—— XIV., Pope, 278

HALFPENNY, Joseph, Father, 237
Halley, George, 96
Hart, Patrick, Father, 240
Hearns, John, Father, 249
Heffernan, Michael, Father, 252

Henrietta Maria, Queen, 44
Henry IV., 32
—— VI., 269
—— VIII., 25, 31, 34, 37
Heverin, Ignatius, Father, 248
Hibernia Dominicana, 69
Hidderton, George, Father, 238
Hilarion of St. Mary, Father, 146
—— of St. Teresa, 151, 247
Hoardley, Archbishop, 148
Hogan, John Baptist, Father, 249
Hospital, St. Vincent's, 174
"House of Studies," 211, 213 *sq.*
Hynes, John, Brother, 241

INCHIQUIN, Lord, 65, 82
Indulgence, Sabbatine, the, 287
Innocent IV., Pope, 4, 5, 12, 207
Ireland, Loyalty to Stuarts, 131
—— Union of, 167
Irish reign of terror, the, 164
Isidore of St. Alexius, Father, 251
—— of St. Michael, Father, 255
—— of St. Joseph, Father, 86, 116
—— of St. Paul, Father, 250
Ita, St., of the Decies, 23

JAMES EDWARD STUART, 139
James I., 41
—— II., 129
—— of St. Bernard, Father, 145, 292, 339
—— of the Resurrection, Father, 249
Joachim, Father, 264
John of St. Matthias, Father, 13, 278
—— canonised, 42
—— death of, 14
—— Father, 257
—— joins the Carmelites, 14
—— Joseph, Father, 259
—— of Jesus Mary, the Venerable, 204

INDEX. 313

John, Patriarch of Jerusalem, 3
—— XXII., Pope, 287
—— of the Cross, St. *See* Father John of St. Matthias
—— (Mullaly), Father, 241
—— (O'Reilly), Father, 255
—— St. Joseph, Father, 261
Joseph of the Annunciation, Father, 258
—— Mary, Brother, 264
—— of St. Martha, Father (Co. Longford), 158, 244
—— (Co. Galway), 250
—— of St. Teresa, 262
—— of St. Teresa, Father, 261
—— St. Francis Xavier, Father, 262
—— St. Mary, Father, 262
—— St., Seminary of, 293 *seq.*
—— St. Teresa, Father, 255

KELLY, Father William, 33
—— Ralph, Archbishop of Cashel, 25
Kennedy, Felim, Father, 237
Kenny, Paul, Father, 239
Kiernan, Father, 105, 234

LACY, Paul, Father, 2
Laud, Archbishop, 76
Lawrence of St. Thomas, Father, 104, 234
—— of St. Teresa, Father, 110 *sqs.* 236
Laws, Penal, 112, 142, 143, 152
Lennon, John, Father, 250
Leo, Father, 171, 257
L'Estrange, Father, 176, 185, 188
"Light and Glory of Ireland," the, 25
Liguori, St. Alphonsus, 224
Limerick, Defence of, 132, 133
—— Treaty of, 133, 276
Lobera, Mother Anna de, 277
Londres, William de, 31
Louis XV., 282
Louvain, Missionary College of, 43, 45

Luke, St., the Evangelist, 3
Lynch, John, Brother, 237

MACAULY, Mother, 174
Mackan, James, Father, 256
MacMahon, Juliana Julia, Mother, 282
MacSweeney Fannid, the, 29
Malachy of Jesus, Father, 235
—— of St. Teresa, Father, 263
Mangan, James, Father, 257
Mannion, Thomas, Father, 250
Marcellus, Father, 240
Mark of St. John Baptist, Father, 253
Mary Anne, Mother, 272
Mary, Father Jerome. *See* Cardinal Gotti
M'Donagh, John, Father, 248
M'Hugo, James, Father, 248
—— Jeffrey, Father, 239
—— Raymond, Father, 240
Memoir of Ireland, a, 191
Michael, Father, 222
Mitigation of Carmelite Rule, 5
—— Fathers of, 17
Molloys, the, 35
Monahan, James, Father, 239
Monasteries, Carmelite, *v.* Abbeys
—— Discalced Carmelite, *v.* Discalced Carmelite
Montalembert, Count de, 194
Monthly Meetings of Archconfraternity of Brown Scapular, 150
Mooney, James, Father, 252
Moore, Lord, 98
Murray, Nicholas, Father, 260

NECROLOGY, the General, 232
Nicholas, Father, 150, 242
Nicholson, Dr., 259
Nogueras, Christopher, Father, 188, 257
Novitiate, the, 205 *sq.*
Nuns, the Teresian, 268 *sqs.*

INDEX.

Nuns, Rule and Constitutions of, 273
—— Life of, 279

OATES, Titus, 126
Oath of Allegiance, 156
Obits, Book of, 232; Lists of, 233
Obituary, the, 232 sqs.
O'Brien of Thomond, 81
—— Simon, Father, 255
O'Bugey, David, 25, 32, 33
O'Connell, Daniel, 178, 197, 258
O'Daugane, Father, 35
O'Ferral, Joseph Michael, Dr., 172-174
O'Flaherty, 36
O'Hanlon, Father Raymond, 175
O'Hara, Father, 161
O'Howleghan, 36
O'Molloy, Hugh, 34
O'Neill, Hugh, 297
—— Owen Roe, 97
—— Sir Phelim, 77, 80, 97
Orange League, 155
—— Lodges, 155
Oratorians, General Chapter of, 222
Order of the Blessed Virgin, 2, 4
O'Reilly, Father Serapion, 163 172
O'Reilly, Hugh, Archbishop, 79
Ormond, Thomas, Earl of, 36
—— Duke of, 81, 126, 141
O'Tothell, Nicholas, 32
Outlaws, the Teresian, 106, 108 sqs.
—— New Generation of, 134 sqs.

PALATIO, Octavian de, 30
Palladius, St., 21, 22
Patrick, Father, 31, 86, 104
—— of St. Brigid, Father, 105,
—— Mary of St. Joseph, Father, 254
—— Province of, 57-61, 302
—— St., 5, 22

Paul of St. Ubaldus, Father, 43
—— of St. Patrick, Father, 255
—— of the Cross, Father, 265
Peel, Sir Robert, 183
Pendrick, Father William, 44
Persecution of Catholics, 41 f., 53, 77
—— of Discalced Carmelites, 37 sq., 49 sq., 67, 77 sq., 89 sqs., 103, 108 sqs., 140 sqs., 143, 164 sqs.
Peter of the Assumption, Father, 250
Peter, Brother, 234
—— Life and Martyrdom of, 100-102
Philip, Father, Superior-General, 229
"Pilgrimage of the Heart," 195
Pippard, Ralph, 30
Pitt, William, 155, 163, 167
Pius V.. Pope, 12
—— VII., Pope, 182
—— IX., Pope, 195, 206
Plunkett, Oliver, Archbishop, 126
Power, Father Seraphim, 154, 240
Power, Joseph, Father, 237
Prayer, efficacy of, 280
—— of St. Gerard, Father, 242
—— of St. John Baptist, Father, 242
—— St. Justin, 253
Prendergast, 36
Province, Constitution of, 57

QUARANTOTTI, Cardinal, 182
Quigley, Father, murder of, 165

RAWSON, John, 36
Raymond, Father, 259
Rebellion, the Irish, 164
—— the Scottish, 147
Reform, Fathers of, 17, 18
—— Teresian, established in Ireland, 44
Regency, the, 155

INDEX. 315

"Regular Life, the," 204
Relly, Father Patrick, 118
Remonstrance, the Grand, 77
Renatus, Joseph, Father, 240
Repeal Movement, 191
Revolution, the French, 166
Ribbonmen, the, 185
Richard II., 32
Rinucini, Cardinal, 64
Roache, John, Father, 256
Robert Mary of St. Joseph, Father, 146
Robert of Jesus Mary, Father, 243
—— of St. Patrick, Father, 253
Roche, John, 33
Roches, the, 35
Rowe, Father John, 65, 128, 235

Salamanca, Theological College of, 222
"Salmanticenses," 222
Saracens, persecution of Carmelites by, 5
Savage, Thomas, Father, 244
Scapular, the Brown, 285 sqs.
—— Archconfraternity of, 149
—— Confraternity of, 24, 306
—— Sodality of, 287 sq.
Science of the Saints, 206
Searle, Father Robert, 32
Sebastian, Father, 224
"Seraphic Doctor"(St. Teresa),8
Serapion, Father, 233, 270, 299, 260
Sheehan, John, Brother, 240
Simon, Father, 235
Sisterhood, Carmelite, established, 268
Sixtus V., Pope, 17, 278
Slane, Richard, 34
Smith, James, Father, 236
"Sons of the Prophet," 3, 17
Soreth, Blessed John, 6, 269, 291
Stanehurst, Nicholas, 33
Statement by Father Agapitus, 236
Stephen, Father, 244.

Stephen, of the Blessed Virgin, Father, 248
Stock, St. Simon, 4, 23, 43, 285
Stone, George, Archbishop, 148
Strafford, Earl of, 53, 76
St. Ruth, General, 132
Sugdæus, John, 30, 32
Sweetman, John, 160, 165
Swift, Dean, 144, 146

TAAFE, Viscount Nicolas, Ambassador, 147
Talbot, Francis, 34
Teresa, Mother, 271
—— of Jesus, St., 1, 6
  Life of, 7
  Death, 10
  reforms the Carmelite Order, 12, 17, 18
  founds Convent of Avila, 12
  canonised, 42
—— St. Simon of, 57
—— temporal association of, 292
—— Tercentenary, 202
Teresians, the, 292
  schools of, 293
  visitation of, 250
Tertiaries, the, 291
Thebaid, the, 23
Theodore, Father, 261
Thomas Aquinas of St. Teresa, Father, life and martyrdom, 89-95, 234
—— of Jesus Mary, Father, 254
—— Mary of St. Elias, Father, 254
—— Aquinas, St., 222
—— of Jesus, the Venerable, 205
—— of the Sacred Stigmata, Father, 250
Thurot, Admiral, 151
Tone, Wolfe, mission to America, 165
Tumulty, Francis, Father, 249
Tyrconnel, Earl of, 130

UBALDUS, Father, 233
Ullathorne, Bishop, 259

INDEX.

Union, repeal of, 180
"United Ireland Society," 156
Urban, Father, 243
—— VIII., Pope, 278
—— of St. Hilarion, Father, 248

VETO, the, 181
Victor, Father, 63, 73, 235
Vesci, Richard de, 33
Visitations, Book of, 75
——. *See* Discalced Carmelites

WALSH, Dr., Archbishop of Dublin, 220

Walsh, John, Father, 258
Ward, Father Patrick, 156
—— John, Father, 238
Wellington, Duke of, 187
Wexford, the Furlongs of, 34
William, Father, 35
—— III., 130, 273
—— IV., 190
Whearty, John, Father, 253
Whelan, William, Bishop, 172
—— Patrick, Father, 257
Wood, project of, 145

YEPES, Juan de, 14
Young Irelanders, 191

THE END.

Printed by BALLANTYNE, HANSON & CO.
Edinburgh & London

SELECTION

FROM

BURNS & OATES'

Catalogue

OF

PUBLICATIONS.

LONDON: BURNS AND OATES, Ld.
28 ORCHARD ST., W.

Latest Publications.

Foundations of Faith: The Existence of God Demonstrated. From the German of Fr. L. von Hammerstein, S.J. With a preface by the Rev. W. L. Gildea, D.D. Crown 8vo, cloth, 6/-.

Pius the Seventh, 1800-1823. By Mary H. Allies. Crown 8vo, cloth, 5s.

Flowers of Devotion. Being a collection of favourite devotions, for Public and Private Use. Compiled from approved sources, and with the *Imprimatur* of His Eminence Cardinal Vaughan. New Edition, printed upon the finest India paper, from new and clear type. 180 pp., size 4½ inches long by 2½ inches wide and less than ¼ inch thick. French morocco, limp, 1s. 6d.; polished paste grain, limp, 2s. 6d; German calf, limp, 4s.; polished morocco, limp, 4s.; Russia, limp, calf lined, 5s.

Rome and England: or, Ecclesiastical Continuity. By the Rev. Luke Rivington, M.A. Crown 8vo, cloth. 3/6.

The Christian Inheritance. By the Right Rev. John Cuthbert Hedley, O.S.B., Bishop of Newport. Second Edition. Crown 8vo, cloth gilt, 430 pp. 6/-

The Life and Letters of Fr. John Morris, S.J. 1826-1893. By Fr. J. H. Pollen, S.J. Quarterly Series. Cloth. 6/-

Controversial Catechism: or, Protestantism Refuted and Catholicism Established. By the Rev. Stephen Keenan. New Edition, with latest Revisions by the Rev. George Cormack, and a Preface by the Right Rev. J. C. Hedley, O.S.B., Bishop of Newport. Cloth. 2s.

Three Daughters of the United Kingdom. A Novel. By Mrs. Innes Browne. Cloth gilt. 5s.

Flora, the Roman Martyr. New One Volume Edition. Crown 8vo, cloth gilt. 6s.

The Formation of Christendom Popular Edition. By T. W. Allies, K.C.S.G.

    Vol. I. The Christian Faith and the Individual. Crown 8vo, cloth 5s.

    Vol. II. The Christian Faith and Society. Crown 8vo, cloth. 5s.

    Vol. III. The Christian Faith and Philosophy. Crown 8vo, cloth. 5s.

No. 2.   1897.

SELECTION
FROM
BURNS AND OATES' CATALOGUE OF PUBLICATIONS.

ALLIES, T. W. (K.C.S.G.)

The Formation of Christendom. Popular Edition.
Vol. I. The Christian Faith and the Individual. Crown
8vo, cloth. £0 5 0
Vol. II. The Christian Faith and Society. Crown 8vo,
cloth. 0 5 0
Vol. III. The Christian Faith and Philosophy. Crown
8vo, cloth. 0 5 0

H. E. CARDINAL VAUGHAN says—" It is one of the noblest historical works I have ever read. Now that its price has placed it within the reach of all, I earnestly pray that it may become widely known and appreciatively studied. We have nothing like it in the English language."

A Life's Decision. Second Edition. Crown 8vo, cloth. 0 5 0
The Throne of the Fisherman, built by the Carpenter's
Son, the Root, the Bond, and the Crown of Christendom. Demy 8vo 0 10 6
The Holy See and the Wandering of the Nations.
Demy 8vo 0 10 6
Peter's Rock in Mohammed's Flood. Demy 8vo . 0 10 6

"It would be quite superfluous at this hour of the day to recommend Mr. Allies' writings to English Catholics. Those of our readers who remember the article on his writings in the *Katholik*, know that he is esteemed in Germany as one of our foremost writers."—*Dublin Review*.

ALLIES, MARY.

Pius the Seventh, 1800-1823. Crown 8vo, cloth, 0 5 0

"It is a subject the handling of which demanded exceptional knowledge and ability, and above all a sympathetic touch; neither the knowledge, ability, nor sympathy have been wanting. The facts of the period are marshalled with masterly skill, and their bearing reviewed with the most admirable clearness. . . . The author writes at once with vigour and grace. She is to be congratulated on the composition of such an exceedingly valuable monograph."—*Catholic Times*.

Leaves from St. John Chrysostom. With introduction
by T. W. Allies, K.C.S.G. Crown 8vo, cloth. . 0 6 0
History of the Church in England, from the beginning of the Christian Era to the accession of
Henry VIII. Crown 8vo, cloth 0 6 0
The Second Part, to the End of Queen Elizabeth's
Reign. Crown 8vo, cloth 0 3 6

ANSWERS TO ATHEISTS: OR NOTES ON
Ingersoll. By the Rev. L. A. Lambert (over 130,000 copies sold in America). Paper £0 0 6
Cloth 0 1 0

BAKER, VEN. FATHER AUGUSTIN.
Holy Wisdom; (Sancta Sophia). Directions for the Prayer of Contemplation, &c. By the Ven. Father F. Augustin Baker, O.S.B. Edited by Abbot Sweeney, D.D. Beautifully bound in half leather. 0 6 0
"We earnestly recommend this most beautiful work to all our readers. We are sure that every community will use it as a constant manual. If any persons have friends in convents, we cannot conceive a better present they can make them, or a better claim they can have on their prayers, than by providing them with a copy."—*Weekly Register.*

BELLASIS, EDWARD. (*Lancaster Herald.*)
Memorials of MR. SERJEANT BELLASIS New and cheaper Edition. 8vo, 250 pp., bound in cloth, with fifteen Portraits and Illustrations 0 6 0
"A noteworthy contribution to the history of the Tractarian Movement."—*Times.*

BOWDEN, REV. H. S. (of the Oratory) Edited by.
Dante's Divina Commedia: Its scope and value. From the German of FRANCIS HETTINGER, D.D. With an engraving of Dante. 2nd Edition. . . 0 10 6
"All that Venturi attempted to do has been now approached with far greater power and learning by Dr. Hettinger, who, as the author of the 'Apologie des Christenthums,' and as a great Catholic theologian, is eminently well qualified for the task he has undertaken."—*The Saturday Review.*

Natural Religion. Being Vol. I. of Dr. Hettinger's Evidences of Christianity. With an Introduction on Certainty. Second edition. Crown 8vo, cloth 0 7 6
"As an able statement of the Catholic Doctrine of Certitude, and a defence, from the Romanist point of view, of the truth of Christianity, it was well worth while translating Dr. Franz Hettinger's 'Apologie des Christenthums,' of which the first part is now published."—*Scotsman.*

Revealed Religion. Being the Second Volume of the above work. With an Introduction on the "Assent of Faith." Crown 8vo, cloth, ... 0 5 0
"It is a book practically invaluable to the educated Catholic who is forced one way or another to read the flippant and most irreligious criticism of the hour, and who, unless supported by some antidote of this kind, must imbibe a good deal of that insidious poison."—*Freeman's Journal.*

BRIDGETT, REV. T. E. (O.SS.R.)
Discipline of Drink, The. An Historical Inquiry into the Principles and Practice of the Catholic Church regarding the Use, Abuse, and Disuse of Alcoholic Liquors, especially in England, Ireland, and Scotland from the 6th to the 16th Century. By Rev. T. E. Bridgett, C.SS.R. With an Introductory Letter by H. E. Cardinal Manning. Fcap. 8vo, cloth. 0 3 6
Our Lady's Dowry; how England Won that Title. New and Enlarged Edition. 0 5 0

BRIDGETT REV. T. E. (C.SS.R.)—continued.

Lyra Hieratica : Poems on the Priesthood. Collected from many sources by the Rev. T. E. Bridgett, C.SS.R. Fcap. 8vo, cloth. (postage 3d.) *net.* . £0 2 6

"The idea of gathering an anthology of Poems on the Priesthood was a happy one, and has been happily carried out. Priests and laity alike owe a debt of gratitude to Father Bridgett for the many beautiful things he has brought together."—*Tablet.*

Ritual of the New Testament. An essay on the principles and origin of Catholic Ritual in reference to the New Testament. Third edition . . . 0 5 0

The Life of the Blessed John Fisher. 2nd Ed. Crown 8vo, cloth, illustrated. 0 7 6

The True Story of the Catholic Hierarchy deposed by Queen Elizabeth, with fuller Memoirs of its Last Two Survivors. By the Rev. T. E. BRIDGETT, C.SS.R., and the late Rev. T. F. KNOX, D.D., of the London Oratory. Crown 8vo, cloth, 0 7 6

"We gladly acknowledge the value of this work on a subject which has been obscured by prejudice and carelessness."—*Saturday Review.*

The Life and Writings of Blessed Thomas More, 2nd Ed. with portrait. 0 7 6

The Wisdom and Wit of Blessed Thomas More . . 0 6 0

"It would be hard to find another such collection of true wisdom and keen, pungent, yet gentle wit and humour, as this volume contains."—*American Catholic Quarterly.*

BRIDGETT, REV. T. E. (C.SS.R.), Edited by.

Souls Departed : Being a defence and Declaration of the Catholic Church's Doctrine touching Purgatory and Prayers for the Dead. By Cardinal Allen. First published in 1565, and now edited in modern spelling. Black cloth, with a Portrait of Cardinal Allen 0 6 0

BROWNLOW, BISHOP.

A Memoir of the late Sir James Marshall, C.M.G., K.C.S.G., taken chiefly from his own letters. With Portrait. Crown 8vo, cloth . . . 0 3 6.

Lectures on Slavery and Serfdom in Europe. Cloth 0 3 6

"The general impression left by the perusal of this interesting book is one of great fairness and thorough grasp of the subject."—*Month.*

Memoir of Mother Rose Columba Adams, O.P., first Prioress of St. Dominic's Convent, and Foundress of the Perpetual Adoration at North Adelaide. Crown 8vo. cloth, with Portrait and Plates . . 0 6 6

"An edifying and touching biography of [one who was both a charming woman and a saintly nun."—*Dublin Review.*

BUCKLER, REV. REGINALD, (O.P.)

The Perfection of Man by Charity. A Spiritual Treatise. Second edition. Crown 8vo. cloth £0 5 0

"The object of Father Buckler's useful and interesting book is to lay down the principles of the spiritual life for the benefit of Religious and Seculars. The book is written in an easy and effective style, and the apt citations with which he enriches his pages would of themselves make the treatise valuable."—*Dublin Review.*

BUTLER, REV. ALBAN.

People's Edition of the Lives of the Saints. In twelve volumes. Each volume containing the Saints of the Month. Superfine paper, cloth extra, each volume   0 1 6

Or the Complete set, in handsome cloth case to match   0 18 0

The lives of the principal Martyrs, Fathers, and other more illustrious Saints, whose memory is revered in the Catholic Church, are here presented to the public. The whole work, comprising over six thousand pages, well printed on good paper, and bound in an attractive style, is by far the cheapest and best edition in the market. Alban Butler's "Lives of the Saints" has long been recognised as a standard work, and it is the most comprehensive Series ever published in the English Language.

CATHOLIC BELIEF: OR, A SHORT AND

Simple Exposition of Catholic Doctrine. By the Very Rev. Joseph Faà di Bruno, D.D. Fifteenth edition . . . . . Price 6d.; post free,   0 0 8½
Cloth, lettered, . . 10d.; . .   0 1 0½
Also an edition printed on better paper and strongly bound in cloth. With Steel Frontispiece. . .   0 2 0

CHALLONER, BISHOP.

Meditations for every day in the year. Revised and edited by the Right Rev. John Virtue, D.D., Bishop of Portsmouth. 7th edition. 8vo . . .   0 3 0
And in other bindings.

DALE, REV. J. D. HILARIUS.

Ceremonial According to the Roman Rite. Translated from the Italian of Joseph Baldeschi. New and Revised Edition. Crown 8vo, cloth . . .   0 6 6

"This work is our standard English directory on the subject. Few functions of any importance are carried on without a glance at it. It is a familiar guide and friend—in short, a classic.'—*Catholic Times.*

The Sacristan's Manual; or, Handbook of Church Furniture, Ornament, &c. Fourth Edition. Crown 8vo, cloth 0 2 6

DEVAS, C. S.

Studies of Family Life: a contribution to Social Science. Crown 8vo 0 5 0

"We recommend these pages and the remarkable evidence brought together in them to the careful attention of all who are interested in the well-being of our common humanity."—*Guardian.*

DRANE, AUGUSTA THEODOSIA, Edited by.

The Autobiography of Archbishop Ullathorne. Demy
8vo, cloth. Second edition £0 7 6
"As a plucky Yorkshireman, as a sailor, as a missionary, as a great traveller, as a ravenous reader, and as a great prelate, Dr. Ullathorne was able to write down most fascinating accounts of his experiences. The book is full of shrewd glimpses from a Roman point of view of the man himself, of the position of Roman Catholics in this country, of the condition of the country, of the Colonies, and of the Anglican Church in various parts of the world, in the earlier half of this century."—*Guardian*.

The Letters of Archbishop Ullathorne. (Sequel
to the *Autobiography*.) 2nd Edit. Demy 8vo, cloth 0 9 0
"Compiled with admirable judgment for the purpose of displaying in a thousand various ways the real man who was Archbishop Ullathorne."—*Tablet*.

EYRE, MOST REV. CHARLES (Abp. of Glasgow)

The History of St. Cuthbert: or, An Account of his
Life, Decease, and Miracles. Third edition. With
maps, charts, &c. handsomely bound in cloth.
Royal 8vo 0 14 0

FABER, REV. FREDERICK WILLIAM, (D.D.)

All for Jesus: or the Easy Ways of Divine Love . 0 5 0
Bethlehem 0 7 0
Ethel's Book: or Tales of the Angels. . . . 0 2 6
Growth in Holiness: or the Progress of the Spiritual
Life 0 6 0
Notes on Doctrinal and Spiritual Subjects, 2 vols. . 0 10 0
Hymns. Complete Edition 0 6 0
Poems. Complete Edition. . . . , . 0 5 0
Sir Lancelot: A Legend of the Middle Ages . . 0 5 0
Spiritual Conferences 0 6 0
The Blessed Sacrament: or the Works and Ways of
God 0 7 6
The Creator and the Creature: or the Wonders of
Divine Love 0 6 0
The Foot of the Cross: or the Sorrows of Mary. . 0 6 0
The Precious Blood: or the Price of our Salvation . 0 5 0
The Easiness of Salvation. (Reprinted from "The
Creator and the Creature.") Cloth, gilt . . 0 1 0
Life and Letters of Frederick William Faber, D.D.,
Priest of the Oratory of St. Philip Neri. By JOHN
EDWARD BOWDEN of the same Congregation. With
Portrait 0 6 0
Father Faber's May Book. Compiled by an Oblate
of Mary Immaculate. Arranged for daily reading,
from the writings of Father Faber. 18mo, cloth,
gilt edges, with steel Frontispiece 0 2 0

FORMBY, REV. HENRY.

Monotheism: in the main derived from the Hebrew
nation and the Law of Moses. The Primitive Religion of the City of Rome. An historical Investigation. Demy 8vo 0 5 0

FRANCIS DE SALES, ST.: THE WORKS OF.

Translated into the English Language by the Very Rev. Canon Mackey, O.S.B., under the direction of the Right Rev. Bishop Hedley, O.S.B.

Vol. I. Letters to Persons in the World. 3rd Ed. . £0 6 0
Vol. II.—The Treatise on the Love of God. Father Carr's translation of 1630 has been taken as a basis, but it has been modernized and thoroughly revised and corrected. 2nd Edition 0 6 0
Vol. III. The Catholic Controversy. . . . 0 6 0
Vol. IV. Letters to Persons in Religion, with introduction by Bishop Hedley on "St. Francis de Sales and the Religious State." 2nd Edition . . . 0 6 0

"We earnestly commend these volumes to all readers, and we desire their widest diffusion, as we desire also that the doctrine and spirit of St. Francis may reign in all our hearts, both of pastors and of people."—*Cardinal Manning* in the *Dublin Review*.

GALLWEY, REV. PETER, (S.J.)

Precious Pearl of Hope in the Mercy of God, The. Translated from the Italian. With Preface by the Rev. Father Gallwey. Cloth 0 4 6
Lectures on Ritualism and on the Anglican Orders, 2 vols. (Or may be had separately.) 0 8 0

GIBBONS, CARDINAL.

The Faith of our Fathers. A Plain Exposition and Vindication of the Church founded by our Lord Jesus Christ. Forty-eighth Revised and Enlarged Edition. With Portrait. Limp cloth, 2s. net (postage 4½d.). Cloth boards, gilt lettered, 3s. net (postage 4½d.).
The Ambassador of Christ. Cloth 0 6 0

GIBSON, REV. H.

Catechism Made Easy. Being an Explanation of the Christian Doctrine. 10th Edition. 2 vols., cloth. . 0 7 6

"This work must be of priceless worth to any who are engaged in any form of catechetical instruction. It is the best book of the kind that we have seen in English."—*Irish Monthly*.

GILLOW, JOSEPH.

Literary and Biographical History, or, Bibliographical Dictionary of the English Catholics. From the Breach with Rome, in 1534, to the Present Time. *Vols. I., II. III. and IV. cloth, demy 8vo* . . *each* 0 15 0
5th, and concluding vol. in preparation.

"The patient research of Mr. Gillow, his conscientious record of minute particulars, and especially his exhaustive bibliographical information in connection with each name, are beyond praise."—*British Quarterly Review*.

The Haydock Papers. Illustrated. Demy 8vo . 0 7 6

"We commend this collection to the attention of every one that is interested in the records of the sufferings and struggles of our ancestors to hand down the faith to their children."—*Tablet*

St. Thomas's Priory ; or, The Story of St. Austin's, Stafford. With Three Illustrations. Tastefully bound in half leather 0 5 0

GLANCEY, REV. M. F.
Characteristics from the Writings of Archbishop Ullathorne, together with a Bibliographical Account of the Archbishop's Works. Crown 8vo, cloth . . £0 6 8

"The Archbishop's thoughts are expressed in choice, rich language. We have perused this book with interest, and have no hesitation in recommending our readers to possess themselves of it."—*Birmingham Weekly Mercury.*

GROWTH IN THE KNOWLEDGE OF OUR LORD.
Meditations for every Day in the Year, exclusive of those for Festivals, Days of Retreat, &c. Adapted from the original of Abbé de Brandt, by Sister Mary Fidelis. A new and Improved Edition, in 3 Vols. Sold only in sets. Price per set, . . . 1 2 6

HAMMERSTEIN, FR. L. VON (S.J.)
Foundations of Faith: The Existence of God Demonstrated. With an Introduction by the Rev. W. L. Gildea, D.D. Crown 8vo, cloth 0 6 0

HEDLEY, BISHOP.
The Christian Inheritance. Second Edition. Crown 8vo, cloth gilt, 430 pp. . . . 0 6 0

"We do not know any book we could more confidently recommend to intelligent inquirers after truth, perplexed by the prevailing unbelief, than this new volume, in which the Bishop of Newport prints some twenty discourses preached by him on various occasions."—*Tablet.*

Our Divine Saviour and other discourses. Second Edition. Crown 8vo, cloth gilt. . . 0 6 0

"This volume is made up of eighteen Discourses, which treat chiefly of the Incarnation, the Mass, the Blessed Sacrament, the Sacramental System and kindred subjects They are not controversial in form, yet they have constant reference to current errors of our day. They are brief, concise, lucid, profoundly philosophical, yet so direct and simple in the arrangement of their thoughts and in their language, that any person of ordinary intelligence can understand and profit by them."—*American Catholic Quarterly.*

A Retreat: consisting of Thirty-three Discourses with Meditations: for the use of Clergy, Religious, and Others. Third Edition. In handsome half-leather binding. Crown 8vo, 428 pp. . . 0 6 0

"The book is one which, beyond the purpose for which it is intended, may be strongly recommended for spiritual reading"—*Month.*

HUMPHREY, REV. W. (S.J.)
The Divine Teacher. A Letter to a Friend. With a Preface in Reply to the English Church Defence Tract "Papal Infallibility." Seventh Edition Demy 8vo, cloth 0 2 6

"We cannot speak in terms too high of the matter contained in this excellent and able volume."—*Westminster Gazette.*

INNER LIFE OF FATHER THOMAS BURKE, O.P.
By a Dominican Friar of the English Province. Dark green buckram, gilt. 0 2 0

In this little work the writer has endeavoured to depict that side of Father Burke's character which, if it is least known, gives the truer as well as the higher idea of the well-known preacher of fifteen years ago.

KEENAN, REV. S.

Controversial Catechism : or, Protestantism Refuted and Catholicism Established. New Edition, with latest revisions by the Rev. George Cormack, and a Preface by the Right Rev. J. C. Hedley, O.S.B., Bishop of Newport, Cloth £0 2 0

Extract from Bishop Hedley's Preface.—"The edition of the 'Controversial Catechism' of the late Rev. Stephen Keenan which is here offered to the public is more than a mere reprint Not only has the text been thoroughly revised, but the innumerable references have been carefully verified, and one or two new chapters have been added."

LIGUORI, ST. ALPHONSUS.

New and Improved Translation of the Complete Works of St. Alphonsus, edited by the late Bishop Coffin :--

Vol. I. The Christian Virtues, and the Means for Obtaining them. Cloth 0 3 0
Or separately :—
 1. The Love of our Lord Jesus Christ . . . 0 1 0
 2. Treatise on Prayer. *(In the ordinary editions a great part of this work is omitted.)* . . . 0 1 0
 3. A Christian's rule of Life 0 1 0
Vol. II. The Mysteries of the Faith—The Incarnation; containing Meditations and Devotions on the Birth and Infancy of Jesus Christ, &c., suited for Advent and Christmas. 0 2 6
Vol. III. The Mysteries of the Faith—The Blessed Sacrament 0 2 6
Vol. IV. Eternal Truths—Preparation for Death . 0 2 6
Vol. V. The Redemption—Meditations on the Passion. 0 2 6
Vol. VI. Glories of Mary. New edition . . . 0 3 6
Reflections on Spiritual Subjects 0 2 6

LILLY, W. S.

Ancient Religion and Modern Thought. Second Edition. Demy 8vo, cloth xxvi.-367 pp. Reduced to 0 6 0
"Contents: The Message of Modern Thought—The Claim of Ancient Religion—Religious and Religion—Naturalism and Christianity—Matter and Spirit.

LIVIUS, REV. T. (M.A., C.SS.R.)

St. Peter, Bishop of Rome ; or, the Roman Episcopate of the Prince of the Apostles. Demy 8vo, cloth 0 12 0

Explanation of the Psalms and Canticles in the Divine Office. By ST. ALPHONSUS LIGUORI. Translated from the Italian by THOMAS LIVIUS, C.SS.R. With a Preface by his Eminence Cardinal MANNING. Crown 8vo, cloth 0 7 6

"Father Livius has in our opinion even improved on the original, so far as the arrangement of the book goes. New priests will find it especially useful."—*Month.*

Mary in the Epistles ; or, The Implicit Teaching of the Apostles concerning the Blessed Virgin. Crown 8vo, cloth 0 5 0

LIVIUS, REV. T. [M.A., C.SS.R.]
 The Blessed Virgin in the Fathers of the First Six
 Centuries. With a Preface by CARD. VAUGHAN.
 Cloth £0 12 0
 "Father Livius could hardly have laid at the feet of our Blessed
 Patroness a more fitting tribute than to have placed side by side
 with the work of his fellow-Redemptorist on the ' Dowry of Mary,'
 this volume, in which we hear the combined voices of the Fathers of
 the first six centuries united in speaking the praise of the Mother of
 God."—*Dublin Review.*

MANNING, CARDINAL. Popular Edition of the Works of
 Four Great Evils of the Day. 7th edition . . 0 2 6
 Fourfold Sovereignty of God. 4th edition . . 0 2 6
 Glories of the Sacred Heart. 7th edition . . 0 4 0
 Grounds of Faith. 11th edition 0 1 6
 Independence of the Holy See. 2nd edition . . 0 2 6
 Internal Mission of the Holy Ghost. 6th edition . 0 5 0
 Miscellanies. 2 vols. . . . . each 0 6 0
 Pastime Papers. 2nd edition 0 2 6
 Religio Viatoris. 5th edition . . . 0 1 6
 Sermons on Ecclesiastical Subjects. . . . 0 6 0
 Sin and its Consequences. 10th edition . . 0 4 0
 Temporal Mission of the Holy Ghost. 4th edition 0 5 0
 True Story of the Vatican Council. 2nd edition . 0 2 6
 The Eternal Priesthood. 12th edition . . 0 2 6
 The Office of the Church in the Higher Catholic
  Education. A Pastoral Letter . . . 0 0 6
 Workings of the Holy Spirit in the Church of England. 0 1 6
 Lost Sheep Found. A Sermon . . . 0 0 6
 Rights and Dignity of Labour . . . 0 0 1

The Westminster Series
 In handy pocket size. All bound in cloth.
 The Blessed Sacrament, the Centre of Immutable
  Truth 0 1 0
 Confidence in God. 0 1 0
 Love of Jesus to Penitents. . . . 0 1 0
 Office of the Holy Ghost under the Gospel . 0 1 0
 Holy Ghost the Sanctifier . . . 0 2 0

MANNING, CARDINAL, Edited by.
 Life of the Curé d'Ars. From the French of the
  Abbé Monnin. Popular Edition. Fcap. 8vo, cloth 0 2 6
 "The authorised translation of the work by the Abbe Monnin, the
 friend and fellow-labourer of the Curé, written by command of the
 Bishop of Belley, and is the only authentic work published."

MEYNELL, ALICE.
 Lourdes: Yesterday, to-day, and to-morrow. Translated from the French of Daniel Barbé by Alice Meynell. With twelve full pages water colour drawings
 by Hoffbauer, reproduced in colours. Royal 8vo,
 blue buckram, gilt 0 6 0

MORRIS, REV. JOHN (S.J., F.S.A.)
 Letter Books of Sir Amias Poulet, keeper of Mary
 Queen of Scots. Demy 8vo . . . net 0 2 6

Two Missionaries under Elizabeth £0 14 0
The Catholics under Elizabeth 0 14 0
The Life of Father John Gerard, S.J. Third edition,
rewritten and enlarged 0 14 0
The Life and Martyrdom of St. Thomas Becket. Second
and enlarged edition. In one volume, large post 8vo,
cloth, pp. xxxvi., 632, ... 0 12 6
or bound in two parts, cloth 0 13 0

"Father Morris is one of the few living writers who have succeeded in greatly modifying certain views of English history, which had long been accepted as the only tenable ones. . . To have wrung an admission of this kind from a reluctant public, never too much inclined to surrender its traditional assumptions, is an achievement not to be underrated in importance."—*Rev. Dr. Augustus Jessopp, in the Academy.*

MORRIS, REV. W. B. (of the Oratory.)

The Life of St. Patrick, Apostle of Ireland. Fourth
edition. Crown 8vo, cloth 0 5 0

"Promises to become the standard biography of Ireland's Apostle. For clear statement of facts, and calm judicious discussion of controverted points, it surpasses any work we know of in the literature of the subject."—*American Catholic Quarterly.*

Ireland and St. Patrick. A study of the Saint's
character and of the results of his apostolate.
Second edition. Crown 8vo, cloth. . . 0 5 0

"We read with pleasure this volume of essays, which, though the Saint's name is taken by no means in vain, really contains a sort of discussion of current events and current English views of Irish character."—*Saturday Review.*

NEWMAN, CARDINAL.

Church of the Fathers. Fcap 8vo, cloth, 361 pp. . 0 4 0
Prices of other works by Cardinal Newman on
application.

PAYNE, JOHN ORLEBAR, (M.A.)

Records of the English Catholics of 1715. Demy 8vo.
Half-bound, gilt top 0 15 0
English Catholic Non-Jurors of 1715. Being a Summary of the Register of their Estates, with Genealogical and other Notes, and an Appendix of
Unpublished Documents in the Public Record
Office. In one volume. Demy 8vo . . 1 1 6
Old English Catholic Missions. Demy 8vo, half-bound. 0 7 0
St. Paul's Cathedral in the time of Edward VI. Being
a detailed Account of its Treasures from a Document
in the Public Record Office. Tastefully printed on
imitation hand-made paper, and bound in cloth . 0 2 6

PERRY, REV. JOHN.

Practical Sermons for all the Sundays of the year.
First and Second Series. Sixth edition. In two
volumes. Cloth 0 7 0

"The price at which it is issued puts it within reach of the most moderate purse. It has been carefully edited, printed in clear type, and neatly bound. We trust its circulation may be so extensive as to verify in Father Perry's regard that which was written of another great servant of God : 'being dead he yet speaketh.' "—*Tablet.*

POPE, REV. T. A. (of the Oratory.)
Life of St. Philip Neri. Translated from the Italian of Cardinal Capecelatro. Second and revised edition.
2 vols. Crown 8vo, cloth £0 12 6

"Altogether this is a most fascinating work, full of spiritual lore and historic erudition, and with all the intense interest of a remarkable biography. Take it up where you will, it is hard to lay it down. We think it one of the most completely satisfactory lives of a Saint that has been written in modern times."—*Tablet.*

PORTER, ARCHBISHOP (S.J.).
The Banquet of the Angels: Preparation and Thanksgiving for Holy Communion. New Edition. 18mo. blue cloth, gilt. 0 2 0
Also bound in a variety of handsome leather bindings suitable for First Communion memorial gifts. From 6s. 6d. to 12s. 6d. *net.*

"This little volume is intended chiefly for people in the world, and contains an excellent series of considerations and meditations suitable for the solemn occasion of Holy Communion."—*Irish Ecclesiastical Record.*

PRACTICAL MEDITATIONS FOR EVERY DAY IN THE YEAR, on the Life of our Lord Jesus Christ. Chiefly for the use of Religious. By a Father of the Society of Jesus. With Imprimatur of Cardinal Manning. New Edition, Revised. In two Volumes. Cloth, red edges . . . , 0 9 0

"These volumes give three different daily points for consideration and application. "A work of great practical utility, and we give it our earnest congratulations."—*Weekly Register.*

QUARTERLY SERIES. Edited by the Rev. John Gerard, S.J. 95 volumes published to date.

Selection.

The Life and Letters of St. Francis Xavier. By the Rev. H. J. Coleridge, S.J. 2 vols. . . . 0 10 6
The History of the Sacred Passion. By Father Luis de la Palma, of the Society of Jesus. Translated from the Spanish. 0 5 0
The Life and Letters of St. Teresa. 3 vols. By Rev. H. J. Coleridge, S.J. . . . . each 0 7 6
The Life of Mary Ward. By Mary Catherine Elizabeth Chalmers, of the Institute of the Blessed Virgin. Edited by the Rev. H. J. Coleridge, S.J. 2 vols. 0 15 0
The Return of the King. Discourses on the Latter Days. By the Rev. H. J. Coleridge, S.J. . . 0 7 6
Pious Affections towards God and the Saints. Meditations for every Day in the Year, and for the Principal Festivals. From the Latin of the Ven. Nicolas Lancicius, S.J. 0 7 6
The Life and Teaching of Jesus Christ in Meditations for Every Day in the Year. By Fr. Nicolas Avancino, S.J. Two vols. 0 10 6
The Hours of the Passion. Taken from the *Life of Christ* by Ludolph the Saxon 0 7 6
The Baptism of the King: Considerations on the Sacred Passion. By the Rev. H. J. Coleridge, S.J. . . 0 7 6

QUARTERLY SERIES—(*selection*) *continued*.

	£	s	d
The Mother of the King. Mary during the Life of Our Lord.	0	7	6
The Mother of the Church. Mary during the first Apostolic Age	0	6	0
The Life of St. Alonso Rodriguez. By Francis Goldie, of the Society of Jesus	0	7	6
Letters of St. Augustine. Selected and rranged by Mary H. Allies	0	6	6
Acts of the English Martyrs, hitherto unpublished. By the Rev. John H. Pollen, S.J.	0	7	6
Life of St. Francis di Geronimo, S.J. By A. M. Clarke.	0	7	6
Aquinas Ethicus; or the Moral Teaching of St. Thomas By the Rev. Joseph Rickaby, S.J. 2 vols.	0	12	0
The Spirit of St. Ignatius. From the French of the Rev. Fr. Xavier de Franciosi, S.J.	0	6	0
Jesus, the All-Beautiful. A devotional Treatise on the character and actions of Our Lord. Edited by Rev. J. G. MacLeod, S.J.	0	6	6
The Manna of the Soul. By Fr. Paul Segneri. New edition. In two volumes.	0	12	0
Saturday dedicated to Mary. From the Italian of Fr. Cabrini, S.J.	0	6	0
Life of Father Augustus Law, S.J. By Ellis Schreiber.	0	6	0
Life of Ven. Joseph Benedict Cottolengo. From the Italian of Don P. Gastaldi.	0	4	6
Story of St. Stanislaus Kostka. Edited by Rev. F. Goldie, S.J. 3rd Edition.	0	4	6
The Lights in Prayer of the Venerable Fathers Louis de la Puente and Claude de la Colombière, and the Rev. Father Paul Segneri. Edited by the Rev. J. Morris, S.J.	0	5	0
Life of St. Francis Borgia. By A. M. Clarke.	0	6	6
Life of Blessed Antony Baldinucci. By Rev. F. Goldie, S.J.	0	6	0
Distinguished Irishmen of the Sixteenth Century. By Rev. E. Hogan, S J.	0	6	0
Journals kept during Times of Retreat. By the late Fr. John Morris, S.J. Edited by Rev. J. Pollen, S.J.	0	6	0
Life of the Rev. Mother Mary of St. Euphrasia Pelletier. By A. M. Clarke.	0	6	0
Jesus: His Life, in the very words of the Four Gospels. A Diatessaron by HENRY BEAUCLERK, S.J. Cloth	0	5	0
First Communion. A Book of Preparation for First Communion. Edited by Father THURSTON, S.J. Second Edition. With Nineteen Illustrations.	0	6	6
The Life and Letters of Fr. John Morris, S.J. By Fr. J. Pollen, S.J. Cloth.	0	6	0
VOLUMES ON THE LIFE OF OUR LORD.			
The Preparation of the Incarnation	0	7	6
The Nine Months. The Life of our Lord in the Womb.	0	7	6
The Thirty Years. Our Lord's Infancy and Early Life.	0	7	6
The Ministry of St. John Baptist	0	6	6

QUARTERLY SERIES—(*selection*) *continued.*

The Preaching of the Beatitudes	£0	6	6
The Sermon on the Mount. Continued. 2 Parts, each	0	6	6
The Training of the Apostles. Parts I., II., III., IV. each	0	6	6
The Preaching of the Cross. Part I.	0	6	6
The Preaching of the Cross. Parts II., III. each	0	6	0
Passiontide. Parts I. II. and III., each	0	6	6
Chapters on the Parables of Our Lord	0	7	6
The Life of our Life. Harmony of the Life of Our Lord, with Introductory Chapters and Indices. Second edition. Two vols.	0	15	0
The Passage of our Lord to the Father. Conclusion of The Life of our Life.	0	7	6
The Works and Words of our Saviour, gathered from the Four Gospels	0	7	6
The Story of the Gospels. Harmonised for Meditation	0	7	6

RENDU, A. (LL.D.)

The Jewish Race in Ancient and Roman History. Translated from the eleventh corrected edition, by Theresa Crook. Crown 8vo, cloth . . . 0 6 0

"Wonderfully well executed."—*Tablet.*
"It has the merits of clearness and condensation."—*Scotsman.*

RIVINGTON, REV. LUKE (M.A.)

Rome and England: or, Ecclesiastical Continuity. Crown 8vo, cloth 0 3 6

"Father Rivington conducts his case with scrupulous fairness, with perfect good temper, and rare courtesy. He is painstaking, scholarly, and consistently logical."—*Pall Mall Gazette.*

ROSE, STEWART.

St. Ignatius Loyola and The Early Jesuits, with more than 100 Illustrations by H. W. and H. C. Brewer and L. Wain. The whole produced under the immediate superintendence of the Rev. W. H. Eyre, S.J. Super Royal 8vo. Handsomely bound in cloth, extra gilt. . . . . . net. 0 15 0

RYDER, REV. H. I. D. (of the Oratory.)

Catholic Controversy: A Reply to Dr. Littledale's "Plain Reasons." Seventh edition . . . 0 2 6

SCHOUPPE, REV. F. X. (S.J.)

Purgatory. Illustrated by the lives and legends of the Saints. Cloth 0 6 0

"We feel absolutely confident that Father Schouppe's work will soon become one of our most popular works on Purgatory, and that we shall ere long have to notice its second edition."—*Tablet.*

STANTON, REV. R. (of the Oratory.)

A Menology of England and Wales; or, Brief Memorials of the British and English Saints, arranged according to the Calendar. Together with the Martyrs of the 16th and 17th centuries. With Supplement, containing Notes, enlarged Appendices, and a new Index. Demy 8vo, cloth 0 16 0

The Supplement, separately 0 2 0

SWEENEY, RT. REV. ABBOT, (O.S.B.)

Sermons for all Sundays and Festivals of the Year. Fourth edition. Crown 8vo, handsomely bound in half leather £0 10 6

' For such priests as are in search of matter to aid them in their round of Sunday discourses, and have not read this volume, we can assure them that they will find in these 600 pages a mine of solid and simple Catholic teaching.'—*Tablet.*

THOMPSON, EDWARD HEALY, (M.A.)

The Life of Jean-Jacques Olier, Founder of the Seminary of St. Sulpice. New and enlarged edition. Post 8vo, cloth, pp. xxxvi. 628 . . . 0 15 0

The Life and Glories of St. Joseph, Husband of Mary, Foster-Father of Jesus, and Patron of the Universal Church. Second edition. Crown 8vo, cloth 0 6 0

Life of Marie Lataste. Cloth 0 5 0

Letters and Writings of Marie Lataste, with Critical and Expository Notes. By two Fathers of the Society of Jesus. Translated from the French. 3 vols . . . . each 0 5 0

ULLATHORNE, ARCHBISHOP.

Autobiography of, (*see* Drane, A. T.) . . . 0 7 6
Letters of, do. ,, ... 0 9 0
Christian Patience: the Strength and Discipline of the Soul. Fifth and Cheaper Edition. Demy 8vo, cloth 0 7 0
The Endowments of Man, Considered in their Relations with his Final End. Fourth and Cheaper Edition. Demy 8vo. cloth 0 7 0
The Groundwork of the Christian Virtues. Fifth and Cheaper Edition. Demy 8vo, cloth . . 0 7 0
Memoir of Bishop Willson, First Bishop of Hobart, Tasmania 0 2 6

WISEMAN, CARDINAL.

Fabiola. A Tale of the Catacombs. New cheap edition. Crown 8vo cloth 0 2 0
Also in cloth gilt lettered. 3s. 6d., cloth richly gilt edges 0 4 0
And a new and splendid edition printed on large quarto paper, embellished with thirty-one full-page illustrations, and a coloured portrait of St. Agnes. Handsomely bound 1 1 0

New Classified Catalogue of Standard Books (96 pages), comprising every class of book in demand among Catholic Readers, post free on application.

BURNS & OATES, LD., 28 Orchard Street, London, W.

www.ingramcontent.com/pod-product-compliance
Lightning Source LLC
Chambersburg PA
CBHW030307240426
43673CB00040B/1085